LEGACY

THE TRUE INGLORIOUS HISTORY OF
PRESIDENT OBAMA

I.S. PETTEICE

Since
1978
Publication
Consultants

PO Box 221974 Anchorage, Alaska 99522-1974
books@publicationconsultants.com—www.publicationconsultants.com

ISBN 978-1-59433-560-0
eISBN 978-1-59433-561-7
Library of Congress Catalog Card Number: 2016933157

Manufactured in the United States of America.

I dedicate *Legacy* to Ambassador Chris Stevens; Officer Sean Smith; CIA Contractor, Tyrone Woods; and CIA Contractor, Glen Doherty. Ambassador Stevens warned our then Secretary of State, Hillary Clinton, of the dangers involved to him and the help that was needed at the American Embassy. Ambassador Stevens and Officer Smith fought valiantly under impossible conditions at Benghazi after the Obama Administration advised them there was nothing to worry about. Before Tyrone Woods and Glen Doherty were killed, they confiscated guns from their enemy and were able to take down 60 terrorists while waiting for America to save them, the rescue that never came. Are we going to let Benghazi rest?

CONTENTS

I

HOW DID IT ALL HAPPEN

Once upon a time there was a man whose name was Thomas Ayers. Thomas Ayers was known as the Godfather of Illinois Politics. While his son Bill Ayers was setting off bombs in America, Thomas Ayers was being promoted to one of the highest profile and prestigious positions in Illinois and the country. He was also handed the keys to the most powerful Nuclear Plants in the country as Chairman of Con Ed.

Many thought Mayor Daley was the Chicago Kingpin until he died. He was just a crooked politician. Thomas Ayers was the man with the power, the "go to" man.

So who sent Obama? The Jews would probably say, Judson Miner. Miner was Jewish.

"'I used to tease Barack that he had Jewish blood,' says Mr. Miner..." (Wall Street Journal, April 28, 2008).

But in all likelihood, who sent Obama was the father of his friends, Former Weather Underground Leader and far-left radical revolutionary, Bill Ayers, Tom Ayers, and the other son, John Ayers.

John Ayers is a national leader in charter school development. At the time Barack Obama was running for the State Senate, a movement was underway from two angles: below in black, Latino and other communities for more local control of schools and from above by business interests who wanted to cut costs.

Thomas Ayers helped found and served as Chairman of the Board of Trustees of Chicago United.

Thomas Ayers was a very close friend to a man named Frank Marshall Davis.

Now Frank Marshall Davis worked with a man named Vernon Jarrett at the communist-sympathizing *Chicago Defender* newspaper.

Frank Marshall Davis, also a Communist, was a friend of Barack Hussein Obama's father, and a mentor of Barack Hussein Obama, Jr.

Obama wrote about his mentor "Frank" (Marshall Davis) in his best-selling memoir *Dreams from My Father* (2005). He mentioned him 22 times in the book by his first name, with various other references as well. The future president recalled a conversation that he had with Davis in the late 70s as the young man prepared to leave Hawaii to go to college on the Mainland.

Davis warned him that college professors would "train you to forget what it is that you already know. They'll train you so good, you'll start believing what they tell you about equal opportunity and the American way and all that sh-t…"

Dr. Paul Kengor, professor and author of the book *The Communist– Frank Marshall Davis: The Untold Story of Barack Obama's Mentor* (2012), notes that Obama took out all overt references to Davis in his audio version of "Dreams From My Father" (which he narrated) as he prepared to run for president. Kengor writes that the future candidate for the highest office in the land "no doubt feared being tied too closely to a man who joined the Communist Party under Stalin and had been so radical that the Federal government placed him on the Security Index [watchlist.]"

The Washington Post reported: "As Obama became a community organizer in college and later grappled with the challenges of race and poverty in Chicago, he visualized Davis and asked, 'What would Frank do? What would Frank think?' Kengor wrote." Obama worked for the ACORN offshoot "Project VOTE" to register black voters in aid of the Senate Campaign of Carol Moseley Braun–who had strong Communist Party USA ties and was Harold Washington's legislative floor leader. Obama helped Carol Moseley Braun win her Senate seat,

and then took it over himself in 2004–backed by the same communist/
socialist alliance that had elected Washington and Moseley Braun.
http://www.keywiki.org/Barack_Obama_and_the_Communist_Party

It would appear the association with Davis, likely affirmed by Valerie
Jarrett (given her family lineage), did shape the president's view of
the role of government. The Federal government has undergone its
largest expansion since the heydays of the Great Society in the 1960s
(and arguably the greatest increase in taxes in over a generation) with
Obama at the helm. http://www.pwesternjournalism.com/fbi-files-
dig-up-shocking-dirt-from-top-obama-advisers-past-that-could-
explain-a-lot/?utm_source=MailChimp&utm_medium=email&utm_
content=top-story&utm_campaign=DailyEmail06.24.15

And, of course, Vernon Jarrett later became the father-in-law of
Iranian-born leftist Valerie Jarrett. Jarrett is Obama's closest White
House advisor and CEO of Habitat Company (slumlord), who
manages the public housing in Chicago. Habitat Co. gets millions
of dollars from the Illinois State Legislature. She was the daughter of
James Edward Bowman and Dorothy Peterson according to Wikipedia
under James Edward Bowman, but Wikipedia under Valerie Jarrett,
lists Barbara Taylor as Valerie Jarrett's mother. They do not list Dr.
Bowman being married twice. Dr. Bowman became The Chair of
Pathology at Nemazee Hospital in Shiraz, Iran and Valerie was born
in Iran. He was the first tenured African-American professor at the
University of Chicago's Biological Sciences Division.

FBI files list Dr. Bowman as having extensive Communist
associations. In 1950, Bowman was in communication with a paid
Soviet agent named Alfred Stern, who fled to Prague after getting
charged with espionage. Bowman was also a member of a Communist-
sympathizing group called the Association of Interns and Medical
Students. After his discharge from the Army Medical Corps in 1955,
Bowman moved to Iran for work, the FBI records show.

Valerie Jarrett, married to William Robert Jarrett, was a lawyer,
worked for the City of Chicago and was the person that hired Michelle
LaVaughan Robinson.

Valerie Jarrett's father-in-law, Vernon Jarrett, was also a Communist
according to FBI documents obtained by Judicial Watch. The agency

considered him a potential Communist saboteur, who was to be arrested in the event of a war with the Soviet Union.

According to Judicial Watch, Jarrett herself is a "liberal extremist" who, like the president, had strong ties to Frank Marshall Davis — a member of the Communist Party with an extensive FBI file.

Michelle LaVaughan Robinson worked at the Sidley Austin law firm (also counsel for Con. Edison). This is the same law firm where former fugitive from the FBI, Bernardine Dohrn, also worked, and where Barack Obama got a summer job, which was arranged by Thomas Ayers.

Bernardine Dohrn, who is married to William Ayers, was once found hiding from the FBI at a San Francisco marina, along with Donald Warden, who changed his name to Khalid al-Mansour.

Khalid al-Mansour (Warden) was a mentor of the Black Panther Party founders, Huey Newton and Bobby Seale, and a close associate of Nation of Islam leader, Louis Farrakhan.

Khalid al-Mansour also was a financial adviser to a Saudi Prince, who donated cash to Harvard, for which Obama got a critical letter of recommendation from Percy Sutton. Sutton was the attorney for Malcolm X, who knew Kenyan politician Tom Mboya. Mboya, who was a close friend of Barack Hussein Obama, Sr., also met Malcolm X when he traveled to Kenya.

Barack Obama, Sr. received his education at the University of Hawaii and his education was paid for by Laubach Literacy Institute, supported by Elizabeth Mooney Kirk. Kirk was a friend of Malcolm X, associated with the Nation of Islam, later headed by Louis Farrakhan. Farrakhan lives very near to Obama, Jr.'s Chicago Mansion, also located very close to the residence of William Ayers and Bernadine Dohrn, who occasionally have been baby sitters for Malia and Sasha Obama, even though they are bomb-making communists.

After Obama, Jr. had attended Occidental College and Columbia University, Obama moved to Chicago and worked for the Industrial Area Foundation that was founded by Marxist and radical agitator, Saul "the Red" Alinsky. Alinsky was the topic of Hillary Clinton's thesis at Wellesley College.

Obama's $25,000 a year salary was funded by the Woods Fund, which was founded by the Woods Family. Their Sahara Coal Company provided coal to Commonwealth Edison, whose CEO was Thomas

Ayers, whose son was William Ayers who served on the board of the Woods Fund along with Obama. (You read that right. "Coal.")

Barack Obama, Jr. also worked with leftist political groups such as the Democratic Socialists of America and Socialists International. It was there that he met Carl Davidson, a member of the Committees of Correspondence for Democracy and Socialism that also sponsored a 2002 anti-war rally at which Obama spoke. The anti-war rally was organized by Marilyn Katz, a former SDS activist, and long-time friend of David Axelrod. Davidson traveled to Cuba during the Vietnam War in an attempt to sabotage the U.S. war effort. He was a member of the Socialist Party until he became President.

The Reverend Jeremiah Wright preached Marxism and Black Liberation Theology. He delivered anti-white, anti-Jew and Anti-American Sermons. Apparently Obama did not attend church on those days because he claimed he did not hear sermons such as "God Damn America." That was about the time Oprah Winfrey left the church because it was too radical for her. I guess Obama didn't notice that the church also gave the anti-Semitic Nation of Islam leader, Louis Farrakhan a lifetime achievement award either.

Then Obama, the non-writer, received $125,000 in advance to write a book about race relations and instead went on what would be one of many vacations with Michelle, to Bali. Then he received a second advance of $40,000 from a different publisher for a manuscript called *Dreams from My Father*, but the writing style strongly reflected that of William Ayers. You know – the one that trampled on the American flag for the cover of the *Chicago* magazine that appeared on every newsstand that Obama claims he never saw.

Next Obama went to work for the law firm of Miner, Banhill and Galland. The Miner firm specializes in negotiating state government contracts to develop low-income housing. They also represent Tony Rezko (another neighbor of Obama in Chicago) and his firm Rezar, and with slumlord, Valerie Jarrett.

The firm's Judson Miner previously was a classmate of Bernadine Dohrn, wife of – William Ayers.

In 1994, Obama represented ACORN and another plaintiff in a lawsuit against Citibank for denying mortgages to blacks (Buycks-Roberson v. Citibank Federal Savings Bank). The lawsuit resulted in banks being blackmailed into approving subprime loans for poor credit risks, a trend that spread nationwide. This led to the collapse of the housing bubble which helped Obama defeat John McCain in the 2008 presidential election.

In 1996 Obama ran for the Illinois State Senate and joined the "New Party," which promoted Marxism. Obama was supported by Dr. Quentin Yong, a socialist who supported a government takeover of the health care system.

In late 1999 Obama purportedly engaged in homosexual activities and cocaine-snorting in the back of a limousine with a man named Larry Sinclair. Sinclair claims he was contacted in late 2007 by Donald Young who was the gay choir director of Obama's Chicago church and who shared information with Sinclair about Obama.

Donald Young was murdered on December 23, 2007, just weeks after Larry Bland, another gay member of the church was murdered, and neither murder have ever been solved. http://bit.ly/1TqTZXv http://bit.ly/1Otfp6q

In 2008 Larry Sinclair held a press conference to discuss his claims, and was arrested immediately after the event, based on a warrant issued by Delaware Attorney General Beau Biden, son of Vice President Joe Biden.

Barack Obama had a long-time association with anti-Semitic Jeremiah Wright.

In the early 2000s, the Rev. Jeremiah Wright of the Trinity United Church of Christ in Chicago kept his eye on the young guys coming up in Trinity. If he spotted someone that acted or looked gay, then Wright would give them kind of a guidance counselor-type direction on how to keep down low – how to do the things they wanted to do, but then also get married and looking 'respectable' – being part of black society.

"To Trinity insiders, the Down Low Club was simply known as "the program."

"That's the terminology. At Trinity, you're urged to 'get with the program,'" explained a male beneficiary of the Down Low Club. "What that means is it's ok to go ahead and have sex with men, just as long as you 'get with the program' and marry a woman, somebody no straight guy would want to marry."

Trinity "helped a lot of blacks get successful and connected." "That's what Wright did for Obama; he connected Obama to the community, and he helped Obama hide his homosexuality." http://bit.ly/1OtfCGB

In 2003, Obama and his wife attended a dinner in honor of Rashid Khalidi, who was leaving his teaching position in Chicago after eight years for a position at Columbia University. Khalidi is a former PLO operative, a harsh critic of Israel, and advocate of Palestinian rights. He is also one who Obama claims he does not know, even though the Obamas have dined on more than one occasion at the home of Khalidi and his wife, Mona and have used them as occasional baby sitters.

The farewell party was graced by such anti-American, anti-Israel attendees as Barack Obama, Bill Ayers, Rev. Jeremiah Wright, Rashid Khalidi and Yasser Arafat.

Obama reportedly praised Khalidi at the decidedly anti-Semitic event, which William Ayers also attended. The event Obama professes he never attended was sponsored by the Arab American Action Network, to which Obama has funneled cash while serving on the board of the Woods Fund with William Ayers. One speaker at the dinner remarked that if Palestinians cannot secure a return of their land, Israel "will never see a day of peace."

To illustrate the point, Khalidi later told the largely pro-Palestinian attendees that Obama deserved their help in winning a U.S. Senate seat, stating: "You will not have a better senator under any circumstances."

Entertainment at the dinner included a Muslim children's dance whose performances just happened to include simulated beheadings with fake swords, and stomping on American, Israeli, and British flags. Obama allegedly told the audience that "Israel has no God-given right to occupy Palestine" and there has been "genocide against the Palestinian people by (the) Israelis."

Characterizing Israel as a "racist" state and "basically an apartheid system in creation," Khalidi during the 1980s so strongly identified with the aims of Yasser Arafat's PLO, which was designated as a terrorist group by the State Department at the time, that he repeatedly referred to himself as "we" when expounding on the PLO's agenda. In the early 1990s, Khalidi was involved with the PLO's so-called "guidance committee." In 1995, Khalidi and his wife Mona founded the Arab American Action Network (AAAN), noted for its contention that Israel's creation in 1948 was a "catastrophe" for Arab people. In 2001 and again in 2002, the Woods Fund of Chicago, with Obama serving on its board, made grants totaling $75,000 to the AAAN.

The Los Angeles Times has a videotape of the event but just happens to refuse to make it public. Obama is influenced greatly by Rashid Khalidi's philosophy as to the Palestinians and Israeli conflict, whose latest book is *Brokers of Deceit*.

Onetime AAAN vice president Ali Abunimah of Electronic Intifada (a website that, like AAAN, refers to Israel's creation as a "catastrophe") once told interviewer Amy Goodman: "I knew Barack Obama for many years as my state senator – when he used to attend events in the Palestinian community in Chicago all the time. I remember personally introducing him onstage in 1999 when we had a major community fund raiser for the community center in Deheisha refugee camp in the occupied West Bank. And that's just one example of how Barack Obama used to be very comfortable speaking up for, and being associated with Palestinian rights and opposing the Israeli occupation."

In June 2007, Abunimah recalled: "When Obama first ran for the Senate in 2004, the Chicago Jewish News interviewed him on his stance regarding Israel's security fence. He accused the Bush administration of neglecting the 'Israeli-Palestinian' situation and criticized the security fence built by Israel to prevent terror attacks: 'The creation of a wall dividing the two nations is yet another example of the neglect of this Administration in brokering peace,' Obama was quoted as saying."

Also in 2007, Abunimah said: "The last time I spoke to Obama was in the winter of 2004 at a gathering in Chicago's Hyde Park neighborhood. He was in the midst of a primary campaign to secure the Democratic nomination for the United States Senate seat he now occupies. But at that time polls showed him trailing. As he came in from the cold and took off his coat, I went up to greet him. He responded warmly and volunteered, 'Hey, I'm sorry I haven't said more about Palestine right now, but we are in a tough primary race. I'm hoping when things calm down I can be more up front.' He referred to my activism, including columns I was contributing to The Chicago Tribune critical of Israeli and U.S. policy, 'Keep up the good work!'"

Reporter, Peter Wallesten revealed the existence of the tape in an article on Obama's pro-Palestinian background. http://bit.ly/1lVme5F

"In the 2004 Illinois Democrat primary race for the U.S. Senate, front-runner Blair Hull was forced out of the race after David Axelrod managed to get Hull's sealed divorce records unsealed, to enable Obama to win the primary, so he could face popular Republican Jack Ryan.

'Jack Ryan's sealed child custody records from his divorce became unsealed, forcing Ryan to withdraw from the race, which enabled the unqualified Obama to waltz into the U.S. Senate, where, after a mere 143 days of work, he decided he was qualified to run for President of the United States." http://bit.ly/1NFDXua

Obama led a make-believe life in which doors were opened and money was provided. Someone was looking out for him at an early age. Whether it was Frank Marshall or George Soros, they saw this handsome half-white, half-Arab young man with an exotic African/Muslim name and led him toward a life of politics.

As a State Representative, he did not vote on anything controversial. He went from the House to the State Senate because he had the Daley machine behind him. But his step to the Senate was short-lived after he became the keynote speaker at the 2004 Democratic Convention that nominated John Kerry when no one had ever heard of him.

He was charismatic and out maneuvered Hillary Clinton in primaries and when the GOP Candidate, John McCain, picked Sarah Pain as his VIP running mate, this practically handed the crown to Obama.

In 2012, Obama ran a second term and promised the Spanish community amnesty to win their vote and the gay community that they could marry. He won their votes and won the election for a second term.

For Obama, it has never been about the Democratic Party or the Republican Party. It has always been about his communist ideology that he learned at an early age from family, mentors, college professors, and extreme leftist friends and colleagues.

He has spent millions to deny access to his true birth records, while even his wife "mentioned they visited the country of his birth, Kenya." She also noted she did not accompany him on the trip to Saudi Arabia on which he bowed to the King. Being a Muslim required him to do so and that the same faith prevented him from taking her with him.

Back in 1961 people of color were called Negroes. So how can the Obama 'birth certificate' state he is "African-American" when the term wasn't even used at that time?

The birth certificate that the White House released lists Obama's birth as August 4, 1961, and lists Barack Hussein Obama as his father. At the time of President Obama's birth, it also shows that his father is aged 25 years old and that Obama's father was born in "Kenya, East Africa".

This would not seem to be anything of concern, except for the fact that Kenya did not even exist until 1963, two whole years after Obama's birth, and 27 years after his father's birth. How could Obama's father have been born in a country that did not yet exist? Until Kenya was formed in 1963, it was known as the "British East Africa Protectorate." http://bit.ly/1PODiFZ

On the Birth Certificate released by the White House, the listed place of birth is "Kapi'olani Maternity & Gynecological Hospital". This cannot be, because the hospital(s) in question in 1961 were called "KauiKeolani Children's Hospital" and "Kapi'olani Maternity Home," respectively. The name did not change to Kapi'olani Maternity & Gynecological Hospital until 1978 when these two hospitals merged. How can this particular name of the hospital be on a birth certificate dated 1961 if this name had not yet been applied to it until 1978? (http://www.kapiolani.org/women-and-children/about-us/default.aspx)

Perhaps a clue comes from Obama's book on his father. He states how proud he is of his father fighting in WW II. Barack Obama's "birth certificate," says his father was 25 years old in 1961 when Obama was born. That should have put his father's date of birth approximately 1936. WW II was basically between 1939 and 1945. Just how many 3-year-olds fight in Wars? Even in the latest stages of WW II his father wouldn't have been more than nine years old. (Richard Silverlieb)

Now more than six full years in the White House and he is still unprepared to be President. He is still unable to deliver the simplest and briefest speech without his ever-present teleprompters.

This is a President that would warn Americans against "jumping to conclusions" about a mass murderer at Fort Hood who shouted "Allahu Akbar." The absurdity of that was lost on no one. He then compounded this by calling the Christmas bomber "an isolated extremist" only to have to admit a few days later that he was part of an al Qaeda plot.

Obama is an elected President who could attempt to close down GITMO even though those released were known to have returned to the battlefield against America. Obama went so far as to instruct the Attorney General to provide the perpetrator of 9/11 a civil trial when no one else would ever consider such an atrocity. And Obama is a person who could wait three days before having anything to say about the perpetrator of another terrorist attack on Americans and then have to give another speech the following day because his first statement was so lame.

II

OUR COUNTRY

Amerika, our once proud and respected country, now broken and mocked by every nation in the world. Every one of our fifty states has filed petitions to secede from the United States "because apparently not everybody got what they wanted out of America's traditional participatory democracy." jason@huffingtonpost.com

America elected a gay, Muslim, Communist, Community Organizer as its President who brought shame, degradation and devastation upon this Country. Barack Obama will go down in history as the worst leader ever to be elected as President of the United States. President Barack Obama will not be known as a man that has accomplished anything to improve America.

In 2012 Americans elected a Republican Congress to fix what was wrong with this Country. But there were too many old, corrupt Congressmen remaining in office that would train the incoming electives in the art of the deal and nothing was being done to curb spending in Washington and weeding out the Communists that were running Congress. The people had hopes that Barack Obama would be impeached and that Obamacare would be repealed and that Congress would stop robbing their Social Security Fund. They hoped that a lid would be put on Socialism and Communism, and we would get a break from Liberals. We had hopes of getting back to following the Constitution that our Honorable Forefathers wrote back in 1776. We wanted America back.

Do you think other countries do not know what is happening in our country?

Residents from every state have filed Petitions to secede from the United States. The Governor of South Carolina said, "Didn't we try that once before?" Yes, they did – in 1860. The Governor of Tennessee said he didn't think that was a valid option for Tennessee. Alabama's Governor Bentley released a statement saying he believed we should have "one nation under God." Texas Governor Rick Perry believes in the greatness of our Union and Obama says you cannot take the Petitions seriously.

On June 25, 2015, Sorcha Faal reported to her Western Subscribers as follows:

"The Ministry of Defense (MoD) is reporting today that President Putin has ordered an atomic-weapon equipped naval strike force comprised of Black Sea and Northern Fleet naval forces to immediately embark to the Gulf of Mexico for what intelligence experts note will be a "Liberation Exercise" designed to protect the lives and property of Texan citizens should they declare their independence from the Obama regime ruled oligarchy that was once known as the United States of America.

'According to this report, this powerful armada will be led by the guided missile cruiser The Moskva (dubbed a "carrier-killer" by NATO) which will be accompanied by the *Pytlivy* escort ship (frigate) and the *Shakhtyor* rescue vessel (tug), all three belonging to the Black Sea Fleet.

'Joining these three Black Sea Fleet vessels for this mission, this report continues, will be the Northern Fleet's K-410 *Smolensk* cruise missile submarine, the K-317 *Pantera* electronic warfare-nuclear attack submarine, and both the B-138 *Obninsk* and B-388 *Petrozavodsk* nuclear attack submarines...all of whom will be stationed outside of the maritime borders of the U.S. in both the Atlantic Ocean and Gulf of Mexico within "striking distance" of Texas.

'Interesting to note about this naval armada is that it includes The *Shakhtyor* rescue vessel; which specializes in submarine rescue operations and has a group of medics with special equipment for prompt assistance to rescued submarine crews whose vessel may have been attacked, and possibly sunk, thus indicating by its presence this scenario is likely to occur. [Note: Under international laws of warfare, it is a crime to attack submarine rescue vessels.]

'Equally ominous to note in this report is it further stating that this naval armada also contains a Naval Spetsnaz Brigade from the Black Sea Fleet that is at "wartime strength" having nearly 1,300 specialized highly specialized fighters capable of deploying in about 100 teams and who are prepared and trained for "insurgency operations" against enemy forces in "hostile terrain".

'MoD experts in this report further state that this naval armada's deployment is a continuation of the Federation's plans for a nuclear first-strike against "Communist Controlled Regions" existing within the United States now being made in order to save that nation from itself by decapitating its elite ruling class, and as we had reported on in our 19 June report, Russia Plans Atomic "First Strike" As "False Flag" Racial Massacre Pushes America to Brink Of Insanity.

'Raising the fears that this naval armada may very well have to be "thrust like a spear" into the defense of Texas and its citizens, this report warns, are the continued war provocations against this State by the Obama regime whose unprecedented and massive "unconventional warfare" plan called Jade Helm, scheduled to begin on 15 July, is but a prelude to martial law being established not only there, but all across America.

'As to why the Obama regime wants/needs to destroy Texas, this report explains, is due to a new law passed in that State that orders the repatriation to them of $1 billion in gold bullion held by the Obama regime at the Federal Reserve in New York.

'And enraging the Obama regime even more against Texas, this report says, are the continued statements of independence being voiced by its lawmakers, included Congressman Giovanni Capriglione who stated about this new law, "We want to show off our strength and resilience. This is to be able to say 'Hey, listen, Texas is unique, it's stable, it's strong and we can show that by letting other states and individuals know that, yes, Texas has a billion dollars in gold. Does your state have a billion dollars in gold?'"

'Unbeknownst, apparently, to this Texas Congressman, this report further warns, is that the Obama regime will never allow any US State to have gold holdings as it threatens their very existence…like the Gadhafi regime of Libya did in 2011 when it announced that payments for its oil could only be made with gold-backed "dinars" [a single African currency made from gold] and it was promptly, and completely destroyed.

'With new polling showing that fully 44% of Texas citizens now believe that the Obama regime intends to attack them and impose martial law, this MoD report continues, the evidence continues to mount that this is exactly what is going to happen.

'Aside from citing from thousands of reports within the US of massive military movements against Texas and other States occurring, MoD intelligence experts in this report state, more recent evidence has been uncovered proving that Obama has issued 19 new secret orders he has kept from both the American people and the US Congress that vastly expands his dictatorial powers.

'In the Obama regimes knowing, and fearing, that the Federation will indeed come to the defense of Texas, this report continues, the US mainstream media (aka lapdogs) have already begun their propaganda campaign against it, which includes a Politico News Service article titled Putin's Plot to Get Texas to Secede which, in part, says:

"Nathan Smith, who styles himself the "foreign minister" for the Texas Nationalist Movement, appeared last Spring at a far-right confab in St. Petersburg, Russia. Despite roaming around in his cowboy hat, Smith managed to keep a low-key presence at the conference, which was dominated by fascists and neo-Nazis railing against Western decadence.

'But at least one Russian newspaper, *Vzglyad*, caught up with the American, noted that TNM is "hardly a marginal group," and quoted Smith liberally on the excellent prospects for a partial breakup of the United States. Smith declared that the Texas National Movement has 250,000 supporters—including all the Texans currently serving in the U.S. Army—and they all "identify themselves first and foremost as Texans" but are being forced to remain Americans. The United States, he added, "is not a democracy, but a dictatorship."

'The Kremlin's famed troll farms took the interview and ran with it, with dozens of bots instantly tweeting about a "Free Texas."

'Not being told to the American people, however, about this issue, this report states, is that the Federation, and its people, view Texas in the same light as they do the recently freed from US-NATO sponsored Ukrainian-Nazi tyranny, Oblast of Crimea, and as best exampled by the Kremlin's report titled Crimea as the Russian Texas that, in part, says:

"The situation unfolding in Crimea has an analogous historical counterpart: Texas. A comparison of Crimea with Texas will demonstrate the relative similarities between the two, arguing that if one accepts the current status of Texas despite its controversial origin story, then they are more than obliged to recognize the future status of Crimea, since the progression of events there have more legitimacy than those which transpired in Texas over 150 years ago."

'As war has now become "inevitable" between the Federation, China and the Obama regime-led United States, this report further warns, with tens-of-thousands of Russian forces preparing for war in the Far East, while thousands of Chinese merchant ships are being retrofitted for military purposes, and the US Navy has assembled two whole carrier battle groups and 200 aircraft off the coast of Guam, NATO's plan to station a further 40,000 troops along the Western border will not be allowed to stand.

'To if a limited nuclear first-strike against the "Communist Regions" of the United States to decapitate the Obama regimes hold on that once free nation, combined with militarily assisting Texas to free itself from those same "oligarchs", this report questions, is not known at this time…but may very well be the only option left to the Federation in the face of such unprecedented propagandist hostelries from the West that now include the indoctrination of Dutch schoolchildren who this past week were forced to see Russia pictured as monster with claws on cartoon map…when the truth, in fact, it is that Russia is the one who is completely surrounded and threatened with destruction.

'And to if the American mainstream press will cease their propaganda and begin telling their people how truly close World War III is, this MoD report concludes, there appears to be no likelihood as just today the editors of Reason.com reported that they are now under assault by the Obama regime, and even more horrifically, Obama's Pentagon this week rewrote their 'Law of War' declaring for the first time in history that any journalist who writes against them are now to be classified as legitimate targets and labeled as "unprivileged belligerents".

'June 25, 2015 © EU and US all rights reserved. Permission to use this report in its entirety is granted under the condition it is linked back to its original source at WhatDoesItMean.Com. Freebase content licensed under CC-BY and GFDL.

'[Ed. Note: Western governments and their intelligence services actively campaign against the information found in these reports so as not to alarm their citizens about the many catastrophic Earth changes and events to come, a stance that the Sisters of Sorcha Faal strongly disagrees with in believing that it is every human beings right to know the truth. Due to our missions conflicts with that of those governments, the responses of their 'agents' against us has been a long-standing misinformation/misdirection campaign designed to discredit and which is addressed in the report "Who Is Sorcha Faal?".]
http://www.whatdoesitmean.com/index1881.htm

III

BARACK OBAMA'S ACCOMPLISHMENTS

I t has been more than six years, and Obama has less than two more years to complete his destruction of America.

In his latest book *Not on my Watch*, author David Risselada, a Marine and a soldier, David begins his narrative with these words: "Our country has changed; we are no longer the bastion of freedom we once were. Somewhere along the line our beloved nation has taken a hard turn left and we have been steadily driving down a road toward totalitarianism. The general public seems to be completely oblivious to it, and those who have noticed are struggling to get others to wake up." In just one paragraph, David summarized two of the biggest problems facing America: 1) the unrelenting onslaught of Marxism, and 2) the apathy of those whose freedom is being undermined by the Marxist agenda. http://bit.ly/1TqUOQc

Before Obama became President he said he wanted to bankrupt the coal industry. Upon taking the oath of office, Obama immediately set his plan of action in motion by imposing a cap and trade system that would be so harsh that electricity costs would skyrocket. When he was unable to get a bill through Congress, Obama bypassed Congress and used Environmental Protection Agency (EPA) rules and regulations to accomplish his goals. The EPA instituted some new regulations that bankrupted and shut down coal plants throughout the East. The share of electricity generated from coal in the United States has plunged by 38% in 2012 from 49% in 2007. While campaigning in 2008, Obama's promised his Cap and Trade policy would make electricity prices skyrocket. Obama said, "So if somebody wants to build a coal plant, they can – it's just that it will bankrupt them."

Did you know that now 1200 new coal-fired plants are planned in other nations with two-thirds of them to be built in India and China and to be exported here? What difference does it make?

The Four Corners Steam Plant, one of the largest coal-fired generating stations in the United States, is located on Navajo land in Fruitland, New Mexico. The plant's five units generate 2,040 megawatts of electricity and are operated by Arizona Public Service Company, which serves about 300,000 homes in New Mexico, Arizona, California, and Texas. As many as 18,000 homes on the Navajo Nation are completely off the grid despite the presence of nearby coal-fired power plants. According to the American Lung Association, the following people in San Juan County are at elevated risk from power plant pollution: 2,885 people with pediatric asthma, 8,442 with adult asthma, 5,219 with COPD, 9,418 with diabetes, 6,607 with cardiovascular disease, 15,612 who are 65 and older, and 27,265 with low incomes. The ALA states that although "[d]angerous levels of air pollution can harm everyone, even healthy adults," those in high-risk categories are particularly vulnerable. Each year the plant emits 157 million pounds of sulfur dioxide, 122 million pounds of nitrogen oxides, 8 million pounds of soot and 2,000 pounds of mercury. http://www.sourcewatch.org/index.php?title=Coal_and_Native_American_tribal_lands.

He cannot, however, stop the American Indians from mining coal. The American Indians have contracts for mining and have tons of coal in reserves. Some tribes have billions of dollars of coal in reserves. Many tribes do realize the damage and pollution to the land and people and are refusing to mine the coal.

Barack Hussein Obama will go down in history as the worst President in History. Up until now Jimmy Carter held that title. Obama imparts the arrogant parody he does not care about America or its citizens. He exhibited great promise of being the finest president ever, but that was not his agenda. He could have achieved an end to all racism, but instead he expanded the ever-widening fracture between the blacks and the whites. Each time there has been difficulty in America, Obama has tossed in the race card to attempt to gain victory for himself. Instead of rising above racism, he slithered under it and provoked more intolerance and discrimination. That in itself is a political sham because he is not an African-American. Bearing in mind that he is half-white, which he rejects; the rest of him being mostly Arab, which he tries to hide, but is exposed by his Arabic surname and Arabic first and middle name. Only a small part of him is African Black from his Luo grandmother, which he pretends he is exclusive.

He is not an African-American and has not a single ancestor that was a slave, or descendants of slaves. His Arab ancestors, however, were slave owners. Slave trading was the main Arab business in East Africa until the British ended it. And he was raised in an Arab school and taught the Arab way of life and knows nothing about how to be an American.

The media has never vetted Obama. As an example, House of Representative member, Steve Scalise, Majority Whip, from the State of Louisiana, and of all things, a Republican - what a shame, and worst of all, when he was campaigning, he spoke in front of an organization known as the White Supremacists – vile constituents, yes – but voters nevertheless. And did the media have a heyday with him.

Then we have Senator Robert Byrd, a Southern Democrat, mind you, who was a member of the Ku Klux Klan. Of course, when Bill Clinton eulogized him at his funeral, Clinton said Byrd just did what any "smart Democrat" would do under the circumstances to get elected, "he joined the Klan." Now, what do you suppose Clinton did to get elected? Well, you could read my books called *The Lyin Kings* or *Sell Your Soul* to get the answer to that question.

Meanwhile, Obama speaks to vile constituents all of the time. And his number one vile de facto vice president, Al Sharpton, visits the White House nearly daily. They both speak to racist groups like the NAACP and the Congressional Black Caucus routinely. Apparently being racist only matters if you are going after Republicans. You are not a racist if you are a Democrat.

You can pretty much say that Obama has destroyed the Clinton political machine and destroyed any chance that Hillary Clinton might have had of winning as President, or any Democrat for that matter. And he has gotten rid of the Kennedys that trolled Washington looking for booze and women. He single-handedly got rid of the Democratic Party. In two election cycles, the Democrats had picked up 14 Senate seats and 52 House seats and the press was touting the death of the Conservative and Republican Parties. In one year, Obama gave the House and Senate back to the Republicans.

Not to mention, Obama with his great leadership has generated the largest sale of arms and ammunition this country has ever seen. Citizens have provided a stimulus to the sporting goods industry where other industries in this country have failed.

Obama has more than another year left to finish his agenda. He has not quite bankrupted the United States, but it is in his agenda to do so. The budget he recently proposed was for four trillion dollars. If Congress does not repeal the Affordable Care Act, just the taxes and money necessary to fund the program will bankrupt the nation. When you have to have the Government pay subsidies to the people so they can pay the premiums for their insurance, it is not affordable, is it? Something is wrong with this picture. The Affordable Care Act is a tax and is designed to keep taxing you – after President Obama finishes his term, of course.

Then Matt Patterson at Newsweek finally spoke out about Obama when the following was printed:

"By Matt Patterson (Newsweek Columnist - Opinion Writer)

'Years from now, historians may regard the 2008 election of Barack Obama as an inscrutable and disturbing phenomenon, the result of a baffling breed of mass hysteria akin perhaps to the witch craze of the Middle Ages. How, they will wonder, did a man so devoid of professional accomplishment beguile so many into thinking he could manage the world's largest economy, direct the world's most powerful military, execute the world's most consequential job?

'Imagine a future historian examining Obama's pre-presidential life: ushered into and through the Ivy League, despite unremarkable grades and test scores along the way; a cushy non-job as a "community organizer;" a brief career as a state legislator devoid of legislative achievement (and in fact nearly devoid of his attention, less often did he vote "present"); and finally an unaccomplished single term in the United States Senate, the entirety of which was devoted to his presidential ambitions.

'He left no academic legacy in academia, authored no signature legislation as a legislator. And then there is the matter of his troubling associations: the white-hating, America-loathing preacher who for decades served as Obama's "spiritual mentor;" a real-life, actual terrorist who served as Obama's colleague and political sponsor. It is easy to imagine a future historian looking at it all and asking: how on Earth was such a man elected president? There is no evidence that he ever attended or worked for any university or that he ever sat for the Illinois bar. We have no documentation for any of his claims. He may well be the greatest hoax in history.

'Not content to wait for history, the incomparable Norman Podhoretz addressed the question recently in the Wall Street Journal: To be sure, no white candidate who had close associations with an outspoken hater of America like Jeremiah Wright and an unrepentant terrorist like Bill Ayers, would have lasted a single day. But because Mr. Obama was black, and therefore entitled in the eyes of liberal Dems to have hung out with protesters against various American injustices, even if they were 'a bit' extreme, he was given a pass. Let that sink in: Obama was given a pass - held to a lower standard because of the color of his skin.

'Podhoretz continues: And in any case, what did such ancient history matter when he was also so articulate and elegant and (as he himself had said) "non-threatening," all of which gave him a fighting chance to become the first black president and thereby to lay the curse of racism to rest?

'Podhoretz puts his finger, I think, on the animating pulse of the Obama phenomenon - affirmative action. Not in the legal sense, of course. But certainly in the motivating sentiment behind all affirmative action laws and regulations, which are designed primarily to make white people, and especially white liberals, feel good about themselves.

'Unfortunately, minorities often suffer so that whites can pat themselves on the back. Liberals routinely admit minorities to schools for which they are not qualified, yet take no responsibility for the inevitable poor performance and high drop-out rates which follow. Liberals don't care if these minority students fail; liberals aren't around to witness the emotional devastation and deflated self-esteem resulting from the racist policy that is affirmative action. Yes, racist. Holding someone to a separate standard merely because of the color of his skin - that's affirmative action in a nutshell, and if that isn't racism, then nothing is.

'And that is what America did to Obama. True, Obama himself was never troubled by his lack of achievements, but why would he be? As many have noted, Obama was told he was good enough for Columbia despite undistinguished grades at Occidental; he was told he was good enough for the US Senate despite a mediocre record in Illinois. He was told he was good enough to be president despite no record at all in the Senate. All his life, every step of the way, Obama was told he was good enough for the next step, in spite of ample evidence to the contrary.

'What could this breed if not the sort of empty narcissism on display every time Obama speaks? In 2008, many who agreed that he lacked executive qualifications nonetheless raved about Obama's oratory skills, intellect, and cool character. Those people - conservatives included - ought now to be deeply embarrassed.

'The man thinks and speaks in the hoariest of clichés and that's when he has his Teleprompters in front of him; when the prompter is absent he can barely think or speak at all. Not one original idea has ever issued from his mouth - it's all warmed-over Marxism of the kind that has failed over and over again for 100 years. (An example is his 2012 campaign speeches which are almost word for word his 2008 speeches)

'And what about his character? Obama is constantly blaming anything and everything else for his troubles. Bush did it; it was bad luck; I inherited this mess. Remember, he wanted the job, campaigned for the task. It is embarrassing to see a president so willing to advertise his own powerless-ness, so comfortable with his own incompetence. (The other day he actually came out and said no one could have done anything to get our economy and country back on track). But really, what were we to expect? The man has never been responsible for anything, so how do we expect him to act responsibly?

'In short: our president is a small-minded man, with neither the temperament nor the intellect to handle his job. When you understand that, and only when you understand that, will the current erosion of liberty and prosperity make sense. It could not have gone otherwise with such an impostor in the Oval Office."

Just in 2015, your taxes quietly went up because of the Democrats. Not one single Republican voted to raise the taxes, only the Democrats. On January 1, 2015,

Medicare tax went from 1.45% to 2.35%
Top Income tax bracket went from 35% to 39.6%
Top Income payroll tax went from 37.4% to 52.2%
Capital Gains tax went from 15% to 28%
Dividend tax went from 15% to 39.6%
Estate tax went from 0% to 55%
A 3.5% Real Estate transaction tax was added.

These taxes were all passed in The Affordable Care Act aka Obamacare. Wait until 2016 when even more taxes will apply.

It has always been Obama and Hillary Clinton's intention to have one global leader with one of them as the head. If that happens, it is good bye America as we know it; good bye America's Constitution; good bye freedom; bankruptcy for America – the end of America.

Americans are beginning to wake up to what is going on in this country and has elected a Republican Congress, but are they strong enough to do what needs to be done? Will Congress impeach this President? Getting rid of this President is the only way Congress will be able to get anything done because this President will veto any Bill that comes to his desk. Will they repeal Obamacare? Will they get rid of the members of Congress that are card-carrying Communists? There are eighty of them that we know about. They have no place in our government. Nor do members of the New Black Panther Party or the Muslim Brotherhood. Will they take care of the immigration problem? Will they reform our welfare problems? Will they take care of our Social Security and Medicare problems?

Well, time has gone by and so far they have done nothing. They have taken the attitude that if they do Obama will veto it anyway.

After six years in office, Obama still cannot say the words "Islamic and Terrorists" in the same sentence. Every act of terrorism in the United States in the past thirty years has been carried out by Islamic Terrorists and the man still refuses to say the words. Where does that leave him? Playing golf or going on another vacation? The only thing Obama has to show for his six years in office is his 2009 Nobel Peace Prize, which no one in America believes he earned. Even in his acceptance speech Obama indicated he was not sure what he had done to earn it.

Now the former Nobel secretary has revealed in his Memoir that the decision to award the Nobel Peace Prize to President Barack Obama in 2009 was one he regretted. He said he felt Obama's failed to live up to the expectations that the prize held. The selection committee initially felt as though it would be a boost for the president. Since when is such a prize given as a boost and not as an earned prize?

After the U.S. had accused Assad's forces of using chemical weapons against Syrians in an attack on Damascus, although he says he had not made a decision yet, Obama was considering using military force against the regime. It was obvious to me that Obama would not make a decision until he flew to Oslo to receive his Nobel Peace Prize award.

And in 2015 Congress should be passing legislation on the Keystone Pipeline, which would provide twenty to 40,000 construction jobs and one hundred thousand indirect jobs and significantly impacts the economy. The U.S. opposition to the Pipeline from Energy Secretary Chu is "it would be desirable to have U.S. gas prices at European levels ($8-$10 gallons), so that alternative fuels would be more competitively priced, but it is not going to happen.

The Obama Administration came out with five sets of anti-coal regulations that are estimated to cost the United States the loss of over one million jobs. In addition, the EPA is zeroing in on anti-fracking regulations to control the utilization of the huge natural gas reserves (over a hundred years' worth) in the U.S. The far left contends that its opposition to the Keystone pipeline is because of possible leaks from the line." http://bit.ly/1XuAiUx

"The President delayed a decision on the Keystone pipeline until after the 2014 mid-term elections. It was because a large Democratic donor, Tom Steyer, pledged to donate over $50,000,000, to the Democrats if he did so.

'After the mid-term elections, the new Republican-led House of Representatives voted to build the pipeline, but the still Democrat-led Senate voted against it. The new Congress in January 2015 in both the Republican-led House and Senate has approved it, but the President will most likely veto it."

'The President is not ending his energy program with the Keystone pipeline. He has been pushing climate change since he has been in office. Even a small child knows there is nothing you can do to change the earth's climate. But Obama is using the Environmental Protection Agency to subvert existing environmental laws and the Constitution unless Congress and the Courts stop an attack that will weaken the business, industrial and energy sectors. It will put our lives at risk when there is not enough electricity to power our homes in various areas of the nation. The cost of electricity will, in the President's words, "skyrocket." http://bit.ly/1XDYWwC

"In the end, President Obama's veto was sustained because the highly public debate over the Keystone XL Pipeline meant that members of Congress had already considered the relevant electoral and ideological forces before the final passage vote. As a result, few members of either the House or the Senate had reason to switch their votes during the veto override attempt." http://www.washingtonpost.com/blogs/monkey-cage/wp/2015/03/05/the-senate-failed-to-override-obamas-veto-of-the-keystone-pipeline-heres-why/

Obama, a man that has no concept of what the Tea Party is, or what it stands for because he is truly not an American himself, said it was a fad and the members were racists even though many of the members are of color.

Obama once said the Constitution gets in the way of his doing what he needs to get done. But he has no intention of letting the Constitution stop his agenda. What he cannot do through Congress he does by Executive Fiat. If he does not like a law, he refuses to enforce it or changes it to suit himself. Despite what Obama has done to destroy America, he still won his second election with promises to grant amnesty to the illegal and publicly declaring support for same-sex marriages. He has already restated his pledge to fast-track his mission to change America fundamentally by expanding the power and scope of the Federal government more than he already has. The left enjoys his rebellious nature and the right sits back and shakes their head.

In his February 2015 State of the Union address, Obama did not rally the Democrats to work with the newly elected Republican Congress. Rather he preferred to throw jabs at the Republicans. And when Obama uses words like "accomplishments," his meanings are along the lines of socialist control. His goal is to transform America. Americans do not matter. It is not significant to him if his actions damage the economy or make America less safe, or even hurt more people than they help. "In the leftist mind, the impersonal collective is paramount." [David Limbaugh]

Barack Obama studied How to Create a Social State under Saul Alinsky.

There are eight levels of control that must be obtained before you can create a socialist state. The first is the most important.

1) Healthcare – Control healthcare and you control the people. Obama has accomplished this feat. He has lied to the people by telling them if you want to keep you doctor, you can. If you want to keep your insurance, you can. Your present insurance rates will not increase. Of course, that did not happen. No one was able to keep their doctor, no one was able to keep their insurance company, and many still do not have insurance because they cannot afford the rates. It was supposed to be affordable for everyone, but even when the government subsidized it, it is not affordable.

2) Poverty – Increase the poverty level as high as possible, poor people are easier to control and will not fight back if you are providing everything for them to live. 4.1% of the nation are on the welfare rolls. 45,753,078 are on food stamps. $131 Billion is spent annually by our government annually on welfare. We make it easy for people to fleece the system and not work.

3) Debt – Increase the debt to an unsustainable level. That way you can increase taxes, and this will produce more poverty. This has happened under Healthcare. The Supreme Court has held that Obamacare is a tax. It was designed to increase in huge increments

in 2016 when Obama goes out of office. Obamacare can be condensed into four sentences.

(a) To insure the uninsured, we first have to uninsure the insured.

(b) Next, we require the newly uninsured to be re-insured.

(c) To re-insure the newly uninsured, they are required to pay extra charges to be re-insured.

(d) The extra charges are required so that the original insured, who became uninsured, and then became re-insured, can pay enough extra so that the original uninsured can be insured, which will be free of charge to them.

This, ladies and gentlemen, is called "redistribution of wealth" ... or, by its more common name, "Socialism."

4) Gun Control – Remove the ability to defend themselves from the Government. That way you can create a police state. Obama has been steadily working on that since he has been in office. With all the riots in the different cities, if he can call martial law, he will call for the confiscation of all guns.

5) Welfare – Take control of every aspect of their lives (Food, Housing, and Income). This also falls under martial law as well as being on the welfare rolls.

6) Education – Take control of what people read and listen to – take control of what children learn in school. This has been going on in our schools for quite some time now. Text books have changed. I have three books published and in each book I have asked if you have read what your children are being taught in school? Your children are not allowed to pray in school any longer, but they are taught prayers of Islam. They are taught the Muslim culture, but not other cultures. When you were young, you trusted your teachers and you are trusting them now. You should not. You should take control of what your children are learning today.

7) Religion – Remove the belief in the God from the Government and schools. You have a right to take control of what your child is learning in school.

8) Class Warfare – Divide the people into the wealthy and the poor. This will cause more discontent, and it will be easier to take (Tax) the wealthy with the support of the poor. Obama is attempting to do this now. This is a socialist tactic. You keep hearing him talk

about taking from the rich and taxing the rich. It does not matter to him that the rich earned their money, and the money belongs to them. He does not say anything about giving up any of his own money.

Does any of this sound like what is happening to the United States at this time?

Alinsky merely simplified Vladimir Lenin's original scheme for world conquest by communism, under Russian rule. Stalin described his converts as "Useful Idiots." The Useful Idiots have destroyed every nation in which they have seized power and control. It is presently happening at an alarming rate in the United States.

If people can read this and still say everything is just fine, they are "useful idiots." Obama said, "Ordinary men and women are too small-minded to govern their own affairs."

"It is difficult to free fools from the chains they revere." Stephen King once said, "we fool ourselves so much we could do it for a living."

Obama does not care about the national debt. He professes to have cut the debt, and it has gone down slightly, but it is still substantially higher than George W. Bush's average annual deficit. And it is projected to skyrocket during the next ten years and Obama knows it. Obama also knows our entitlements will consume our entire budget within fifteen years, but he impedes any action that is taken to remedy the problem.

For some reason, Obama, and his minions are doing everything they can to drive this country into bankruptcy or further. Our founders in writing our Constitution were trying to prevent this very action.

For the first time in America's history, our sovereign debt (Government debt, especially that held in bonds denominated in foreign currencies) was downgraded from a Triple A rating under Obama's reign.

Under Obama, our budget deficit to fund government operations for the year (10% of GDP) has been the highest since World War II.

And under Obama, our Federal debt is highest since just after World War II. (The gross amount of debt outstanding issued by the US Treasury-$18 Trillion +). (67% of GDP).

Again, under Obama's reign, Federal Spending (25% of GDP).

Under Obama's watch, long-term unemployment (45.9% of total) is the highest since the 1930s. According to a report by Urban.Org, the long-term unemployed tend to be less educated and are more likely to be non-white, unmarried, disabled, and impoverished. They also tend to have worked previously in the construction industry and construction occupations. Also, it is found that the longer someone spends being unemployed, the harder it becomes to find a new job.

Since Obama's time in office, only 49% of U.S. taxpayers owed and are paying income tax. Federal employees are among the highest-paid employees in the country; however, according to the Internal Revenue Service, nearly 312,000 Federal workers and retirees owed more than $3.5 billion in back taxes as of Sept. 30, 2011.

George Soros, who is fond of saying the wealthy should pay more, a billionaire himself, according to Blomberg, probably owes the IRS in the ballpark of $7 Billion in tax revenue. That could make a huge dent in our deficit. http://bit.ly/1NkHO9E Being a close friend of the President, naturally he will not be paying the IRS any time soon.

The same goes for Al Sharpton, who, according to the New York Post, owes $4.7 Million in back taxes. Sharpton is a regular visitor to the White House, so do you think he will be pressed to pay any taxes?

While Obama has been in office, 47% of the population is receiving one or more Federal benefits payments, the highest in American history.

Obama is the fourth President to violate the War Powers Act. The United States Congress passed the War Powers Act in 1973, when it was believed that several previous presidents, including John F. Kennedy, Lyndon Johnson and Richard Nixon (who was still the president at the time) exceeded their authority when they sent troops to Vietnam without congressional approval. The War Powers Act itself requires U.S. forces are to be withdrawn from foreign lands where they are involved in hostilities in sixty days unless Congress ratifies their deployment. Obama submitted a report to Congress that his administration was not in violation of the Act despite the fact that the 60-day deadline for congressional approval of the Libyan operations was past due. But, as usual, Congress caved and did nothing.

Obama is the first President that has been held in contempt of court for illegally obstructing oil drilling in the Gulf of Mexico. A New Orleans Judge ruled that the Obama Administration acted in contempt by continuing its deepwater drilling moratorium after the policy was struck down.

Does anyone know where the money went for those shovel-ready jobs? First, there was no such thing as a shovel-ready job. And the money did not go where it was supposed to go, or where it is supposed to go. It did go into the pockets of the politicians. Roads are bad, and bridges did need to be rebuilt in some areas. But the big unions did get the money and so did the politicians. When Obama signed the stimulus bill in 2009, he promised it would provide "help for those hardest hit by our economic crisis." The states hurt the most, the ones with more foreclosures, unemployment, and bankruptcy, got less money than richer states closer to power. Washington, D.C. got the most stimulus money: $7,602 per capita.

Rich Democrat donors also got payback. Well, you remember the "green" energy company, Solyndra, who defaulted on more than half a billion dollars of our money while Obama mega-donor George Kaiser finagled his interest ahead of ours. There were other beneficiaries of Obama's largesse for suspicious transactions, which include Larry Page and Sergey Brin for Tesla Motors, NRG Solar owners Warren Buffet and Steve Cohen, and Siga Tech owner Ronald Pearlman. All told, more than 75 percent of stimulus grants and money for such "businesses" found their way to big Obama supporters.

Even crony Capitalist, Al Gore, got his nose in the trough. His investment in Fisker Automotive scored a $528 million loan guarantee. Can you imagine the risks you could take if someone gave you $528 million that you were not personally on the hook to repay? Of course, all these businesses are in the tank, or on their way.

Obama is the first President to by-pass Congress and implement the Dream Act through executive fiat. And he is the first President to order a secret amnesty program that stopped the deportation of illegal immigrants across the U.S., including those with criminal convictions.

He also is the first President to demand a company hand-over $20 billion to one of his political appointees. He does not mind spending someone else's money. He demanded that BP Oil set up a slush fund of $20 billion to pay the damages for the oil spill. Some unfortunate words have been used like "Shakedown," and "Are we living in Cuba or

Venezuela?" And, "I thought we had laws in this country? Since when does the President of the United States arbitrarily get to decide how much money a privately owned company has to give the government? What happens if BP wouldn't go along? Would the CEO have woken up with a horse's head in his bed? Would Obama have seized his company Hugo Chavez style?"

Again, Obama is the first President to tell a CEO of a major corporation (GM) to resign. The Obama Administration asked Rick Wagoner. The Chairman and CEO of General Motors Corp., to step down and he agreed. The White House confirmed that Wagoner was leaving at the government's behest.

Additionally, he is the first President to terminate America's ability to put a man in space. Since Obama has been in office, he has presided over a dismantling of the space program and has conceded our global position as the unequivocal leader in space.

Under Obama's term, for the first time in American history, a law was signed by an auto-pen without Obama being present because Obama was in Europe on a week-long trip.

Another first example is that Obama threatened insurance companies if they publicly spoke out on the reasons for their rate increases. Obama's Secretary of Health, then Kathleen Sebelius, threatened to block insurers who criticize Obamacare out of the market by not approving their policies for sale. Sebelius said that insurers were attributing their rate increases to Obamacare, and she said there would be zero tolerance for this misinformation.

Equally important, Obama is the first President to tell a major manufacturing company in which state it was allowed to locate a factory. Boeing originally planned to build a 787 Dreamliner Factory in Washington State, but negotiations fell through with the International Association of Machinists when the Union refused to remove a long-term no-strike clause. The Union had struck four times since 1989 and had cost Boeing as much as $1.8 Billion in revenue. So who can blame Boeing for choosing South Carolina, a right-to-work state, where the workers are not forced to join a union? And then enters Obama's National Labor Relations Board, who files suit against Boeing in an attempt to force them to locate their factory in Washington State.

As of 2011, Obama was the first President to appoint forty-five Czars to replace elected officials in his office. Obama, by 2015, may have appointed as many as eighteen or twenty more. A Czar enjoys power and authority in the administration but does not have to undergo investigation or be subjected to vetting and confirmation by the Senate. These Czars exercise considerable control over government operations; even Senate controlled officers. You can refer to my book *Soundoff* for more details.

"Barack Obama's unconstitutional use of Czars to help run his administration have proven to be corrupt or radical (or sometimes both). No wonder the Obama administration fights tooth and nail to allow these Czars to operate in secret. Nevertheless, Judicial Watch managed to develop a comprehensive list of Czars as part of efforts to ensure government accountability." [Written by Judicial Watch]

Barack Obama is the first President to surround himself with radical left-wing anarchists. When Obama makes a controversial appointment, it has nothing to do with his lack of vetting. It is a pattern. The media might call it a series of errors, but do not be fooled. The Obama team nominates those who share their goal of profoundly changing America. They know exactly what they are doing.

Also, Obama is the first President to hide his birth, medical, educational and travel records. The Western Center for Journalism reported that Obama's legal team has now spent well over $1.4 million dollars blocking access to documents of which every American should have access. Can you think of any reason Obama would spend that much money to hide his records? Well, perhaps it is because these records will shed light on his citizenship and birth. Is it not strange that the United States can track one single cow, not in this country, but to Canada, that is carrying mad cow disease, yet no one can find Obama's records, or bothers to look for them? Why is it that even after six years Obama is still getting a pass from the media?

Here we have a President, who put millions of Americans into a mortgage crisis with thousands of dollars of lost equity.

We have a President releasing terrorists from Gitmo because they are Muslims, and he wants to make peace with all Arab nations; never mind that these terrorists have gone back out and committed terrorist acts again against America.

We have a President that if a black man is killed while robbing a convenience store, this President will memorialize him at his funeral and pay reparations to his parents for his life.

We have a President that if a white man or woman is killed by a black man he will go on vacation or play golf and not respond in kind.

We have a President that when a Mexican has a rap sheet for seven felony drug charges murders a white woman, the President decides to visit a State Prison. He talks to several prisoners imprisoned for drug charges because they remind him of his youth when he smoked pot and since they did not get a second chance and did not have the support structure he had when he was growing up, the President decides to release many prisoners that were in prison on drug charges, some of which were drug kingpins.

We have a President that makes education a priority in this country, but in a recent State of the Union address proposed to tax college savings plans for his new programs. This amounts to nothing more than confiscation through taxation.

Throughout America, police are seizing cash from innocent citizens without ever charging them with a crime. Bankers conspire with the IRS to seize the accounts of innocent citizens with no notification, no court order, and no charge of a crime.

On the more negative side, Obama is the first President to go on multiple "global apology tours." Each time Obama visited countries throughout the Middle East he criticizes America. He went to Egypt (he is no longer welcome there), Saudi Arabia, Turkey, and Iraq. He will not go to Israel, who is supposed to be our Ally. He told those countries that America has shown arrogance and was dismissive and derisive. Obama said that "on occasion America dictated to other nations."

Not surprisingly, we have Obama the spender, who is the first President to fly in a personal trainer from Chicago at least once a week at taxpayer expense. The Washington D.C. Yellow Pages has fifty-six entries under fitness trainers who can either walk or ride their bike to the White House. Why is it that Obama has to fly his fitness trainer in from Chicago a couple of times a week? Mr. and Mrs. Obama try to exercise at least an hour every day and the fitness trainer said he visits them two to four times a week.

Obama is the only President we have had to side with a foreign nation (Mexico) over one of the American fifty states (Mexico vs. Arizona).

And do you remember when Obama said our military men and women should pay for their own private insurance because they "volunteered to go to war and knew the consequences." Then he tells the members of the military that they were unpatriotic for balking at the last suggestion. http://bit.ly/1rE7c5B

In October 2011, Obama thought he would help out our economy and make it easier for homeowners to refinance their FHA mortgages through Fannie May and Freddie Mac. To dodge congressional opposition, Obama issued an Executive Order setting up new rules that posted larger losses than expected, sought $6 billion in additional aid.

In July 2011, Obama was before the National Council of La Raza. President Obama said when it came to bypassing Congress on immigration that the idea of "doing things" on his own was "very tempting."

In September 2011. Obama told the Congressional Hispanic Caucus that he would like to work his way around Congress.

In July 2011, at the time of the debt limit debate, Obama asked lawyers if there was a way to interpret the Fourteenth Amendment so as to get around Congress. Obama wanted to establish a "long-term extension of the Federal borrowing limit" on his own.

Libya war – In Article I, Section 8 (Powers of Congress) of the US Constitution, there is the phrase "To declare War…" But Obama said the U.S. actions in Libya did not amount to war, so he did not need the approval of Congress. And he ignored the War Powers Act.

Obama then decreed, through Kathleen Sebelius, Secretary of Health and Human Services, that church-affiliated institutions would have to cover free birth control for employees, even if that decree violated moral and ethical beliefs. A law professor at Princeton, said, "They pursue this agenda with a religious zeal because, in fact, the ideology in which abortion is a "right" and "sexual freedom" is a core value of their religion."

Once again, Obama was trying to bypass the Constitution that says "Congress shall make no law respecting an establishment of religion or prohibiting the free exercise thereof…."

It does not matter if you are a Democrat, a Republican, a conservative or a liberal. Surely at some point you have given some thought of the attitude, mindset or character of Barack Obama.

He gives anti-Christian statements;

   a. He is a Pro-Islam apologist;
   b. He is reluctant to support those fighting against ISIS;
   c. He fires any military commander that disagrees with him;
   d. He traded five Islamic terrorists for one military defector.

America has been asking whose side is Obama on?

As of 17 March 2014, following is a list of the commanding generals fired by Obama. Just think of their education and all of the years of service these men gave for their country; and to be fired by a community organizer.

Commanding Generals fired:

General John R. Allen-U.S. Marines Commander International Security Assistance Force [ISAF] (Nov 2012)
Major General Ralph Baker (2 Star)-U.S. Army Commander of the Combined Joint Task Force Horn in Africa (April 2013)
Major General Michael Carey (2 Star)-U.S. Air Force Commander of the 20th US Air Force in charge of 9,600 people and 450 Intercontinental Ballistic Missiles (Oct 2013)
Colonel James Christmas-U.S. Marines Commander 22nd Marine Expeditionary (July 2013)
Major General Peter Fuller-U.S. Army Commander in Afghanistan (May 2011)
Major General Charles M.M. Gurganus-U.S. Marine Corps Regional Commander of SW and I Marine Expeditionary Force in Afghanistan (Oct 2013)
General Carter F. Ham-U.S. Army African Command (Oct 2013)
Lieutenant General David H. Huntoon, Jr. (3 Star)-U.S. Army 58th Superintendent of the US Military Academy at West Point, NY (2013)
Command Sergeant Major Don B Jordan-U.S. Army 143rd Expeditionary Sustainment Command (suspended Oct 2013)
General James Mattis-U.S. Marines Chief of CentCom (May 2013)

Colonel Daren Margolin-U.S. Marine in charge of Quantico's Security Battalion (Oct 2013)

General Stanley McChrystal-U.S. Army Commander Afghanistan (June 2010)

General David D. McKiernan-U.S. Army Commander Afghanistan (2009)

General David Petraeus-Director of CIA from September 2011 to November 2012 & U.S. Army Commander International Security Assistance Force [ISAF] and Commander U.S. Forces Afghanistan [USFOR-A] (Nov 2012)

Brigadier General Bryan Roberts-U.S. Army Commander 2nd Brigade (May 2013)

Major General Gregg A. Sturdevant-U.S. Marine Corps Director of Strategic Planning and Policy for the U.S. Pacific Command & Commander of Aviation Wing at Camp Bastion, Afghanistan (Sept 2013)

Colonel Eric Tilley-U.S. Army Commander of Garrison Japan (Nov 2013)

Brigadier General Bryan Wampler-U.S. Army Commanding General of 143rd Expeditionary Sustainment Command of the 1st Theater Sustainment Command [TSC] (suspended Oct 2013)

Commanding Admirals fired:

Rear Admiral Charles Gaouette-U.S. Navy Commander John C. Stennis Carrier Strike Group Three (Oct 2012)

Vice Admiral Tim Giardina(3 Star, demoted to 2 Star)-U.S. Navy Deputy Commander of the US Strategic Command, Commander of the Submarine Group Trident, Submarine Group 9 and Submarine Group 10 (Oct 2013)

Naval Officers fired: (All in 2011)

Captain David Geisler-U.S. Navy Commander Task Force 53 in Bahrain (Oct 2011)

Commander Laredo Bell-U.S. Navy Commander Naval Support Activity Saratoga Springs, NY (Aug 2011)

Lieutenant Commander Kurt Boenisch-Executive Officer amphibious transport dock Ponce (Apr 2011)

Commander Nathan Borchers-U.S. Navy Commander destroyer *Stout* (Mar 2011)

Commander Robert Brown-U.S. Navy Commander Beachmaster Unit 2 Fort Story, VA (Aug 2011)

Commander Andrew Crowe-Executive Officer Navy Region Center Singapore (Apr 2011)

Captain Robert Gamberg-Executive Officer carrier *Dwight D. Eisenhower* (Jun 2011)

Captain Rex Guinn-U.S. Navy Commander Navy Legal Service office Japan (Feb 2011)

Commander Kevin Harms- U.S. Navy Commander Strike Fighter Squadron 137 aboard the aircraft carrier Abraham Lincoln (Mar 2011)

Lieutenant Commnder Martin Holguin-U.S. Navy Commander mine countermeasures *Fearless* (Oct 2011)

Captain Owen Honors-U.S. Navy Commander aircraft carrier *USS Enterprise* (Jan 2011)

Captain Donald Hornbeck-U.S. Navy Commander Destroyer Squadron 1 San Diego (Apr 2011)

Rear Admiral Ron Horton-U.S. Navy Commander Logistics Group, Western Pacific (Mar 2011)

Commander Etta Jones-U.S. Navy Commander amphibious transport dock Ponce (Apr 2011)

Commander Ralph Jones-Executive Officer amphibious transport dock *Green Bay* (Jul 2011)

Commander Jonathan Jackson-U.S. Navy Commander Electronic Attack Squadron 134, deployed aboard carrier Carl Vinson (Dec 2011)

Captain Eric Merrill-U.S. Navy Commander submarine *Emory S. Land* (Jul 2011)

Captain William Mosk-U.S. Navy Commander Naval Station Rota, U.S. Navy Commander

Naval Activities Spain (Apr 2011)

Commander Timothy Murphy-U.S. Navy Commander Electronic Attack Squadron 129 at Naval Air Station Whidbey Island, WA (Apr 2011)

Commander Joseph Nosse-U.S. Navy Commander ballistic-missile submarine Kentucky (Oct 2011)

Commander Mark Olson-U.S. Navy Commander destroyer *The Sullivans* FL (Sep 2011)

Commander John Pethel-Executive Officer amphibious transport dock New York (Dec 2011)

Commander Karl Pugh-U.S. Navy Commander Electronic Attack Squadron 141 Whidbey Island, WA (Jul 2011)

Commander Jason Strength-U.S. Navy Commander of Navy Recruiting District Nashville, TN (Jul 2011)

Captain Greg Thomas-U.S. Navy Commander Norfolk Naval Shipyard (May 2011)

Commander Mike Varney-U.S. Navy Commander attack submarine *Connecticut* (Jun 2011)

Commander Jay Wylie-U.S. Navy Commander destroyer *Momsen* (Apr 2011)

Naval Officers fired: (All in 2012):

Commander Alan C. Aber-Executive Officer Helicopter Maritime Strike Squadron

Commander Derick Armstrong- U.S. Navy Commander missile destroyer *USS The Sullivans* (May 2012)

Commander Martin Arriola- U.S. Navy Commander destroyer *USS Porter* (Aug 2012)

Captain Antonio Cardoso- U.S. Navy Commander Training Support Center San Diego (Sep 2012)

Captain James Cobell- U.S. Navy Commander Oceana Naval Air Station's Fleet Readiness Center Mid-Atlantic (Sep 2012)

Captain Joseph E. Darlak- U.S. Navy Commander frigate *USS Vandegrift* (Nov 2012)

Captain Daniel Dusek-U.S. Navy Commander USS Bonhomme Commander David Faught-Executive Officer destroyer *Chung-Hoon* (Sep 2012)

Commander Franklin Fernandez- U.S. Navy Commander Naval Mobile Construction Battalion 24 (Aug 2012)

Commander Ray Hartman- U.S. Navy Commander Amphibious dock-landing ship *Fort McHenry* (Nov 2012)

Commander Shelly Hakspiel-Executive Officer Navy Drug Screening Lab San Diego (May 2012)

Commander Jon Haydel- U.S. Navy Commander *USS San Diego* (Mar 2012)

Commander Diego Hernandez- U.S. Navy Commander ballistic-missile submarine *USS Wyoming* (Feb 2012)

Commander Lee Hoey- U.S. Navy Commander Drug Screening Laboratory, San Diego (May 2012)

Commander Ivan Jimenez-Executive Officer frigate *Vandegrift* (Nov 2012)

Commander Dennis Klein- U.S. Navy Commander submarine *USS Columbia* (May 2012)

Captain Chuck Litchfield- U.S. Navy Commander assault ship *USS Essex* (Jun 2012)

Captain Marcia Kim Lyons- U.S. Navy Commander Naval Health Clinic New England (Apr 2012)

Captain Robert Marin- U.S. Navy Commander cruiser *USS Cowpens* (Feb 2012)

Captain Sean McDonell- U.S. Navy Commander Seabee reserve unit Naval Mobile Construction Battalion 14 FL (Nov 2012)

Commander Corrine Parker- U.S. Navy Commander Fleet Logistics Support Squadron 1 (Apr 2012)

Captain Liza Raimondo- U.S. Navy Commander Naval Health Clinic Patuxent River, MD (Jun 2012)

Captain Jeffrey Riedel- Program manager, Littoral Combat Ship program (Jan 2012)

Commander Sara Santoski- U.S. Navy Commander Helicopter Mine Countermeasures Squadron 15 (Sep 2012)

Commander Kyle G. Strudthoff-Executive Officer Helicopter Sea Combat Squadron 25 (Sep 2012)

Commander Sheryl Tannahill- U.S. Navy Commander Navy Operational Support Center [NOSC] Nashville, TN (Sep 2012)

Commander Michael Ward- U.S. Navy Commander submarine USS Pittsburgh (Aug 2012

Captain Michael Wiegand- U.S. Navy Commander Southwest Regional Maintenance Center (Nov 2012)

Captain Ted Williams- U.S. Navy Commander amphibious command ship *Mount Whitney* (Nov 2012)

Commander Jeffrey Wissel- U.S. Navy Commander of Fleet Air Reconnaissance Squadron 1 (Feb 2012)

Naval Officers fired: (All in 2013):

Lieutenant Commander Lauren Allen-Executive Officer submarine Jacksonville (Feb 2013)

Reserve Captain Jay Bowman-U.S. Navy Commander Navy Operational Support Center [NOSC] Fort Dix, NJ (Mar 2013)

Captain William Cogar-U.S. Navy Commander hospital ship Mercy's medical treatment facility (Sept 2013)

Commander Steve Fuller-Executive Officer frigate *Kauffman* (Mar 2013)

Captain Shawn Hendricks-Program Manager for naval enterprise IT networks (June 2013)

Captain David Hunter-U.S. Navy Commander of Maritime Expeditionary Security Squadron 12 & Coastal Riverine Group 2 (Feb 2013)

Captain Eric Johnson-U.S. Navy Chief of Military Entrance Processing Command at Great Lakes Naval Training Center, IL (2013)

Captain Devon Jones-U.S. Navy Commander Naval Air Facility El Centro, CA (July 2013)

Captain Kevin Knoop-U.S. Navy Commander hospital ship Comfort's medical treatment facility (Aug 2013)

Lieutenant Commander Jack O'Neill-U.S. Navy Commander Operational Support Center Rock Island, IL (Mar 2013)

Commander Allen Maestas-Executive Officer Beachmaster Unit 1 (May 2013)

Commander Luis Molina-U.S. Navy Commander submarine *Pasadena* (Jan 2013)

Commander James Pickens-Executive Officer frigate *Gary* (Feb 2013)

Lieutenant Commander Mark Rice-U.S. Navy Commander Mine Countermeasures ship *Guardian* (Apr 2013)

Commander Michael Runkle-U.S. Navy Commander of Mobile Diving and Salvage Unit 2 (May 2013)

Commander Jason Stapleton-Executive Office Patrol Squadron 4 in Hawaii (Mar 2013)
Commander Nathan Sukols-U.S. Navy Commander submarine *Jacksonville* (Feb 2013)
Lieutenant Daniel Tyler-Executive Officer Mine Countermeasures ship *Guardian* (Apr 2013)
Commander Edward White-U.S. Navy Commander Strike Fighter Squadron 106 (Aug 2013)
Captain Jeffrey Winter-U.S. Navy Commander of Carrier Air Wing 17 (Sept 2013)
Commander Thomas Winter-U.S. Navy Commander submarine *Montpelier* (Jan 2013)
Commander Corey Wofford- U.S. Navy Commander frigate *Kauffman* (Feb 2013)

Retired Army Lt. Gen. William G. "Jerry" Boykin, founding member of Delta Force and later Deputy Undersecretary of Defense for Intelligence under President George W. Bush said, "I believe there is a purging of the military. The problem is worse than we have ever seen." "Morale is at an unprecedented low."

Retired Navy Capt. Joseph John, a Naval Academy graduate who served three tours of duty in Vietnam, served as an al-Qaida expert for the FBI, and was a commanding officer with SEALs embedded on special operations said, "The "bigger picture" is that "the U.S. armed forces have been under relentless attack by the occupant of the Oval Office for five years."

Ret. Army Maj. Gen. Paul E. Vallely commented, "Obama seeks to "seize control over national security" and, bypassing Congress, singlehandedly weaken the U.S. military. Obama is purging the military by firing top-level commanders and that his ultimate goal is to "destroy U.S. military superiority" to the "advantage of our global enemies."

Retired Army Maj. Gen. Patrick Brady, recipient of the U.S. military's highest decoration, the Medal of Honor added, "There is no doubt [Obama] is intent on emasculating the military and will fire anyone who disagrees with him" over such issues as "homosexuals, women in foxholes, the Obama sequester."

J.D. Gordon, a retired Navy commander and a former Pentagon spokesman in the Office of the Secretary of Defense said, "Obama administration is rushing to unload senior officers whom he believes have become "political pawns" dismissed for questionable reasons."

It was Retired Army Maj. Gen. Patrick Brady, recipient of the U.S. military's highest decoration, the Medal of Honor who said "Just when you thought the leadership of this government could not get any worse, it does." "Never in history has an administration spawned another scandal to cover the current one."

And the Coast Guard Reserve speaking on condition of anonymity said, "I spend most of my 'drills' doing online training on things like 'diversity' and 'preventing sexual harassment' these days." "It's becoming a joke. This country is in trouble."

Retired Air Force pilot Lt. Col. Robert "Buzz" Patterson, senior military aide to President Bill Clinton, also asserts that Obama's national security policies are weakening the military and endangering the country's safety.

It is unknown why dozens of high-ranking military officers have been dismissed from their positions in the past few years during a time of peace. Is it because Obama is shaping his own personal military power through FEMA? Or was it only because these officers did not have the same vision for America?

In my book *The Lyin Kings* I wrote about FEMA's Concentration Camps and 600 million rounds of hollow point bullets, but I just recently read where the use of guillotines for "governmental purposes" was lobbied for and passed in the U.S. Congress. The information received is that 15,000 are currently stored in Georgia and 15,000 in Montana. What does the Government need with 30,000 guillotines?

Have you read this Bible verse? "And I saw thrones, and they sat upon them, and judgment was given unto them: and I saw the souls of them that were beheaded for the witness of Jesus, and for the word of God, and which had not worshipped the beast, neither his image, neither had received his mark upon their foreheads, or in their hands; and they lived and reigned with Christ a thousand years. – Revelations 20:4."

Obama has always seen himself as more of a world ruler than as the President of the United States. No other President has ever gone to another country and apologized for the United States, the greatest country in the world.

If you listened to his apology speech in Germany in 2009, you know he has something against Israel. If you believe him to be a Muslim, you know he has something against Israel. If you believe his father was a

Muslim, and he was brought up in Indonesia and went to a Muslim school, you know he has something against Israel.

It would have been nice if Obama had apologized to Israel for his remarks in Germany. It would have been nice if Obama had apologized to Israel for the remarks that he made to French President Nicolas Sarkozy when he and Obama were overheard talking before an open microphone about Israeli Prime Minister Benjamin Netanyahu. At a G20 summit in 2011 Sarkozy said, "I cannot bear Netanyahu, he's a liar," and Obama responded, "You're fed up with him, but I have to deal with him even more often than you," Obama replied, according to the French interpreter.

Instead, Obama calls Sandra Fluke and tells her how proud of her he is that she testified before the House Democrats in favor of Obama's contraception mandate in the healthcare law. Obama called to offer Fluke support and said her parents should be proud of her.

Fluke became well-known after conservative talk show host Rush Limbaugh called her a "slut" and a "prostitute" for wanting people to pay for her contraception.

In my book *The Lyin Kings*, I exposed both Hillary Clinton and Barack Obama as members of the Illuminati. You can easily Google "Illuminati" on the internet, and it lists both Clinton and Obama as members, as well as numerous movie stars. When Obama throws parties at the White House, the movie stars in attendance are all Illuminati members. They greet each other with various secret Illuminati signals. Below is a photograph of Obama giving an Illuminati signal to another member.

Dylann Storm Roof, a 21-year-old white man, went to an African-American church in Charleston, South Carolina with the intent to kill, and did kill nine people in the congregation.

"According to a childhood friend, Roof went on a rant about the shooting of Trayvon Martin and the 2015 Baltimore protests that were sparked by the death of Freddie Gray while Gray was in police custody. He also often claimed that "blacks were taking over the world." Roof reportedly told friends and neighbors of his plans to kill people, including a plot to attack the College of Charleston, but his claims were not taken seriously.

'One of the friends who briefly hid Roof's gun away from him said, "I don't think the church was his primary target because he told us he was going to the school. But I think he couldn't get into the school because of the security ... so I think he just settled for the church." An African-American friend of his said that he never witnessed Roof expressing any racial prejudice, but also said that a week before the shooting, Roof had confided in him that he would commit a shooting at the college." http://bit.ly/1OP9AkX

But Obama, who never gives up an opportunity to give a speech, or incite racism even more, jumped in the arena and volunteered to memorialize each of the nine victims.

Of course, believing you should never let a good crisis go to waste, he could not just let his speech be about the victims and their families. He had to speak about gun violence, racial inequality, a broken criminal justice system, how to make a better community, how we shouldn't slip into a comfortable silence again, and to settle for symbolic gestures without following up with the hard work of more lasting change is how we lose our way. He called the confederate flag a symbol of "systemic oppression and racial subjugation," and called for the South to "take down that flag."

What is important to note is (1) if a 21-year-old black youth entered a white church and killed nine white people, would this have even been reported in the news, let alone would the president and vice president and Congress have attended the funeral? (2) It has been reported that the Department of Justice is paying the families of these victims $29 Million in reparations. That comes to about $3½ Million for each family. Why are they being paid by our government for their loss? Is it so that they won't start a protest? Now blacks are yelling they should be paid because they are descendants of slaves.

The truth of it all is that if instead of enacting more gun controls, South Carolina had repealed the prohibition against concealed carrying weapons in churches, these lives could perhaps have been saved. South Carolina law, Title 23, Chapter 31(8) prohibits the carrying of lawfully concealed firearms in – (8) church or other established religious sanctuary unless express permission is given by the appropriate church official or governing body.

Mike Gallagher, An American radio host and conservative political commentator, and the host of The Mike Gallagher Show, had this to say about Barack Obama.

"Many listeners have asked about the, "Obama: It Was You," essay that someone sent me. Here it is:

President Obama: This is why you didn't go to France to show solidarity against the Muslim terrorists:

It was you who spoke these words at an Islamic dinner - "I am one of you."

It was you who on ABC News referenced - "My Muslim faith."

It was you who gave $100 million in U.S. taxpayer funds to re-build foreign mosques.

It was you who wrote that in the event of a conflict -"I will stand with the Muslims."

It was you who assured the Egyptian Foreign Minister that - "I am a Muslim."

It was you who bowed in submission before the Saudi King.

It was you who sat for 20 years in a Liberation Theology Church condemning Christianity and professing Marxism.

It was you who exempted Muslims from penalties under Obamacare that the rest of us have to pay.

It was you who purposefully omitted - "endowed by our Creator" - from your recitation of The Declaration of Independence.

It was you who mocked the Bible and Jesus Christ's Sermon on the Mount while repeatedly referring to the 'Holy' Quran.

It was you who traveled the Islamic world denigrating the United States of America.

It was you who instantly threw the support of your administration behind the building of the Ground Zero Victory mosque overlooking the crater of the World Trade Center.

It was you who refused to attend the National Prayer Breakfast, but hastened to host an Islamic prayer breakfast at the White House.

It was you who ordered Georgetown Univ. and Notre Dame to shroud all vestiges of Jesus Christ before you would agree to go there to speak, but in contrast, you have never requested that the mosques you have visited adjust their decor.

It was you who appointed anti-Christian fanatics to your Czar Corps.

It was you who appointed rabid Islamists to Homeland Security.

It was you who said that NASA's "foremost mission" was an outreach to Muslim communities.

It was you who as an Illinois Senator was the only individual who would speak in favor of infanticide.

It was you who were the first President not to give a Christmas Greeting from the White House, and went so far as to hang photos of Chairman Mao on the White House tree.

It was you who curtailed the military tribunals of all Islamic terrorists.

It was you who refused to condemn the Ft. Hood killer as an Islamic terrorist.

It is you who has refused to speak-out concerning the horrific executions of women throughout the Muslim culture, but yet, have submitted Arizona to the UN for investigation of hypothetical human-rights abuses.

It was you who when queried in India refused to acknowledge the true extent of radical global Jihadists, and instead profusely praised Islam in a country that is 82% Hindu and the victim of numerous Islamic terrorists' assaults.

It was you who funneled $900 Million in U.S. taxpayer dollars to Hamas.

It was you who ordered the USPS to honor the Muslim holiday with a new commemorative stamp.

It was you who directed our UK Embassy to conduct outreach to help "empower" the British Muslim community.

It was you who embraced the fanatical Muslim Brotherhood in your quest to overthrow the Egyptian President, Hosni Mubarak.

It was you who funded mandatory Arabic language and culture studies in Grammar schools across our country.

It is you who follows the Muslim custom of not wearing any form of jewelry during Ramadan.

It is you who departs for Hawaii over the Christmas season so as to avoid past criticism for not participating in seasonal White House religious events.

It was you who was uncharacteristically quick to join the chorus of the Muslim Brotherhood to depose Egypt's Hosni Mubarak, formerly America's strongest ally in North Africa; but, remain muted in your non-response to the Brotherhood led slaughter of Egyptian Christians.

It was you who appointed your chief adviser, Valerie Jarrett, an Iranian, who is a member of the Muslim Sisterhood, an off-shoot of the Muslim Brotherhood."

IV

NEW BLACK PANTHERS
AND RACISM

" I look to a day when people will not be judged by the color of their skin, but by the content of their character." Martin Luther King, Jr.

The New Black Panthers have been around for quite some time, and Eric Holder was not about to prosecute them when he was in office, although Malik Shabazz and his group should have been investigated as domestic terrorists.

The Black Panthers (not the same as "The New Black Panthers") believed that the Federal Government owed them.

Their 1966 Platform read as follows:

Focusing on the 1972 Platform, everything the Black Panthers would like, they want for free. They say nothing about working, or what they will do in return. They just believe they are entitled to free stuff from the government. And most of what the asked for, they received.

1. We want freedom. We want power to determine the destiny of our Black and oppressed communities. We believe that Black and oppressed people will not be free until we are able

to determine our destinies in our own communities ourselves, by fully controlling all the institutions which exist in our communities.

2. We want full employment for our people. We believe that the Federal government is responsible and obligated to give every person employment or a guaranteed income. We believe that if the American businessmen will not give full employment, then the technology and means of production should be taken from the businessmen and placed in the community so that the people of the community can organize and employ all of its people and give a high standard of living

3. We want an end to the robbery by the white man of our Black Community. "We believe that this racist government has robbed us and now we are demanding the overdue debt of forty acres and two mules. Forty acres and two mules was promised 100 years ago as restitution for slave labor and mass murder of black people. We will accept the payment as currency which will be distributed to our many communities. The Germans are now aiding the Jews in Israel for the genocide of the Jewish people. The Germans murdered six million Jews. The American racist has taken part in the slaughter of over twenty million black people; therefore, we feel that this is a modest demand that we make."

Their 1972 Platform reads as follows:

3. We want an end to the robbery by the capitalist of our Black and oppressed communities. "We believe that this racist government has robbed us and now we are demanding the overdue debt of forty acres and two mules. Forty acres and two mules were promised 100 years ago as restitution for slave labor and mass murder of Black people. We will accept the payment in currency which will be distributed to our many communities. The American racist has taken part in the slaughter of over fifty million Black people. Therefore, we feel this is a modest demand that we make."

4. We want decent housing, fit for the shelter of human beings. We believe that if the landlords will not give decent housing to

our Black and oppressed communities, then the housing and the land should be made into cooperatives so that the people in our communities, with government aid, can build and make decent housing and the land should be made into cooperatives so that the people in our communities, with government aid, can build and make decent housing for the people.

5. We want education for our people that exposes the true nature of this decadent American society. We want education that teaches us our true history and our role in the present-day society. We believe in an educational system that will give to our people a knowledge of self. If you do not have knowledge of yourself and your position in the society and the world, then you will have little chance to know anything else.

6. We want completely free health care for all Black and oppressed people. We believe that the government must provide, free of charge, for the people, health facilities which will not only treat our illnesses, most of which have come about as a result of our oppression, but which will also develop preventative medical programs to guarantee our future survival. We believe that mass health education and research programs must be developed to give all Black and oppressed people access to advanced scientific and medical information, so we may provide ourselves with proper medical attention and care.

7. We want an immediate end to police brutality and murder of Black people, other people of color, all oppressed people inside the United States. We believe that the racist and fascist government of the United States uses its domestic enforcement agencies to carry out its program of oppression against Black people, other people of color and poor people inside the United States. We believe it is our right, therefore, to defend ourselves against such armed forces, and that all Black and oppressed people should be armed for self-defense of our homes and communities against these fascist police forces.

8. We want an immediate end to all wars of aggression. We believe that the various conflicts which exist around the world stem directly from the aggressive desires of the U.S. ruling circle and government to force its domination upon the oppressed

people of the world. We believe that if the U.S. government or its lackeys do not cease these aggressive wars that it is the right of the people to defend themselves by any means necessary against their aggressors.

9. We want freedom for all Black and poor oppressed people now held in U.S. Federal, state, county, city and military prisons and jails. We want trials by a jury of peers for all persons charged with so-called crimes under the laws of this country. We believe that the many Black and poor oppressed people now held in U.S. prisons and jails have not received fair and impartial trials under a racist and fascist judicial system and should be free from incarceration. We believe in the ultimate elimination of all wretched, inhuman penal institutions, because the masses of men and women imprisoned inside the United States or by the U.S. military are the victims of oppressive conditions which are the real cause of their imprisonment. We believe that when persons are brought to trial that they must be guaranteed, by the United States, juries of their peers, attorneys of their choice and freedom from imprisonment while awaiting trials.

10. We want land, bread, housing, education, clothing, justice, peace and people's community control of modern technology.

When in the course of human events, it becomes necessary for one people to dissolve the political bands which have connected them with another, and to assume, among the powers of the earth, the separate and equal station to which the laws of nature and nature's God entitle them, a decent respect to the opinions of mankind requires that they should declare the causes which impel them to the separation.

We hold these truths to be self-evident, that all men are created equal; that they are endowed by their Creator with certain unalienable rights; that among these are life, liberty, and the pursuit of happiness. That, to secure these rights, governments are instituted among men, deriving their just powers from the consent of the governed; that, whenever any form of government becomes destructive of these ends, it is the right of the people to alter or to abolish it, and to institute a new government, laying its foundation on such principles, and organizing its powers in such form, as to them shall seem most likely to effect their safety and happiness. Prudence, indeed, will dictate that governments long established should not be changed for light and transient causes; and, accordingly, all experience hath shown that mankind are more disposed to suffer, while evils are sufferable, than to right themselves by abolishing the forms to which they are accustomed. But, when a long train of abuses and usurpations, pursuing invariably the same object, evinces a design to reduce them under absolute despotism, it is their right, it is their duty, to throw off such government, and to provide new guards for their future security.

*This document transcribed from The Black Panther Intercommunal News Service May 13, 1972: p. B of the supplement to the newspaper.

Black Panther Community Programs
Black Panther Party Community Programs
1966 - 1982

1. Alameda County Volunteer Bureau Work Site
2. Benefit Counseling
3. Black Student Alliance
4. Child Development Center
5. Consumer Education Classes
6. Community Facility Use
7. Community Health Classes
8. East Oakland CIL (Center for Independent Living) Branch
9. Community Pantry (Free Food Program)
10. Drug/Alcohol Abuse Awareness Program
11. Drama Classes
12. Disabled Persons Services/Transportation and Attendant
13. Drill Team
14. Employment Referral Service
15. Free Ambulance Program
16. Free Breakfast for Children Programs
17. Free Busing to Prisons Program
18. Free Clothing Program
19. Free Commissary for Prisoners Program
20. Free Dental Program
21. Free Employment Program
22. Free Food Program

23. Free Film Series
24. Free Furniture Program
25. Free Health Clinics
26. Free Housing Cooperative Program
27. Food Cooperative Program
28. Free Optometry Program
29. Community Forum
30. Free Pest Control Program
31. Free Plumbing and Maintenance Program
32. Free Shoe Program
33. GED Classes
34. Geriatric Health Center
35. GYN Clinic
36. Home SAFE Visits
37. Intercommunal Youth Institute (becomes OCS by 1975)
38. Junior and High School Tutorial Program
39. Legal Aid and Education
40. Legal Clinic/Workshops
41. Laney Experimental College Extension Site
42. Legal Referral Service(s)
43. Liberation Schools
44. Martial Arts Program
45. Nutrition Classes
46. Oakland Community Learning Center
47. Outreach Preventative Care
48. Program Development
49. Pediatric Clinic
50. police patrols
51. Seniors Against a Fearful Environment
52. SAFE Club
53. Sickle Cell Anemia Research Foundation
54. Son of Man Temple (becomes Community Forum by 1976)
55. Sports
56. Senior Switchboard
57. The Black Panther Newspaper
58. Teen Council
59. Teen Program

60. U.C. Berkeley Students Health Program
61. V.D. Preventative Screening & Counseling
62. Visiting Nurses Program
63. WIC (Women Infants, and Children) Program
64. Youth Diversion and Probation Site
65. Youth Training and Development

1 through 65 are all government programs given freely with few exceptions. Perhaps they were not back in 1966 and 1972.

I was unaware that the Black Panthers or New Black Panthers did not have freedom. We are all living in the United States of America, and they have as much freedom as the rest of us have. It seems to me they keep themselves bound by their own practices.

The New Black Panther Party was founded in 1989 in Dallas, TX and reorganized in 1998 under the leadership of the late Khallid Abdul Muhammad and has become one of the fastest growing Black Nationalist Organizations in the country. With a youthful leadership and contingency, the New Black Panther Party demands respect for its dedication to the progression of the black nation. The New Black Panther Party is a Revolutionary organization with an Afrikan-centered ideology

Despite its name, NBPP is not an official successor of the Black Panther Party. Members of the original Black Panther Party have insisted that the newer party is illegitimate and have firmly declared, "There is no new Black Panther Party".

Hashim Nzinga currently leads the New Black Panther Party. Malik Zulu Shabazz announced on an October 14, 2013, online radio broadcast that he was stepping down and that Nzinga, then national chief of staff, would replace him. Chawn Kweli, who, initially, served as NBPP national spokesman replaced Nzinga as national chief of staff. Still, the NBPP upholds Khalid Abdul Muhammad as the de facto father of the movement. When former Nation of Islam (NOI) minister Khalid Abdul Muhammad became the national chairman of the NBPP from the late 1990s until his death in 2001, He, Shabazz, and many other, breakaway members of the NOI followed Minister Muhammad to the NBPP during this period. Nzinga served as personal assistant to Minister Muhammad.

In April 2010, Malik Zulu Shabazz appointed French Black leader Stellio Capo Chichi as the representative of the movement in France. Capo Chichi has been holding the position of head of the francophone branch of NBPP.

Malik Zulu Shabazz, having shown his self to be little more than a "gangbanger in a suit" holds the distinction of being fired by former Washington, D.C. Mayor Marion Barry for being too radical. You have to be a real piece of work to be too radical to work for a mayor who was a confirmed drug addict and criminal—and Shabazz was. Someone once said Shabazz makes Al Sharpton almost look good. Shabazz praises those who riot, loot and burn and claims that these are the only tactics that will bring justice to the black community

When not in Baltimore inciting wayward young black men to loot, burn, and riot, Shabazz passes his time as the National President of Black Lawyers for Justice. Shabazz claims to advocate Anti-Zionism (including claims that Jews dominated the African slave trade and were behind the 9/11 attacks on the Twin Towers in New York, City) at http://bit.ly/1HCT7Oe

Speaking of Baltimore, their population is 68% black. Their police department is 68% black. Their fire department is 58% black. Their school district is 86% black. Their school teachers are 72% black. Their city council is 90% black. Their Mayor is black. Their Chief of Police is black. 54% of their population is on welfare. And they believe the whites are the reason they are living in poverty? Did I miss something here?

Poverty is no excuse for destructive behavior. Poverty is no excuse for criminal behavior. Poverty does not cause crime. If it did, all poor people would be criminals. These criminals were driven by anger, resentment, no moral scruples, pent up rage, a lack of positive parental guidance, a lack of religious guidance. These men and boys lacked traits such as honesty, integrity and positive work ethics that should have been instilled in them. They do not learn this in gangs. It can only be taught by parenting.

Gangs teach youngsters to fight, kill, steal, do drugs, sell drugs, and break any law that gets in the way of their criminal lifestyle. They also teach them to view the police as the enemy.

Liberals and Liberal Government officials do more damage than good to the youngsters in our country. I hope you are proud of what you did in Ferguson and Baltimore.

The Anti-Defamation League, the Southern Poverty Law Center, and the U.S. Commission on Civil Rights consider the New Black Panthers to be a hate group. http://bit.ly/1HCTit2

If the black man will go to school and at least get a high school education, he can gain full employment and get a guaranteed income. The Federal government is not responsible for you. You are responsible for you. The Constitution gives us all equal rights. Stand up and work for those rights as the rest of us do. Women do it, why can't a black man do it. The Federal government does not owe you a living. You owe that to yourself. Go out, get an education, and get a job. Get a dream and fulfill your dream.

If you get an education and get jobs, you can get your housing and will not have to live in government projects. Stop having babies to get government handouts. The government does not owe you decent housing. It aids you in giving you decent housing, but that does not make you entitled. Where do you think the money comes from for all the handouts you receive? It comes from all of the people that go to work every day and pays taxes. If they stop working and decide they want handouts too, then the handouts will have to stop because there won't be anyone left to pay taxes. At the moment, 47% of all the people in the United States are on welfare.

You need education on how to get along in the world, how to live in the world, and how to make money in the world. Once you learn to read and write and some math, the library is full of books that will teach you about your history. Your role in present-day society is to love your neighbor, not how to be a black man.

Black people have made their own oppression. Not one black person today has been a slave, nor have their parent(s), nor have their grandparents. Forget about slavery and move on. You all have had every opportunity to get an education and yet you seem to prefer to be in gangs instead of getting an education. Perhaps your parent(s) are to blame because they have not encouraged you or made the children study and go to school. Young girls get pregnant at an early age. They receive welfare checks because they either do not know who the father of their child is, or the father will not marry them, or he will not support the child. The government does not owe you free medical treatment. You are no better than the white people that do not have the money to pay for medical services. Now there is Obamacare, and they pay subsidies if you cannot pay for health insurance.

The United States Supreme Court has ruled "that President Obama's healthcare law allows the government to provide nationwide tax subsidies to help poor and middle-class people buy health insurance, a sweeping vindication that endorsed the larger purpose of Mr. Obama's signature legislative achievement.

'The court's three most conservative members — Justices Antonin Scalia, Clarence Thomas and Samuel A. Alito Jr. — dissented. Justice Scalia called the majority's reasoning "quite absurd."

'President Obama spoke about the Supreme Court's decision allowing nationwide tax subsidies to help poor and middle-class people buy health insurance. By Associated Press on Publish Date June 25, 2015. Photo by Stephen Crowley/The New York Times.

'The court's decision reflects the philosophy that judges should endure whatever interpretive distortions it takes to correct a supposed flaw in the statutory machinery," he wrote.

'"It is up to Congress to design its laws with care," he added, "and it is up to the people to hold them to account if they fail to carry out that responsibility."

'Justice Scalia announced his dissent from the bench, a sign of bitter disagreement. His summary was laced with notes of incredulity and sarcasm, which sometimes drawing amused murmurs in the courtroom as he described the "interpretive somersaults" he said the majority had performed to reach the decision." http://nyti.ms/1GKjJbT

You have a right to defend your home in the case of someone coming in to rob you. But you better think again when you call the police force and government agencies racist and fascist and especially when you are asking for all this free stuff. You have no rights against the United States Armed Forces or the Police Forces. It has been my experience that if the police force is after you it is because you are in the wrong, not because of oppression. Even in Ferguson, that boy was wrong.

I used to work in the judicial system and never once did I see an unfair or partial trial. As a matter of fact, it was always the opposite.

The system always gave every latitude to the Defendant to prove his innocence. But when a man does wrong, no matter what his color, he will be arrested and judged accordingly. It is true, however, that black men do makeup 40.2% of the prison population. Most of the prisoners cannot afford attorneys, and an attorney is appointed to represent them. You lose that freedom of choice because the government only employs so many attorneys, and you do not get to decide who you want to represent you. But you cannot blame the system because you went out and committed a crime.

To quote Pat Buchanan, Senior Advisor to Presidents Richard Nixon and Gerald Ford, "First, America has been the best country on earth for black folks. It was here that 600,000 black people, brought from Africa in slave ships, grew into a community of 40 million. They were introduced to Christian salvation and reached the greatest levels of freedom and prosperity blacks have ever known.

'Wright ought to go down on his knees and thank God he is an American.

'Second, no people anywhere has done more to lift up blacks than white Americans. Untold trillions have been spent since the '60s on welfare, food stamps, rent supplements, Section 8 housing, Pell grants, student loans, legal services, Medicaid, Earned Income Tax Credits and poverty programs designed to bring the African-American community into the mainstream.

'Governments, businesses, and colleges have engaged in discrimination against white folks — with affirmative action, contract set-asides, and quotas — to advance black applicants over white applicants.

'Churches, foundations, civic groups, schools and individuals all over America have donated time and money to support soup kitchens, adult education, day care, retirement and nursing homes for blacks.

'We hear the grievances. Where is the gratitude?

'Barack talks about new "ladders of opportunity" for blacks.

'Let him go to Altoona and Johnstown and ask the white kids in Catholic schools how many were visited lately by Ivy League recruiters handing out scholarships for "deserving" white kids.

'Is white America responsible for the fact that the crime and incarceration rates for African-Americans are seven times those of white America? Is it white America's fault that illegitimacy in the African-American community has hit seventy percent and the black dropout rate from high schools in some cities has reached fifty percent?

'Is that the fault of white America or, first and foremost, a failure of the black community itself?

'As for racism, its ugliest manifestation is in interracial crime, and especially interracial crimes of violence. Is Barack Obama aware that while white criminals choose black victims 3 percent of the time, black criminals choose white victims 45 percent of the time?

'Is Barack aware that black-on-white rapes are 100 times more common than the reverse, that black-on-white robberies were 139 times as common in the first three years of this decade as the reverse?

'We have all heard ad nauseam from the Rev. Al about Tawana Brawley, the Duke rape case, and Jena. And all turned out to be hoaxes. But about the epidemic of black assaults on whites that are real, we hear nothing.

'Sorry, Barack, some of us have heard it all before, about forty years and forty trillion tax dollars ago." http://buchanan.org/blog/pjb-a-brief-for-whitey-969

I agree with Buchanan. Listen up! It is time for you to play a different tune. Stop whining. The whites are tired of paying your way. Get a job and support yourself and get some self-respect. You have listed 65 programs that you want for free, and you are getting nearly all of them – for free. What are you giving in return? It is time for you to give back to society.

New Black Panther Party Chairman Malik Zulu Shabazz once said, "black America must decide who will represent you. You must decide if you will choose the ballot as a means to change, or the bullet, demanding change does come by any means necessary."

Shabazz also said, "I have hopes he (Obama) will change the U.S. government's position toward the Israeli-Palestinian conflict because our position has been unwarranted bias. Time and time again the U.S. vetoed resolutions in the U.N. Security Council condemning [Israeli] human rights violation. … I hope he shifts policy." http://www.wnd.com/2011/10/351545/

Following the Obama election, the New Black Panther Party group was charged with voter intimidation because their members were standing outside of a Philadelphia voting precinct dressed in paramilitary attire. Malik Shabazz was carrying a nightstick in a fashion in which a witness described as the most brazen form of voter intimidation he had ever seen. The Justice Department dismissed the charges, and it was speculated that Obama may have been involved. Malik Shabazz visited the White House private residence in July 2009.

You will often read newspaper stories that refer to a "fringe organization," which in actuality is the New Black Panther Party. They were involved in the Trayvon Martin case when they offered a $10,000 bounty for George Zimmerman.

When Obama was campaigning in Selma, Alabama in 2007, the Black Panthers marched behind Obama with raised fists in the "Black Power" salute. Then-Senator Hillary Clinton and Al Sharpton were at the same event, but the Panthers were there to support Obama. No media ever reported it.

Speaking to WND, Shabazz boasted he met Obama when the politician attended the 42nd anniversary of the voting rights marches in Selma in 2007. "I have nothing but respect for Obama and his pastor," said Shabazz, referring to Jeremiah Wright, Obama's former pastor of nearly 20 years. Below is a photograph of Senator Obama with the New Black Panthers in Selma in 2007.

Shabazz said in 2008 that aside from promoting black rights, he also supports Obama because he may take what he called a "less-biased" policy on the Israeli-Palestinian conflict. http://bit.ly/1l4XEzb

Our government has done an investigation as to the deep ties of the people within the Black Panther Party and the New Black Panther Party and their affiliation with terror organizations such as Hezbollah. The Black Panthers and the New Black Panther Party have a Marxist doctrine and have unified much of the common objectives and like-minded attitudes to Islam.

On Obama's 2008 Campaign website (moonbattery.com) there was a profile on the New Black Panthers along with a picture of their symbol. Why would someone running for President of the United States promote a hate group, a terrorist organization that advocates black militants to form an army that shocks the conscious of The People.

The fact that a candidate associates and supports such a group and the media never mentions it is beyond comprehension. The Media, as usual, gave Obama a free pass, and the Department of Justice, as usual, gave the New Black Panthers another free pass.

While studying at Yale, Hillary Clinton, monitored a Black Panthers trial in New Haven to make sure there was no legal abuse. Clinton then wrote a summary report that was turned over to the ACLU.

Later that year Mrs. Clinton went to Oakland, California to work for a radical law firm that represented another Black Panther named Abdul Alim Musa, an American, who was first known as Clarence Reams.

Musa was raised in Oakland, California and maintained a deep friendship with Eldridge Cleaver and Pete O'Neal both of which sought a campaign and coordination with like-minded radicals in Algeria where American forces are currently fighting al Qaeda operatives. Musa is a supporter of the Islamic Republic and the Ayatollah Khomeini and has made several trips to Iran in the late 1970s and early in 1980.

In 1970, the Federal Bureau of Investigation published that the Black Panther Party was the most dangerous and violent of all extremist groups. Eldridge Cleaver as a member of the BPP had very close ties to Al Fatah, Arab Guerillas in the 1970s. Additionally, Cleaver met with the North Vietnamese as with the Premier of China Chou En Lai along with up to 60 additional members of the BPP. Later, Eldridge Cleaver developed a friendship with Professor Gates. We should remember Professor Gates from the 'beer summit' event held at the White House by Barack Obama recently.

Being mentored by Louis Farrakhan, a Muslim, and Malik Zulu Shabazz, the New Black Panthers, have maintained an aggressive and militant pro-black agenda in addition to a full anti-Semitic mission throughout the United States. Khalid Muhammad with Louis Farrakhan reached out to Muammar el-Qaddafi of Libya for friendship and joint business ventures in the United States. Qaddafi was a target by world leaders to step down from his dictatorship in Libya while opposition rebels for more than a year sought to find and kill Qaddafi and late in 2011 he was captured and died.

The New Black Panther Party's deceased chairman, Khalid Abdul Muhammad, a former Nation of Islam leader claimed that "there is a little bit of Hitler in all white people." Muhammad was once considered Louis Farrakhan's most trusted adviser and gave speeches referring to the "white man" as the "devil.

In a 1993 speech condemned by the U.S. Congress and Senate, Muhammad, lionized on the NBPP site, referred to Jews as "bloodsuckers," labeled the Pope a "no-good cracker" and advocated the murder of white South Africans who would not leave the nation subsequent to a 24-hour warning. He was dismissed as Farrakhan's Aide for these remarks. http://www.wnd.com/2011/10/351545/#Eegl7z2b6Rxk4p27.99

Islam, in preparing a revolution against the United States, were indebted to Black Panther Party members such as Bobby Seale, Huey Newton, Eldridge Cleaver, and Malcolm X. Other names that keep popping up in all investigations are Hillary Clinton, Barack Obama, Professor Gates, and Attorney General Eric Holder, who quietly implements a policy of freedom for all terrorists.

http://bit.ly/1RjaMg9

All New Black Panther Party members must memorize the group's rules, such as that no party member "can have a weapon in his possession while drunk or loaded off narcotics or weed," and no member "will commit any crimes against other party members or black people at all."

Some interesting statistics:

"In 1988 when Jesse Jackson was running for the Democratic nomination, 23 percent of white Democrats said they wouldn't vote for a black president, compared to 19 percent of white Republicans.

'In 2008, when Obama was a candidate rather than a president, the numbers were about equal (5%) among Republicans and Democrats.

'In 1990, 65 percent of white Democrats and 71 percent of white Republicans said they'd object to an interracial marriage of a close relative.

'From 1990 to 2008, white Republicans were just slightly more likely than white Democrats to say they considered blacks to be more "unintelligent" than "intelligent." However, the numbers have fallen over time, and the small partisan gap erased itself in 2010 and 2012, under Obama's presidency. [Under Obama, I would not be surprised to see this number go way up, given that he was supposed to be so smart.]

'A 1989 poll shows that approximately 63% of white Republicans and 63% of white Democrats believed that blacks lack the motivation to pull themselves out of poverty.

'In 2004, approximately the same percentage (32%) of white Republicans and white Democrats opposed a close relative marrying a black person.

'In 2006, 37% of white Republicans and 36% of white Democrats said blacks are "more lazy" than "hard-working."

'The 2009 survey showed that the percentage of white Democrats and white Republicans who oppose living in a half black neighborhood is tied at 20%.

'A 2008 survey shows the percentage of whites who say they do not feel close to blacks at 10% for both parties.

'In 2004, 18% of white Republicans, and 15% of white Democrats said they believed the Federal government was spending too much money on improving conditions for blacks.

'On average, between the 2004 and 2006 editions of the surveys — the last two before Obama was either a president or a candidate — the index of negative racial attitudes stood at 22 percent for white Democrats and 26 percent for white Republicans. Those values are within the margin of error.

NOTEWORTHY:

'If there's a discouraging trend, it's not so much that negative racial attitudes toward blacks have increased in these polls, but that they've failed to decrease under Obama, as they did so clearly for most of the past three decades.

'I completely get most of these statistics. Sure there are some knuckle-dragging Neanderthals who are just race bigots, but most of them are "old school" folks, with one foot in the grave and another on a banana peel. By the way, if you poll black people, you would get some astoundingly racist statistics against whites.

'Thanks for all the racial healing, Barack Obama." http://bit.ly/1HCTQiz

A black man can complain all he wants, but there is a certain amount of advantage to being black. For instance, Barack Obama would not be President if he were not black. Many, many people admit they would not have voted for him if he were not black. You can call that a racist statement and I will call the people that voted for him for that reason racist, but it is a fact.

Many blacks would never finish school if they were not black because they are graded on the curve. They do not study as hard as whites, they do not put forth as much effort in class as whites, they do not care as much whether they pass their grade as whites. White parents pound into their children that they must study and get good grades and that it is not acceptable to fail a grade and have to take the class over again. I do not believe the same concern is passed on to the black children. Their concern is not act white.

There are a few blacks that excel in America. Unfortunately, our President is not one of them. I believe he has the intelligence, but he has never used that gift. He has a different agenda.

President Barack Obama described himself as "impatient" for more progress on race relations in the U.S. But he pushed back against critics like Tavis Smiley who have criticized him for telling the African-American community to wait on said progress.

"There's no reason for folks to be patient. I'm impatient," Obama said to CNN's Candy Crowley in an interview that aired on a Sunday morning."

It appears to me that Obama and Al Sharpton are the biggest race baiters we have in this country. Then you have Eric Holder, who implies that most police officers are racists. "It means that we as a nation have failed," Holder continues, according to Breitbart. "It's as simple as that. We have failed." "It is extremely odd for Holder — and Obama — to constantly act as if Americans have failed on the issue of racism. It's almost as if they are addicted to using race as a political tool, and refuse to move forward and put the past behind them." http://bit.ly/1OBY0GI

Is Barack Obama a racist? Yes. In his book *Dreams from My Father*, he said, "I ceased to advertise my mother's race at the age of 12 or 13, when I began to suspect that by doing so I was ingratiating myself to whites." Yet Obama took a white girl to his senior prom. http://ti.me/1HCUexm

"I found a solace in nursing a pervasive sense of grievance and animosity against my mother's race." White people!

"There was something about her that made me wary, a little too sure of herself, maybe and white."

"It remained necessary to prove which side you were on, to show your loyalty to the black masses, to strike out and name names."

"I never emulate white men and brown men whose fates didn't speak to my own. It was into my father's image, the black man, son of Africa, that I'd packed all the attributes I sought in myself: the attributes of Martin and Malcolm, DuBois and Mandela.

From "Audacity of Hope," he said, "I will stand with the Muslims should the political winds shift in an ugly direction."

Here's a black journalist's opinion of the Obamas.

Even if you love Obama, you might take a few minutes to read this because it is unvarnished in its implications for them and our country.

Mychal Massie is a journalist that is not afraid like so many are to be branded a racist simply because he is black. How beautiful and liberating the truth can be when our minds are opened for all who care to see and be free.

The summary below of Barack and Michelle Obama's 5-year reign in the White House is by far the best I've ever read as it squarely hits the nail on the head. And it took a black reporter writing it to make it as effective as it is. A white man's account would be instantly criticized by the liberal media as pure racism. But, how can anyone scream "racist" when an exacting description of the Obamas is penned by a well-known journalist of color?

(Mychal Massie is a respected writer and talk show host in Los Angeles.)

"The other evening on my twitter, a person asked me why I didn't like the Obamas. Specifically, I was asked: I have to ask, why do you hate the Obamas? It seems personal, not policy related. You even dissed (disrespect) their Christmas family picture.'

'The truth is I do not like the Obamas, what they represent, their ideology, and I certainly do not like his policies and legislation. I've made no secret of my contempt for the Obamas. As I responded to the person who asked me the aforementioned question, I don't like them because they are committed to the fundamental change of my/our country into what can only be regarded as a Communist state.

'I don't hate them per definition, but I condemn them because they are the worst kind of racialists, they are elitist Leninists with contempt for traditional America.

'They display disrespect for the sanctity of the office he holds, and for those who are willing to admit same, Michelle Obama's raw contempt for white America is contemptuous.

'I don't like them because they comport themselves as emperor and empress. I expect, no I demand respect, for the Office of President, and a love of our country and her citizens, from the leader, entrusted with the governance of same. President and Mrs. Reagan displayed an unparalleled love for the country and her people. The Reagans made Americans feel good about themselves and about what we could accomplish.

'Obama's arrogance by appointing 32 leftist czars and constantly bypassing congress is impeachable. Eric Holder is probably the MOST incompetent and arrogant DOJ head to ever hold the job. Could you envision President Reagan instructing his Justice Department to act like jack-booted thugs?

'Presidents are politicians and all politicians are known and pretty much expected to manipulate the truth, if not outright lie, but even using that low standard, the Obamas have taken lies, dishonesty, deceit, mendacity, subterfuge and obfuscation to new depths. They are verbally abusive to the citizenry, and they display an animus for civility.

'I do not like them because they both display bigotry overtly, as in the case of Harvard Professor Louis Gates, when he accused the Cambridge Police of acting stupidly, and her code speak pursuant to now being able to be proud of America.

'I view that statement and that mind set as an insult to those who died to provide a country where a Kenyan, his illegal alien relatives, and his alleged progeny, could come and not only live freely but rise to the highest, most powerful, position in the world.

'Michelle Obama is free to hate and disparage whites because Americans of every description paid with their blood to ensure her right to do that. I have a saying, that "the only reason a person hides things, is because they have something to hide." No president in history has spent over a million dollars to keep his records, and his past sealed.

'And what the two of them have shared has been proven to be lies. He lied about when and how they met. He lied about his mother's death and problems with insurance. Michelle lied to a crowd pursuant to nearly $500,000 bank stocks they inherited from his family. He has lied about his father's military service, about the civil rights movement, ad nausea. He lied to the world about the Supreme Court in a State of the Union address.

'He berated and publicly insulted a sitting Congressman. He has surrounded himself with the most rabidly radical, socialist academicians today. He opposed rulings that protected women and children that even Planned Parenthood did not seek to support. He is openly hostile to business and aggressively hostile to Israel.

'His wife treats being the First Lady as her personal American Express Black Card (arguably the most prestigious credit card in the world). I condemn them because as people are suffering, losing their homes, their jobs, their retirements, he and his family are arrogantly showing off their life of entitlement - as he goes about creating and fomenting class warfare.

'I don't like them, and I neither apologize nor retreat from my public condemnation of them and his policies. We should condemn them for the disrespect they show our people, for his willful and unconstitutional actions pursuant to obeying the Constitutional parameters he is bound by, and his willful disregard for Congressional authority.

'Dislike for them has nothing to do with the color of their skin; it has everything to do with their behavior, attitudes, and policies. And I have open scorn for their constantly playing the race card.

'I could go on, but let me conclude with this. I condemn in the strongest possible terms the media for refusing to investigate them, as they did President Bush and President Clinton, and for refusing to label them for what they truly are. There is no scenario known to man, whereby a white president and his wife could ignore laws, flaunt their position, and lord over the people, as these two are permitted to do out of fear for their color.

'As I wrote in a syndicated column titled, "Nero in The White House" - "Never in my life, inside or outside of politics, have I witnessed such dishonesty in a political leader.

'He is the most mendacious political figure I have ever witnessed. Even by the low standards of his presidential predecessors, his narcissistic, contumacious arrogance is unequalled. Using Obama as the bar, Nero would have to be elevated to sainthood.

'Many in America wanted to be proud when the first person of color was elected president, but instead, they have been witness to a congenital liar, a woman who has been ashamed of America her entire life, failed policies, intimidation, and a commonality hitherto not witnessed in political leaders. He and his wife view their life at our expense as an entitlement - while America's people go homeless, hungry and unemployed. [Confirmed on http://bit.ly/1XuCb3E

When Jesse Jackson was asked how he felt about being lumped into the category of being a race baiter, he didn't have a problem. He compared himself to Dr. Martin Luther King and said Dr. King was considered to be a race baiter and a Communist.

And while the riots were going on in Ferguson, Missouri, which is several states away from Oberlin College in Ohio and even further away from Columbia Law School in New York, black students postponed their final exams because they were traumatized by the riots going on in Ferguson. They demanded that African-American students be completely exempt from failing this semester because they are so deeply affected during "times like this."

The Ohio College has said they will allow the professors flexibility in "emergency incomplete requests," but have not given a "flat out pass" to all black students. A petition was circulated among the students and received more than 1300 signatures. Sounds racist to me.

The New Black Panthers, blacks on welfare, gangstas, and all blacks crying po mouth, for that matter, could take a big lesson from Morgan Freeman. Freeman has the right attitude and is not a racist.

Officially, February is Black History Month. Morgan Freeman appeared on "60 Minutes" and gave his views on Black History Month. When Journalist Mike Wallace asked his view, Freeman's response was "Ridiculous."

"Why?" asked the veteran news reporter.

"You're going to relegate my history to a month?" asked Freeman. "What do you do with yours? Which month is white history month? No, come on, tell me," he continued.

"Well, I'm Jewish," responded Mike Wallace.

'Freeman kept pressuring for an answer. "Okay. Which month is Jewish history month?"

'There isn't one," replied Wallace.

"Oh. Oh, why not? Do you want one?" asked Morgan Freeman in response.

'Wallace said "No."

"I don't either," explained Freeman. "I don't want a Black History Month. Black history is American history."

'Mike Wallace then shifted the conversation to the broader topic of racism. "How are we going to get rid of racism and — ?"

'Morgan Freeman's answer should be something that all conservatives can applaud (H/T CNS News).

"Stop talking about it. I'm going to stop calling you a white man, and I'm going to ask you to stop calling me a black man," said Freeman.

"I know you as Mike Wallace. You know me as Morgan Freeman. You want to say, 'Well, I know this white guy named Mike Wallace.' You know what I'm saying?" he asked.

'That interview took place in 2005, but it looks like Morgan Freeman's fairly conservative views on race have stayed consistent since then.

'Last year, Freeman appeared on CNN and was interviewed by Don Lemon. The topic of racism came up again.

"Today? No. You and I. We're proof," replied Freeman. "Why would race have anything to do with it? Put your mind to what you want to do and go for that. It's kind of like religion to me. It's a good excuse for not getting there."

'That view is incredibly refreshing. While people like President Barack Obama and former Attorney General Eric Holder seem to believe that they are defined by their skin color and that black Americans are unable to succeed on their own, Morgan Freeman has taken a stand for a better path.

'He's 100 percent right on this issue, and America could use more common-sense thinking like Freeman's." http://bit.ly/21rFAj0

"I have met few more racist than our own President. To quote: "We can't equate what is happening now to what was happening 50 years ago...and if you talk to your parents, grandparents, uncles, they'll tell you that things are better, not good in some places, but better," said Obama

'Obama is advising young people to be persistent because "typically progress is in steps, it's in increments."

"In dealing with something "as deeply rooted as racism or bias in any society, you've got to have vigilance but you have to recognize that it's going to take some time, and you just have to be steady so that

you don't give up when you don't get all the way there," Obama said."
http://bit.ly/1LLaWWg

Obama is a man that should be ending racism in this country instead of inciting it and meeting with men like Al Sharpton, who is one of the biggest race hustlers in this country. Obama is a man that should rise above racism and color because he is the President and is supposed to be a leader, a "man," not a black man. But instead he plays the role of a black man of 150 years ago. Instead of being a unifier, he is a divider.

Michelle Obama could also be attempting to end racism but is also insecure about her color. She has been the First Lady for over six years and recently gave a commencement address at Tuskegee University in which she addressed the hurdles of racism she faced en route to becoming the first African-American First Lady.

She could just as easily have shared ways of how her race helped her get into Princeton was probably because of affirmative action; perhaps the reason she became an associate of a law firm was probably because of diversity, and they needed a woman, and a woman of color.

How can you even talk about racism when so many white people put you in the position that you are living in today, and you are so privileged?

Instead, she stands up before America and hatefully states that this is the first time in her life that she is proud to be an American when her husband became President of the United States. But that pride is short-lived. Remember the 911 ceremony when it was believed the First Lady said "All this for a flag."

How long must America pay for our forefather's transgressions of slavery? Not every American owned slaves, yet every white American is being blamed. How many more years will you cry for our blood when you were not made a slave, when your parent was not a slave, when your grandparent was not a slave, but just because you are black? Whites do not care if you are black. It is you that care if you are black. It is you that is holding you back.

The City of Chicago is proposing a five and a half million-dollar reparation package for those who suffered under the ruthless rule of police commander Jon Burge from 1972 to 1991. According to the Chicago Tribune, the Plan was backed by Mayor Rahm Emanuel and would supply victims with free college tuition, counselling for drug abuse and psychological issues, and include a formal apology from the city.

Fox News' Charles Payne, who is black, said he is afraid nationwide slavery reparations might be next.

"The news in my mind is a glimpse of really much bigger news that is going to come from the White House," he said. "I think that there's going to be an official apology from the White House for slavery in America and then there's going to be a major push to get cash. And I'm talking lots of cash."

Payne, who is black, argued that it would be counterproductive to dwell on the tragedies of the past. He speculated that President Obama would make his push for slavery reparations next year.

"I think it would be a major mistake," Payne said. "Instead, Obama should discuss and focus on all of the progress we have made and how all Americans need to move forward for better days for all of our kids." http://huff.to/1Ti1YFB

When will the blacks decide they are men and start acting like men and stop whining? If you are trustworthy, you will be trusted. Get away from your gangs and your prejudices and decide what you want to do with your life and do it. Obama and Sharpton are two of the biggest names in the country, and they are still crying racism. That is a real shame. They would have respect if they were not crying racism and whining. When they stop crying racism, they will become their own man and stop blaming everything on everybody else. What kind of country would we have today if Obama had the attitude of Morgan Freeman?

You respect Dr. Martin Luther King, but you do not listen to what he says. You watch all of Morgan Freeman's movies. Will you listen to what he said?

"Dr. Ben Carson said on Hugh Hewitt's radio show today that he believes race relations in the U.S. have gotten much worse under President Obama. Hewitt asked him if things are "going to get worse" before they get better when it comes to race in the United States.

'And Carson said, "I believe that things were better before this president was elected. And I think that things have gotten worse because of his unusual emphasis on race." http://bit.ly/1PYgCnI

African-American boys have the notion if they read too much or if they speak proper English that they are "acting white." There is no such thing as acting white if you want to do away with racism.

You are either a gentleman, or you are a lady. It does not matter what color you are. This is the only way you are going to climb out of your squalor, stop feeling sorry for yourself and succeed at something in your life. The idea that you have to dress a certain way, wear your hair a certain way, talk a certain way, or walk a certain way to prove that you are black must end. You are the one being racist. Just be a gentleman, talk like you have an education, and remember that your name is all that you have in life and take care of it.

One thing we do not have today is honest dialog when it comes to race in America. I read where one college professor said, and I quote, "I am especially concerned about the black students I encounter because a higher percentage of them come from impoverished backgrounds. The black students who concern me most are those who because of the victimhood mentality that has been pushed on them since first grade in America's public schools have developed a negative attitude toward education specifically and life in general. For example, I am encountering an increasing number of black students who view learning to speak proper English as "talking white"; something they disdain and even mock in other black students. As a college professor I can attest to the fact that speaking proper English hardly qualifies as "talking white," since few of my white students speak proper English."

This also concerns me. Since when is speaking proper English "talking white." That has to be a racist term. People of color want to be treated the same as white people, yet they do not want to act the same as white people. How does talking trash make them educated? How does it take away their confusion and negative attitudes about life and getting a head in life? Do they want to hang on to their poverty stricken life and attitudes, or do they want to seek out a life of success? To do so will mean to let go of some old attitudes. White people have to do that also. You have to assume personal responsibility for your life and not make excuses. It does not matter what color you are.

"Sad to say but poor people—no matter their race—who accept the victimhood mentality as gospel, will remain stuck at the bottom of the socio-economic ladder." http://bit.ly/20pQPVX/

Racism and discrimination are not what are holding you back. Your attitudes are holding you back. You live in a culture of moral decay.

You think it is okay to have children without parents or marriage. Then you do not teach the children right from wrong or anything about working or goal setting. You cannot give them any of the tools for success because you do not have them yourself. Go to church and listen to the Minister if you are not going to read the Bible yourself. You will at least learn right from wrong.

The dependency upon the government for your entire life is not the answer for you and gives your children the wrong impression. Your daughter sees mom spending her life at home with no ambition but raising kids and drawing government assistance. When she grows up, her life will be the same. Your son sees dad spend his life in prison and when he is thirteen he goes to juvenile hall and from there moves up to prison life. That is not the way to encourage your children to have a better life than you have.

Give your children a chance to have a better life. Give them the tools to do better than you did for yourself. If you cannot do it for them, then give them up for adoption so they will get that chance. Break that selfish cycle of dependence.

In 2012, when conservative legal watch dog group, Judicial Watch, sued the Department of Justice in Federal Court to enforce a Freedom of Information Act (FOIA) request for documents pertaining to the New Black Panthers case, the Federal Court held that political appointees appointed by President Obama did interfere with the Department of Justice's prosecution of the New Black Panther Party.

The Department of Justice then claimed that Judicial Watch was not entitled to attorney's fees since "none of the records produced in this litigation evidenced any political interference whatsoever in" how the Department of Justice handled the New Black Panther Party case. But the U.S. Supreme Court held that "The documents reveal that political appointees within the Department of Justice were conferring about the status and resolution of the New Black Panther Party case in the days preceding the DOJ's dismissal of claims in that case, which would appear to contradict Assistant Attorney General Perez's testimony that political leadership was not involved in that decision. Surely the public has an interest in documents that cast doubt on the accuracy of government officials' representations regarding the possible politicization of agency decision-making. In sum, the Court concludes that three of the four fee entitlement factors weigh in favor of awarding fees to Judicial Watch. Therefore, Judicial Watch is both eligible and entitled to fees and costs, and the Court must now consider the reasonableness of Judicial Watch's requested award."

Obama held a summit on Ferguson, and yet he nominated a man who represented a cop killer to lead the Justice Department's Civil Rights Division. Obama is a Liberal and very much anti-law and order.

Obama's choice of former head of the NAACP Legal Defense Fund, attorney Debo Adegbile zealously defended Mumia Abu-Jamal, who was convicted 30 years ago of murdering a Philadelphia police officer. Adegbile helped Abu-Jamal get his death sentence overturned. Obama's choice was so bad that even Harry Reid and other Democrats blocked the nomination.

"There will be no true justice in America until the racist regime of Barack Obama is gone." http://theblacksphere.net/2014/12/guess-obama-wanted-lead-doj-civil-rights-division/

Finally, the following is an email that I received that was circulating and was written supposedly by a dying black male. We all would have been proud to have known him.

"I wanted to clear up a few black and white questions and answers. The things I state are facts. They are not downloaded from some media website, not propaganda, just observations from an 80-year-old black man born in America.

'I was told by my parents (yes, a married man and woman with my last name) that I was a nigger. We lived in "Nigger Town" in a small Texas town, no A/C, grass growing through the floor, no car, no TV. We washed our bodies with lye soap that my mother made by hand. I thought I was a nigger until I graduated high school, went to college, did an enlistment in the Army and got a job. I am now retired, own my own home, have six children by ONE WOMAN and we all have the same last name. I have a Bachelor's Degree in Liberal Arts and a Master's Degree in Sociology. My retirement, VA disability from combat in the Korean War (I only have one leg) and part-time pay in a local college, is about $125,000 a year. From dirt poor nigger, to old, black, proud American.

'Yes, I am black, and I can say "nigger", because I understand the true meaning of the word. Let's clear up a few things about the Michael Brown incident.

'Fact: It is not called "shoplifting or stealing," it's called "robbery," which is a felony. Brown stole something and assaulted someone that means ROBBERY. It's on video, and it's a fact. Not shoplifting, not theft, not "lifting" a few cigars, but ROBBERY!

'Michael Brown, like Trayvon, was portrayed by the media as a "little black boy", cute little headphones and his cap and gown photo gunned down by a ruthless police assassin, executed by "whitey". First, I have never seen a cop drag a person into their car's driver door to arrest them. So, let us be clear, Michael Brown was a nigger; a sorry assed, criminal, hoodlum, nigger. Nobody wants to say that, but I will. He had a criminal record a mile long, was known for numerous assaults, robberies, including the one you saw with your own eyes and still refuse to call it a robbery. He was, like so many others, living a life that he thought he was "entitled" to, just for being alive. Gangsta rap, weed, drinking, guns and those stupid-assed low profile rims makes him some kind of bad-ass nigger.

'I have fought communist Chinese and North Korean soldiers in the 1950s with more honor than that nigger. Yep, I peeled potatoes and shot communists. That's the only job a nigger soldier could get.

'Rodney King? Black Riots!

'Trayvon? Black Riots!

'Hurricane Katrina? Black Riots! Stealing TV's, designer clothes, etc.

'O.J. Simpson kills white man and white woman - found not guilty? Did white folks riot? Nope!

'In fact, when is the last time white people rioted? Civil War, maybe?

'That's because they are, relatively, civilized people, much like many black Americans. Protesting is one thing, hell, I'm all for it. Even if you are an ignorant idiot you have a right to protest.

'Stop only showing the young black "cap and gown" photos of Michael. Charles Manson may have a few of those laying around, as well. Show the nigger "gangsta" photos of the "poor unarmed teenager" (grown man) pics that have been removed from his Facebook page, holding the loaded pistol, smoking weed, with a mouthful of money.

'Militarization? The stupid-assed media that publicizes this has no idea what "militarization" really is. Cops wear helmets and vests and drive armored vehicle because unemployed niggers thrown bricks at them, moron!

'You put on an "Adam 12" uniform and walk down the streets of Ferguson during the criminal riots. I can guarantee that you'll jump into the first armored "military tank" that you see.

'You only "want the police" when you "need the police" otherwise, you mock and fear what you do not understand about the police. And by the way, the police are trained to take your shit, but I wouldn't fuck around with those Army National Guard, they aren't as well disciplined "culturally" to take your shit like police do every day. They will ventilate your black asses with M-16's with military precision and extreme prejudice.

'And finally, the way we protest and demand justice, is run down the streets breaking shit, looting stores, and acting like a bunch of untrained monkeys? Hell, after Rodney King, criminal niggers were actually killing people, thinking they were entitled to be worse criminals than they already were.

'For those black criminals that do that, you are a disgrace to your race, inflamed by idiots like Al Sharpton, instead of listening to logic from proud black Americans, like Bill Cosby (not so proud anymore, after all these allegations coming out about him), Samuel Jackson (questionable), Colin Powell (a RINO to the Republican Party), Allen West, me, etc. (And may I add Dr. Ben Carson? Boomer).

'You blame white people for your ignorance, criminal acts, unemployed laziness, etc.

You blame white people for 89% of the prisons in America being full of blacks. They did nothing wrong, the racists white cops framed them all, right? No chance at school, no chance for college, military, employment?

'Bull Shit!

'More niggers kill niggers, than niggers killing whites, whites killing niggers, and whites killing whites - combined. I find this astounding.

'It's not white peoples' faults, the Emancipation Proclamation was signed by a white man years ago. You can go to school, get a job, buy a house, and vote, just like white folks! You are not a slave, you are not discriminated against! Slavery is abolished and nobody alive today was alive when it was popular. Get over it! You are discriminated against because you are a criminal, sorry-assed nigger. Otherwise, black Americans are treated like everyone else.

'If you choose to create "baby daddy and baby mama" and fake disabilities as an excuse for laziness to draw social security disability instead of husband, wife, family, job, mortgage, it's your fault, not white folks. And there are a lot of proud black Americans that will tell you the same, as I am one of them!

'Remember, the way you act on the camera is remembered by everyone who sees it. They will never forget it. It shows them how you, as the black race responds to a situation that don't particularly go the way you think they should. It will become a reference standard, something they expect from you when the next media report doesn't go your way. Stop being stupid niggers and be a proud black American. My parents raised me well, but they were wrong about one thing, I am not a nigger.

'I will not be around long. While my mind is still sharp, and my aim is still good, my body is eating away with cancer. It started in the prostate and is spreading rapidly. After I die, I have asked my children to publish my writings and include my name. Although I am not expecting any miracles I can only hope that Americans will stop blaming color, start blaming criminals see people for what they really are. We have too many countries that want us dead. We should not be fighting each other."

I can only interject one thing here. It seems to be a common complaint and misconception among blacks that they are poverty ridden, and whites live a comfortable life. That is totally wrong, so it has to be an attitude problem in how we are all brought up. When I read how this man was reared, it was no different than the way I was brought up. Is it because we both had two parents to help us have a future dream? Do children with only one parent have nothing to look forward to in life but despair because that is what they see from their mother? Does mom never encourage them to get good grades in school so they can grow up and live a better life than she has had? Has mom ever read them stories to encourage them to dream?

The black is the least educated – 13 percent of the population. It is the most criminal and the most dependent on government charity. And guess what? They dominate national politics. Everything revolves around what blacks want, demand, do, or cannot do.

"Courses of instruction in the schools, academic rigor, codes of dress, rules regarding unceasing obscenity, all must be set to suit them, as must be examinations for promotion in fire departments, the military, and police forces. Blacks must be admitted to universities for which they are not remotely qualified, where departments of Black Studies must be established to please them. Corporate work forces, federal departments, and elite high-schools must be judged not on whether they perform their functions but on whether they have the right number of blacks."

We try never to offend or upset the blacks.

"If a white shoots a black to defend himself, it becomes national news for weeks, or months, and riots follow. But when blacks engage in their unending racial attacks on whites, the media demurely look the other way. The attackers are never black. They are "teens." Reporters who say otherwise are likely to be fired. In effect, the thirteen percent censor the national press." [Black Power: A Done Deal by Fred Reed]

And does a black man know it is okay to be black without acting like a nigger? Do you know you can be a black gentleman – just a man? If you want acceptance, then start acting acceptable. Stop the rioting. Do what you know in your heart is the right thing to do.

At one time, the government was supplying larger cities with weapons and armor vehicles. Our government had already given our local Police Departments free armored trucks known as MRAPS to patrol the streets. The Pentagon was getting ready to unload 13,000 more to different police departments throughout the country. Obama has not given up on confiscating your guns.

Now Obama is taking action to demilitarize the police, with an announced ban on the use of Federal funds to provide certain military-type equipment to local police forces. According to The New York Times, the new Federal proposal will keep local police from acquiring "armored vehicles, the highest-caliber firearms and ammunition, and camouflage uniforms." This came about as a result of the findings of the task force from the Ferguson riots.

Obama wants to give police officers a softer look. He wants to make the police look less intimidating and "racist." Again the Federal Government is intruding in the State level where it does not belong.

"According to Leftists, black neighborhoods don't have a crime problem. Black criminals are just trying to do business, and the cops keep getting in the way. Such is the logic of America's racist black president.

'Why else would Obama speak last year to the Congressional Black Caucus about the disparities in arrests in black neighborhoods? He can't blame the pimp overseers, lest they upset the system.

'These war zones are there for a reason. The black denizens must be at the ready to burn a city down, or the Left could lose their ability to terrorize the nation." http://theblacksphere.net/2015/06/obama-loves-black-thugs-political-otherwise/

Do black communities manufacture anything other than fear and hatred? There are so many gangs, and drug dealing is so prevalent that most blacks do not consider it a crime. When a black gets picked up on a drug arrest, other blacks just consider he was "trying to make a living."

Stop being black men. Just be men. Just be a man. Can you do that? Do you even want to do that? Don't associate with a gang, don't hang out just to try to be somebody. Just be the person you are – just be the "**man**" you are. Be a better person today than you were yesterday. Be proud of the man that you are. Be someone that you can be proud to know.

Quit referring to yourself as a black man, or an African-American, or a Negro. Refer to yourself as an American. You do not have to refer to the color of your skin. You probably were not born in Africa. If necessary to refer to yourself at all, just say "I'm an American." That makes us all equal.

Now, be a contributor to society. Crime, prostitution, rap, out of wedlock pregnancies and massive abortions are not contributions.

Michael Richards was right when he spoke of "just being an American." Some of you may remember Richards in his role as Kramer on TV's Seinfeld. He gave a speech in Court after making racial comments in his comedy act. He said, "There are African Americans, Mexican Americans, Asian Americans, Arab Americans, etc. And then there are just Americans. You pass me on the street and sneer in my direction. You call me 'White boy,' 'Cracker,' 'Honkey,' 'Whitey,' 'Caveman'... And that's OK... But when I call you, Nigger, Kike, Towel head, Sand-nigger, Camel Jockey, Beaner, Gook, or Chink ... You call me a racist.

You say that whites commit a lot of violence against you.... So why are the ghettos the most dangerous places to live?

You have the United Negro College Fund. You have Martin Luther King Day. You have Black History Month. You have Cesar Chavez Day. You have Ma'uled Al-Nabi. You have the NAACP. You have BET.... If we had WET (White Entertainment Television), we'd be racists. If we had a White Pride Day, you would call us racists. If we had White History Month, we'd be racists.

If we had any organization for only whites to 'advance' our lives, we'd be racists.

We have a Hispanic Chamber of Commerce, a Black Chamber of Commerce, and then we just have the plain Chamber of Commerce. Wonder who pays for that??

A white woman could not be in the Miss Black American pageant, but any color can be in the Miss America pageant.

If we had a college fund that only gave white students scholarships... You know we'd be racists.

There are over 60 openly proclaimed Black Colleges in the United States, yet if there were 'White colleges', that would be a racist college.

In the Million Man March, you believed that you were marching for your race and rights. If we marched for our race and rights, you would call us racists.

You are proud to be black, brown, yellow and orange, and you're not afraid to announce it. But when we announce our white pride, you call us racists.

You rob us, car jack us, and shoot at us. But, when a white police officer shoots a black gang member or beats up a black drug dealer running from the law and posing a threat to society, you call him a racist.

I am proud...... But you call me a racist.

Why is it that only whites can be racists?"

V

ILLEGALS

Obama, actually believing he is King, or Emperor, brags to an audience of illegal immigrants in Nashville, Tennessee and Chicago. He tells them that his executive orders while they are technically possible to reverse, he does not believe it is "politically feasible."

"It's true a future administration might try to reverse some of our policies," Obama said. "But I'll be honest with you — the American people basically have a good heart and want to treat people fairly and every survey shows that if, in fact, somebody has come out and subjected themselves to a background check, registered, paid their taxes, the American people support allowing them to stay."

I don't know about you, but if someone in my presence says "I'll be honest with you," or "trust me," you know you need a pair of boots or a lawyer.

Obama took unilateral executive action to defer deportations for millions of illegal immigrants, effectively granting amnesty.

He thinks he can dictate who can and cannot criticize his actions. He admits he has changed the law himself.

Obama intimated that criticism of his actions was based on hateful racism, both of himself and of illegal immigration. He said only Native Americans have a right to be critical of illegal immigration policies.

I guess this administration believes Americans are all stupid. The "Native Americans" that they are referring to were here before the establishment of the United States, and are not connected with the United States; therefore they actually do not have a "right" to say anything about United States immigration policy.

He said he would take care of the illegal immigrants and his support is all-encompassing. He does not care how many of them are felons or have been on the welfare rolls for 20 years without applying for citizenship. They voted for him in the last election and he owes them.

However, Congress has a different view and will not be passing a bill to fund the amnesty programs. Congress at least listened to America on the issue that the borders should be closed first. Whether that will happen or not will remain to be seen, but they are not cooperating with Obama on his amnesty program, at least at the present time.

Though Obama received 71% of the Hispanic vote, Americans overwhelmingly disapprove and oppose illegal immigration and support legal immigration. But Obama still believes he owes the Hispanics.

Senator John McCain said that illegal immigrants will have to pay back taxes and pay for their citizenship, so he does not see a scenario where it would cost us money.

There are an estimated eleven million illegal immigrants living in the United States today. That is an increase of one-third up from 2005 when there was 8.5 million according to the Center for American Progress. Eighty-Six percent have been living in the United States for seven years or longer.

327,000 illegal immigrants were apprehended at the border by the U.S. Border Patrol Agents in 2011 when they were seeking employment in the United States.

Eighty percent of illegal immigrants are from Mexico and Latin America. Nine percent are from Asia. Eleven percent are from Europe, Canada, Africa, and other countries.

$11.2 Billion was paid by illegal immigrants in taxes in 2010 according to the Institute on Taxation and Economic Policy. About half of all illegals pay some form of Federal taxes.

$4.2 Billion is the amount the Federal Government paid to individuals with children in 2005 whose tax bills dip below zero. The Additional Tax Child Credit (ACTC) is heavily claimed by illegal aliens according to Factcheck.Org.

$4.3 Billion is the annual estimated cost to taxpayer-provided health care for uninsured illegal aliens as of 2010 according to the Center for Immigration Studies. About half of that goes to the people with incomes below 133 percent of poverty.

$48.6 Billion is the estimated cost to taxpayers of covering 3.1 million amnestied immigrants during the budget period 2014-2019 in which Medicaid expansion takes effect, according to the same source.

$2.6 Trillion is an estimated cost that could result from putting roughly ten million adult illegal aliens on a guaranteed pathway to citizenship made in 2007 by the Heritage Foundation.

$40 billion is the annual cost of educating illegals and their offspring in this country according to the Center for Immigration Studies.

$1.5 trillion is the amount that would be added to this country's cumulative GDP over 10 years with a comprehensive immigration reform plan that includes legalization for all illegal aliens currently living in the U.S. according to the Center for American Progress.

$4.5 billion to $5.4 billion is the amount of additional net tax revenue that would accrue to the Federal Government over three years if all current illegal aliens were legalized.

$23,482 is the current cost of apprehending, detaining, processing, and transporting one individual in deportation proceedings.

There are five "gateway" states where large populations of illegal aliens have settled: California, Florida, Illinois, New York and Texas.

One million is the estimated number of illegal immigrants deported under the Obama administration's immigrant enforcement program, Secure Communities, which checks the status of immigrants booked into county jails in participating jurisdictions.

It has just been announced that Obama is offering housing in America to 100,000 Syrian refugees by 2017.

"The Daily Caller reports:

'Each refugee is offered a placement grant of $1,850 from the Department of State (a family of 6 would receive $11,100). This includes: pre-arrival, reception, initial housing food, clothing, referral services and social programs. The benefit eligibility is for those refugees who have been in the U.S. for up to three months.

'Refugees who've been in the United States up to seven years are also offered medical financial assistance through Medicaid as well as through the State Children's Health Insurance Program (SCHIP)." http://conservativepost.com/obama-doesnt-have-money-for-vets-and-marines-but-check-what-he-did-for-refugees/

Passage of the DREAM Act would add $329 Billion to the U.S. economy, according to the Center for American Progress.

What happened to all of the immigrant children that came streaming into the United States – that were invited by Obama? You know they were not sent back home. Seven Hundred and Sixty of them were dropped into Tennessee without anyone's knowledge or any warning. Tennessee Governor Bill Haslam was fit to be tied.

"It is unacceptable that we became aware via a posting on the HHS website that 760 unaccompanied children have been released by the Office of Refugee Resettlement to sponsors in Tennessee without my administration's knowledge," the governor wrote in a strongly-worded letter to President Obama. "I still have not been contacted and have no information about these individuals or their sponsors other than what was posted on the HHS website," he wrote.

It's been the Obama administration's standard operating procedure to release the illegals into states without notifying local or state government officials. If Obama is truly acting in the best interests of the nation – why is he cloaking this nefarious scheme in a shroud of secrecy? http://fxn.ws/UIUpz9

Iowa had a different idea about it. Obama just said "Up yours Iowa." Iowa shoved it back.

The Governor of Iowa announced that Iowa was not going to take any illegal children. Obama overruled him and sent him 124 teens between the ages of 13 and 19. Their plane landed in Des Moines. The Governor drove to the airport and chartered a United plane from Chicago and within eight hours all of the teens were loaded onto the plane and on their way to Honduras where the plane was unloaded. Four social workers from Iowa made sure they made it to the terminal.

The Social Workers told the Honduras officials "here are your teens, they have no papers, you let them come illegally to America, Iowa refuses to take them. Iowa did not hear one thing from Washington.

Our prisons are full of Illegals who have committed felonies. You can go any place on our internet and find pictures of Hispanics desecrating our flag or flying the Mexico flag instead of the American flag. How many really want to assimilate and become Americans?

There has been a lot of discussion this year about immigration and a lot of confusion about the Fourteenth Amendment.

"Liberals argue that the 14th Amendment infers automatic citizenship upon any person born within the United States, even if the person's parents are in the country illegally.

'This isn't what was intended by the 14th Amendment, as proven by the words of the very man who authored the amendment in 1866, Michigan Sen. Jacob M. Howard.

'Howard explained in writing exactly what the scope of the law was when he introduced it, making it quite clear that it was referring to granting citizenship to the recently freed slaves only, not foreigners or even Native Americans.

'According to The Federalist Papers Project, Howard wrote, in part, "that every person born within the limits of the United States, and subject to their jurisdiction, is by virtue of natural law and national law a citizen of the United States."

'But Howard continued, "This will not, of course, include persons born in the United States who are foreigners, aliens, who belong to the families of ambassadors or foreign ministers accredited to the government of the United States, but will include every other class of persons." http://bit.ly/1N1kqyG

VI

MUSLIMS AND MUSLIM BROTHERHOOD

P resident-elect Obama chooses the leader of a Muslim Brotherhood-affiliated group to recite a prayer during his January 2009 inauguration:

Obama selected Ingrid Mattson – then-president of the Islamic Society of North America (ISNA), a Muslim Brotherhood-linked group that had previously been named as an unindicted co-conspirator in a Hamas terror-funding case – to recite a prayer during his inauguration ceremonies in January 2009. The Muslim Brotherhood, which is the ideological forebear of both Hamas and al Qaeda, openly promotes the establishment of a worldwide Islamic caliphate and is bitterly hostile towards Israel. Not only did Obama fail to ask Mattson to explain ISNA's links to the Brotherhood and Hamas, but he sent his senior adviser, Valerie Jarrett, to be the keynote speaker at ISNA's national convention later that year.

Dr. Emanuel Tanya, a well-known and well-respected psychiatrist, once said in an e-mail: A man whose family was German aristocracy prior to World War II, owned a number of large industries and estates. When asked how many German people were true Nazis, the answer he gave could guide our attitude toward fanaticism. 'Very few people were true Nazis,' he said, 'but many enjoyed the return of German pride, and many more were too busy to care. I was one of those who just thought the Nazis were a bunch of fools. So, the majority just sat back and let it all happen. Then, before we knew it, they owned us, and we had lost control, and the end of the world had come.' 'My family lost everything. I ended up in a concentration camp and the Allies destroyed my factories.'

'We are told again and again by 'experts' and 'talking heads' that Islam is a religion of peace and that the vast majority of Muslims just want to live in peace. Although this unqualified assertion may be true, it is entirely irrelevant. It is meaningless fluff meant to make us feel better and meant to somehow diminish the specter of fanatics rampaging across the globe in the name of Islam.'

'The fact is that the fanatics rule Islam at this moment in history. It is the fanatics who march. It is the fanatics who wage any one of 50 shooting wars worldwide. It is the fanatics who systematically slaughter Christian or tribal groups throughout Africa and are gradually taking over the entire continent in an Islamic wave. It is the fanatics who bomb, behead, murder, or honor-kill. It is the fanatics who take over mosque after mosque. It is the fanatics who zealously spread the stoning and hanging of rape victims and homosexuals. It is the fanatics who teach their young to kill and to become suicide bombers.'

'The hard, quantifiable fact is that the peaceful majority, the 'silent majority,' is cowed and extraneous. Communist Russia was comprised of Russians who just wanted to live in peace, yet the Russian Communists were responsible for the murder of about 20 million people. The peaceful majority were irrelevant. China's huge population was peaceful as well, but Chinese Communists managed to kill a staggering 70 million people.'

'The average Japanese individual prior to World War II was not a War mongering sadist. Yet, Japan murdered and slaughtered its way across South East Asia in an orgy of killing that included the systematic murder of 12 million Chinese civilians; most killed by sword, shovel, and bayonet. And who can forget Rwanda, which collapsed into butchery? Could it not be said that the majority of Rwandans were 'peace loving'?

'History lessons are often incredibly simple and blunt, yet for all our powers of reason, we often miss the most basic and uncomplicated of points: peace-loving Muslims have been made irrelevant by their silence. Peace-loving Muslims will become our enemy if they don't speak up, because like my friend from Germany , they will awaken one day and find that the fanatics own them, and the end of their world will have begun.' 'Peace-loving Germans, Japanese, Chinese, Russians, Rwandans, Serbs, Afghans, Iraqis, Palestinians, Somalis, Nigerians, Algerians, and many others have died because the peaceful majority did not speak up until it was too late.' 'Now Islamic prayers have been introduced in Toronto and other public schools in Ontario, and, yes, in Ottawa, too, while the Lord's Prayer was removed (due to being so offensive?). The Islamic way may be peaceful for the time being in our country until the fanatics move in.'

'In Australia, and indeed in many countries around the world, many of the most commonly consumed food items have the halal emblem on them. Just look at the back of some of the most popular chocolate bars, and at other food items in your local supermarket. Food on aircraft have the halal emblem just to appease the privileged minority who are now rapidly expanding within the nation's shores.'

'In the U.K, the Muslim communities refuse to integrate and there are now dozens of "no-go" zones within major cities across the country that the police force dare not intrude upon. Sharia law prevails there, because the Muslim communities in those areas refuse to acknowledge British law.'

'As for us who watch it all unfold, we must pay attention to the only group that counts - the fanatics who threaten our way of life."

Muslim parents of the Montreal, Canada suburb of Dorval, demanded the abolition of pork from the school canteens. They quickly received a note of refusal from the Mayor and Town Clerk of the City stating: "Muslims must understand that they have to adapt to Canada and Quebec, its customs, its traditions, its way of life, because that's where they chose to immigrate. "They must understand that they have to integrate and learn to live in Quebec. "They must understand that it is for them to change their lifestyle, not the Canadians who so generously welcomed them. "They must understand that Canadians are neither racist nor xenophobic, they accepted many immigrants before Muslims. America should take notice, not only for Muslim but all other immigrants.

We have the most transparent administration in history holding secret meetings at the White House with "American Muslim Leaders." Although the media made a request for a list of names of those that attended, nothing was forthcoming.

I have not kept it a secret that I believe Obama is a Muslim. He is certainly a follower of the Islamic faith and ideology. He walks very softly around the Muslim Community and throws the Christians under the bus every chance he gets. It has been said, however, "he is probably just a narcissistic atheist, agnostic, or secular humanist, as he seems to worship at the altar of himself."

There is still no doubt he is a supporter of the Islamic faith and defends the actions of radical Islamists. By his very actions, Obama shows himself to be more in sympathy and support for Islam than Christianity and no longer attempts to hide it. He said, "The USA is not a Christian Nation." You are wrong - we are a Christian Nation founded on Judeo-Christian values allowing all religions in America to worship and practice freely... something that Islam would never do.

Obama constantly refers to "the Muslim World." I know of Muslim countries. Do you know of a Muslim world? I am not the only one that believes Obama is a Muslim. I feel certain of that. Throughout his campaign, Obama repeatedly referred to his Muslim family members, his ties to Indonesia, his Muslim villages, and his Arabic name.

Dr. Peter Hammond's book: *Slavery, Terrorism, and Islam: "The Historical Roots and Contemporary Threat* goes into detail about Islam as follows:

"Islam is not a religion, nor is it a cult. In its fullest form, it is a complete, total, 100% system of life.

'Islam has religious, legal, political, economic, social, and military components. The religious component is a beard for all of the components.

'Islamization begins when there are sufficient Muslims in a country to agitate for their religious privileges.

'When politically correct, tolerant, and culturally diverse societies agree to Muslim demands for their religious privileges, some of the other components tend to creep in as well.

'Here's how it works:

'As long as the Muslim population remains around or under 2% in any given country, they will be for the most part regarded as a peace-loving minority, and not as a threat to other citizens.

This is the case in:

United States – Muslim 0.6%
Australia – Muslim 1.5%
Canada – Muslim 1.9%
China – Muslim 1.8%
Italy – Muslim 1.5%
Norway – Muslim 1.8%

'At 2% to 5%, they begin to proselytize from other ethnic minorities and disaffected groups, often with major recruiting from the jails and among street gangs. This is happening in:

Denmark – Muslim 2%
Germany – Muslim 3.7%
United Kingdom – Muslim 2.7%
Spain – Muslim 4%
Thailand – Muslim 4.6%

'From 5% on, they exercise an inordinate influence in proportion to their percentage of the population. For example, they will push for the introduction of halal (clean by Islamic standards) food, thereby securing food preparation jobs for Muslims. They will increase pressure on supermarket chains to feature halal on their shelves – along with threats for failure to comply.

This is occurring in:

France – Muslim 8%
Philippines – Muslim 5%
Sweden – Muslim 5%
Switzerland – Muslim 4.3%
The Netherlands – Muslim 5.5%
Trinidad & Tobago – Muslim 5.8%

'At this point, they will work to get the ruling government to allow them to rule themselves (within their ghettos) under Sharia, the Islamic Law.

'The ultimate goal of Islamists is to establish Sharia law over the entire world.

'When Muslims approach 10% of the population, they tend to increase lawlessness as a means of complaint about their conditions.

In Paris, we are already seeing car-burnings. Any non-Muslim action offends Islam and results in uprisings and threats, such as in Amsterdam, with opposition to Mohammed cartoons and films about Islam. Such tensions are seen daily, particularly in Muslim sections in:

Guyana – Muslim 10%
India – Muslim 13.4%
Israel – Muslim 16%
Kenya – Muslim 10%
Russia – Muslim 15%

'After reaching 20%, nations can expect hair-trigger rioting, jihad militia formations, sporadic killings, and the burnings of Christian churches and Jewish synagogues, such as in:

Ethiopia – Muslim 32.8%

'At 40%, nations experience widespread massacres, chronic terror attacks, and ongoing militia warfare, such as in:

Bosnia – Muslim 40%
Chad – Muslim 53.1%
Lebanon – Muslim 59.7%

'From 60%, nations experience unfettered persecution of non-believers of all other religions (including non-conforming Muslims), sporadic ethnic cleansing (genocide), use of Sharia Law as a weapon, and Jizya, the tax placed on infidels, such as in:

Albania – Muslim 70%
Malaysia – Muslim 60.4%
Qatar – Muslim 77.5%
Sudan – Muslim 70%

'After 80%, expect daily intimidation and violent jihad, some State-run ethnic cleansing, and even some genocide, as these nations drive out the infidels, and move toward 100% Muslim, such as has been experienced and is on-going in:

Bangladesh – Muslim 83%
Egypt – Muslim 90%
Gaza – Muslim 98.7%
Indonesia – Muslim 86.1%
Iran – Muslim 98%
Iraq – Muslim 97%
Jordan – Muslim 92%
Morocco – Muslim 98.7%
Pakistan – Muslim 97%
Palestine – Muslim 99%
Syria – Muslim 90%
Tajikistan – Muslim 90%
Turkey – Muslim 99.8%
United Arab Emirates – Muslim 96%

'100% will usher in the peace of 'Dar-es-Salaam' – the Islamic House of Peace. Here there's supposed to be peace, because everybody is a Muslim, the Madrasses are the only schools, and the Koran is the only word, such as in:

Afghanistan – Muslim 100%
Saudi Arabia – Muslim 100%
Somalia – Muslim 100%
Yemen – Muslim 100%

'Unfortunately, peace is never achieved, as in these 100% states the most radical Muslims intimidate and spew hatred, and satisfy their blood lust by killing less radical Muslims, for a variety of reasons.

'Before I was nine, I had learned the basic canon of Arab life. It was me against my brother; me and my brother against our father; my family against my cousins and the clan; the clan against the tribe; the tribe against the world, and all of us against the infidel. – Leon Uris, 'The Haj.'

'It is important to understand that in some countries, with well under 100% Muslim populations, such as France, the minority Muslim populations live in ghettos, within which they are 100% Muslim, and within which they live by Sharia Law. The national police do not even enter these ghettos. There are no national courts, nor schools, nor non-Muslim religious facilities. In such situations, Muslims do not integrate into the community at large. The children attend madrassas. They learn only the Koran. To even associate with an infidel is a crime punishable with death. Therefore, in some areas of certain nations, Muslim Imams and extremists exercise more power than the national average would indicate.

'Today's 1.5 billion Muslims make up 22% of the world's population. But their birth rates are higher than the birth rates of Christians, Hindus, Buddhists, Jews, and all other believers. Muslims will exceed 50% of the world's population by the end of this century.

'Well, boys and girls, today we are letting the fox guard the henhouse.

'The wolves will be herding the sheep!

'NOTE: Has anyone ever heard a new government official being identified as a devout 'Catholic, a devout Jew or a devout Protestant...? Just wondering.

'Devout Muslims being appointed to critical Homeland Security positions?

'Doesn't this make you feel safer already??

'That should make the United States much safer, huh!!

'Was it not "Devout Muslim men" that flew planes into U.S. buildings only ten years ago?

'We must never forget this.

'Was it not a Devout Muslim man who killed 13 at Fort Hood? (He killed "From within" -don't forget that).

'Also: This is very interesting, and we all need to read it from start to finish. Maybe this is why our American Muslims are so quiet and not speaking out about any atrocities. This question was sent to a friend who worked in Saudi Arabia for 20 years. The following is his reply:

'Can a good Muslim be a good American?

'Theologically - no . . . Because his allegiance is to Allah, The moon God of Arabia

104

'Religiously, no. Because no other religion is accepted by His Allah except Islam (Quran, 2:256)(Koran)

'Scripturally, no. Because his allegiance is to the five Pillars of Islam and the Quran.

'Geographically, no. Because his allegiance is to Mecca, to which he turns in prayer five times a day.

'Socially, no. Because his allegiance to Islam forbids him to make friends with Christians or Jews..

'Politically, no. Because he must submit to the mullahs (spiritual leaders), who teach annihilation of Israel and destruction of America, the great Satan.

'Domestically, no. Because he is instructed to marry four Women and beat and scourge his wife when she disobeys him (Quran 4:34)

'Intellectually, no. Because he cannot accept the American Constitution since it is based on Biblical principles, and he believes the Bible to be corrupt.

'Philosophically, no. Because Islam, Muhammad, and the Quran do not allow freedom of religion and expression.. Democracy and Islam cannot co-exist. Every Muslim government is either dictatorial or autocratic.

'Spiritually, no. Because when we declare 'one nation under God,' the Christian's God is loving and kind, while Allah is never referred to as Heavenly father, nor is he ever called love in The Quran's 99 excellent names.

'Therefore, after much study and deliberation. ... Perhaps we should be very suspicious of all Muslims in this country. - - - They obviously cannot be both 'good' Muslims and good Americans. Call it what you wish, it's still the truth. The more who understand this, the better it will be for our country and our future. The religious war is bigger than we know or understand.

'Can a Muslim be a good soldier?

'Army Maj. Nidal Malik Hasan opened fire at Ft. Hood and Killed 13. He is a good Muslim!

'Footnote: The Muslims have said they will destroy us from within."

Internal Muslim Brotherhood documents captured by the FBI name Islamic Society of North America (ISNA) as one of 29 American-Muslim organizations with ties to the Muslim Brotherhood.

The Brotherhood gave birth to both al Qaeda and Hamas.

"It's also easy to know what the Brotherhood's agenda is because they told us in their own documents," They said their work in America is a kind of grand jihad, in eliminating and destroying Western civilization from within. And most importantly, they say they want to do it at the hands not just of the believers – the Muslim Brotherhood supporters – but at the hands of the unbelievers – us."

Obama has a continuing relationship with ISNA and publicly brags about it.

There was a time with John McCain jumped on Michelle Bachman for requesting that the Muslim influence on the Obama Administration be investigated because Huma Abedin was Deputy Chief of Staff to Secretary of State Hillary Clinton and had access to top secret information – and had deep ties to the Muslim Brotherhood.

It was okay for Muslim groups like CAIR and ISNA to go in and purge hundreds of pages of "offensive" words and phrases like "jihad" and "Islamist" from FBI training materials. But it was not okay for Conservative groups who were labeled as "McCarthyites" to call for an investigation, and it was quickly shut down. http://www.westernjournalism.com/muslim-brotherhood-infiltrates-the-white-house/#mRVSOtsziqTKzToI.99

Representative Keith Ellison is the first Muslim to be elected to Congress. He was raised Roman Catholic. One of his brothers is a pastor of a Baptist church in Detroit. His grandfather worked as a member of the NAACP in Louisiana. He said when he looked at his spiritual life he looked at what might inform social change, justice in society, and he found Islam. His wife is not Muslim, but his four children are raised Muslim.

Communist sympathizer, Valerie Jarrett was born in Shiraz, Iran to American parents, James E., and Barbara Taylor Bowman. Her grandfather, Robert Robinson Taylor was accredited as the first African American Architect. Her father ran a children's hospital in Shiraz. Her parents were both African-American. Jarrett also speaks Persian and French. She married William Robert Jarrett, a Chicago Sun-Times Reporter in 1983. She began working for Chicago Mayor Harold Washington in 1987. She was Deputy Chief of Staff for Mayor

Richard Daley in 1991 when she hired Michelle Robinson, who was then engaged to Barack Obama.

Jarrett is one of the three senior advisers to President Obama. She holds the retitled position of assistant to the president for intergovernmental affairs and public engagement, managing the White House Office of Public Engagement, Office of Intergovernmental Affairs and Office of Urban Affairs. Add everything connecting her to Muslims

Huma Abedin – "quoting former federal prosecutor Andrew C. McCarthy writing at National Review this week – Huma Abedin "worked for many years at a journal that promotes Islamic supremacist ideology that was founded by a top al-Qaida financier, Abdullah Omar Naseef." That would be for at least seven years (1996-2003), by the way, during which Abedin also worked for Hillary Clinton.

'Let this sink in for just a moment. The journal Huma worked for – which promotes Islamic supremacism and was founded by al-Qaida financer Naseef, who also headed the Muslim World League, a leading Muslim Brotherhood organization – is called the Journal of Muslim Minority Affairs. It was edited first by Huma's father, Syed Abedin, and now by her mother, Saleha Abedin. Saleha is a member of the Muslim Sisterhood. Mother Abedin also directs an organization (the International Islamic Committee for Woman and Child) that comes under the umbrella of the Union for Good, another U.S.-designated terrorist organization. As McCarthy reminds us, "the Union for Good is led by Sheikh Yusef al-Qaradawi, the notorious Muslim Brotherhood jurist who has issued fatwas calling for the killing of American military and support personnel in Iraq as well as suicide bombings in Israel."

'Given these alarming professional and family associations, it is hard to imagine how Huma Abedin ever received the security clearance necessary to work closely with the Secretary of State. But she did, and from her powerful post, she undoubtedly exerted influence over U.S. policy-making. (In his National Review piece, McCarthy lists specific actions that bespeak a shift in U.S. foreign policy to favor the Muslim Brotherhood.)

'Isn't the Abedin-Clinton national security story at least as newsworthy as her husband, Anthony Weiner's private parts?" http://www.wnd.com/2013/07/huma-abedin-muslim-brotherhood-princess/#XZEkl1vWypDIWA3v.99

In April 2009, President Obama appointed Los Angeles Deputy Mayor Arif Alikhan as Assistant Secretary for Policy Development at the Department of Homeland Security. Two weeks before he received this appointment, Alikhan (who once called the jihadist terror group Hezbollah a "liberation movement") had participated in a fund raiser for the Muslim Public Affairs Council (MPAC), which, like ISNA, is linked to the Muslim Brotherhood. Assistant Secretary for Policy Development for Homeland Security, Arif Alikhan, is a Muslim. "Arif Alikhan" is the Deputy Executive Director of Homeland Security, Law Enforcement, and Fire/EMS at Los Angeles World Airports. He was appointed by Obama to the new position in October 2011 and is responsible for the 1,200 sworn police officers and civilian security officers that protect Los Angeles International Airport, Ontario International Airport, and Van Nuys Airport. He is also responsible for all fire and emergency medical services at LAWA's three airports. Arif Alikhan was born in 1968 after his parents immigrated to North America from Pakistan (mother) and India, (father) in the late 1960s.

Homeland Security Advisor, Mohammed Elibiary, is a Muslim. According to Breitbart, Elibiary is a senior member of the Department of Homeland Security Advisory Council. Elibiary also supports brokering a U.S. partnership with the Muslim Brotherhood terrorist group.

Obama advisor and founder of the Muslim Public Affairs Council, Salam al-Marayati, is a Muslim. Al-Marayati seems a polite, moderate Arab-American Muslim, is a frequent media spokesperson for American Muslims and was the Clintons' guest at the White House several times. He espouses American ideals and has reached out to the Christian and Jewish communities. An Iraqi-American, Al-Marayati co-founded and became director of the Los Angeles-based MPAC, the Muslim Public Affairs Council, in 1988 to bring help integrate Muslims into American politics and give them a voice.

While Al-Marayati is not as radical as his MPAC colleagues–Maher H. Hathout and former board member Mahdi Bray-or as his coalition organizations such as CAIR, he is not a moderate. Consider some of his positions:

Al-Marayati tries to normalize Islam by showing that he shares the values of the US Constitution. Al-Marayati also argues that separation of church and state, "is not the only acceptable form of government" and in essence endorses sharia.

He objects to Islam alone being identified with terrorism and denies Wahabism poses any dangers. "There are radical Christian, Jewish and Hindu movements, too, which are also capable of slaughtering innocents (The Lord's Resistance Army in Uganda, Baruch Goldstein and the settler extremists in Israel, the Hindutva motivated pogroms in India)."

Al-Marayati equated jihad (holy war) with Patrick Henry's 'Give me liberty or give me death." He equates terrorists to "American freedom fighters a hundred years ago [who] were also regarded as terrorists by the British." 1996

Hezbollah's attacks on Israel in the 1990s were "not terrorism. That is legitimate resistance." PBS News Hour 1999

Israel was "established by force, violence and terrorism" and is "racist, chauvinistic, and militaristic." Statement signed by MPAC1993.

Israel's defensive action against terrorism "is nothing more than war to steal lands from Palestinians, to decimate their leadership, to humiliate the Palestinian people." Alan Keyes Show 4/15/02

Terrorism is the work of only a "few extremists" and Israel "cannot be allowed" to use their actions "to derail the Road Map." MPAC Statement on the Road Map

"If we're going to look at suspects [for 9/11], we should look to the groups that benefit the most... we should put the state of Israel on the suspect list because I think this diverts attention from what's happening in the Palestinian territories so that they can go on with their aggression and occupation and apartheid policies." Al-Marayati, on KCRW 9/11/01

"Flaws in State Department Global Terrorism Report.....it flouts both reason and justice to ignore large-scale state-sponsored terrorism when perpetrated by Israel, to focus solely on the acts of Palestinians." MPAC statement May 18, 2001.

"The US government has once again demonstrated its double standard....American Muslim charities have lost practically all presumption of innocence... while other groups have conducted the most egregious conduct in financing extremism with impunity. In the case of pro-Israel charities... the impression (is given) that indicted war criminals (i.e., Sharon) have been provided American tax shelter....MPAC challenges the US Treasury Department to open an investigation of these irregularities...." MPAC Statement January 27, 2003.

"Jewish unlawfulness is tolerated because powerful brokers can dictate terms in Congress and the Administration." [11] MPAC-affiliated magazine, *The Minaret*, 1994

MPAC co-sponsored pro-Palestinian rallies in 2000 where MPAC speakers chanted "Khaybar, Khaybar, oh Jews, the Army of Muhammed is coming for you!"; posters called for "Death to Israel" and literature called for the destruction of the Jews and Israel. http://bit.ly/1lsgJdZ

Obama's Sharia Czar, Imam Mohamed Magid, of the Islamic Society of North America is a Muslim. Mohamed Magid is the Obama administration's go-to guy for Muslim outreach and advises on international affairs and counterterrorism. He is a regular visitor to the White House (even when the administration wants to conceal it). Magid attends important administration speeches on the US Middle East policy at the State Department. He counsels the Department of Justice to criminalize defamation of Islam. He entertains the deputy national security adviser at his DC-area mosque. He serves on the Department of Homeland Security's Countering Violent Extremism Working Group. He also advises the FBI and many other Federal agencies. http://bit.ly/1Qb0cGU

Dawud Walid, another Muslim is popular with the Obama Administration and took two taxpayer-financed trips overseas on behalf of the State Department. (1) "Dawud Walid is back from his second consecutive government-financed travel to Mali to "build religious and cultural ties between American religious and civic leaders with Malian counterparts. According to a transcript posted on his web site, Walid told his Malian hosts that "America has evolved to be one of the world's most tolerant societies regarding religious expression and practice."

"But State Department money also financed Walid's trashing of American treatment of American Muslims. "Since the tragedy of September 11, 2001, American Muslims have been subjected to increased discrimination from racial and religious profiling by law enforcement, a rise in hate crimes, work-place discrimination, to the recent trend of some citizens and elected officials protesting the construction of new mosques. Late last year, an Imam named Luqman

Ameen Abdullah was shot twenty-one times including twice in the back during a raid by law enforcement agencies. The raid occurred based on an investigation of Abdullah's mosque, which ended up proving no links to terrorism or treason," Walid said in Bamako, Mali." http://bit.ly/1l504xN

As of February 2015, Rashad Hussain was an American attorney, and Special Envoy and Coordinator for Strategic Counterterrorism Communications. Before that time, he was U.S special envoy to the Organization of Islamic Cooperation (OIC), the second largest intergovernmental body after the UN, with 57 member states. Hussain, a Muslim of Indian heritage, has served in the White House Counsel's Office and on the National Security Council as a political appointee of the Obama Administration. Hussain was born in Wyoming and was raised in Plano, Texas, the son of Indian-born U.S. citizens. The Religion News Service said that rather than noting that Hussain has memorized the Quran, "Muslims abroad are more likely to take note of his White House credentials, and access to the Oval Office, as he seeks partnerships in education, health, science, and technology."

Eboo Patel is a member of President Barack Obama's inaugural Advisory Council on Faith-Based Neighborhood Partnerships. He is an American Ismaili Muslim of Gujarati Indian heritage and founder and president of the Interfaith Youth Core, a Chicago-based international nonprofit that aims to promote interfaith cooperation.

And last but not least, our closet Muslim himself, Barack Hussein Obama. It's questionable if Obama ever officially took the oath of office when he was sworn in. He didn't repeat the oath properly to defend our nation and our Constitution.

The Egyptian magazine *Rose al-Youssef* has identified at least six Brotherhood-tied agents of influence who have worked into positions in the Obama administration. "The weekly publication, founded in 1925, said the operatives have turned the White House "from a position hostile to Islamic groups and organizations in the world to the largest and most important supporter of the Muslim Brotherhood," an Egyptian-based jihadist movement that supports Hamas and al-Qaida."

As I stated previously in *The Lyin Kings*, President Obama backed the Muslim Brotherhood takeover of Egypt. Secret Service records showed hundreds of visits to the White House since 2009. The Brotherhood and Obama have the same goal: to destroy the West. Our government has done a lot in empowering the Brotherhood's American network under the guise of "Islamic outreach."

The six named people include Arif Alikhan, assistant secretary of Homeland Security for Policy development; Mohammed Elibiary, a member of the Homeland Security Advisory Council; Rashad Hussain, the U.S. special envoy to the Organization of the Islamic Conference; Salam al-Marayati, co-founder of the Muslim Public Affairs Council (MPAC); Imam Mohamed Magid, president of the Islamic Society of North America (ISNA); and Eboo Patel, a member of President Obama's Advisory Council on Faith-Based Neighborhood Partnerships.

Does it bother anyone that a Muslim is now in control of our strategy against ISIS? That is what Rashad Hussain now does as an empowered Center for Strategic Counterterrorism Communications, currently a small component of the U.S. State Department, he will spearhead the new campaign to fight the ISIS propaganda machine.

"Hussain, a devout Muslim, has a history of participating in events connected with the Muslim Brotherhood," reported Cal Thomas in an article published by Townhall.

'Citing Egypt's *Rose El-Youssef* magazine, The Investigative Project on Terrorism reported that Hussain "maintained close ties with people and groups that [the magazine] says comprise the Muslim Brotherhood network in America." http://bit.ly/1NkKnZi

Egypt suggests that Alikhan provides the direct link between the Obama administration and the Arab Spring revolutions of 2011.

"Elibiary, who has endorsed the ideas of radical Muslim Brotherhood luminary Sayyid Qutb, may have leaked secret materials contained in Department of Homeland Security databases, according to the magazine. He, however, denies having any connection with the Brotherhood.

'Elibiary also played a role in defining the Obama administration's counterterrorism strategy. The magazine asserts that Elibiary wrote the speech Obama gave when he told former Egyptian President Hosni Mubarak to leave power but offers no source or evidence for the claim."

According to the magazine. Rashad Hussain maintains very close ties with people and groups that comprise the Muslim Brotherhood in America. Magid heads the ISNA, which founded the Muslim Brotherhood members.

"Rose El-Youssef says Patel maintains a close relationship with Hani Ramadan, the grandson of Brotherhood founder Hasan al-Banna and is a member of the Muslim Students Association, which it identifies as "a large Brotherhood organization." http://bit.ly/1wGvJnB

Also during the early part of his presidency, Obama appointed Dalia Mogahed – a pro-Sharia Muslim – as his chief adviser on Islamic affairs. Dalia Mogahed is an advisor on all matters Islamic whom Obama has appointed to the Council on Faith-Based and Neighborhood Partnerships. She describes her role in the Obama administration as a communicator to the president and other public officials of "what it is Muslims want." In other words, she is Obama's Muslim czar. As such, her particular brand of Islam warrants some scrutiny.

Together with such luminaries as Feisal Abdul Rauf, former Secretary of State Madeleine Albright, and diplomat Dennis Ross, Mogahed was a leading voice in the Leadership Group on U.S.-Muslim Engagement, which in September 2008 had issued a 154-page recommendation paper – the Obama administration eventually adopted a number of those suggestions (on how to improve America's relationship with Muslims globally). The paper specifically called on the U.S. to engage opposition parties (including the Muslim Brotherhood) in Egypt and to use intermediaries to engage Hamas – in hopes of moderating the terror group.

In early October 2009, Mogahed was interviewed on a British television program hosted by Ibtihal Bsis, a member of the extremist Hizb ut Tahrir party, which seeks to facilitate the non-violent destruction of Western democracy and the creation of a worldwide Islamic state governed by Sharia Law. Bsis and another guest (also a member of Hizb ut Tahrir) stated that Sharia should be "the source of legislation" for all nations in the world; they also repeatedly condemned the "man-made law" and the "lethal cocktail of liberty and capitalism" that existed in Western societies. Mogahed did not dispute any of their assertions. Instead, she stated that the Western view of Sharia was "oversimplified," and that the majority of Muslim women around the world associated Islamic Law with "gender justice." "I think the reason so many women support Sharia is because they have a very different understanding of Sharia than the common perception in Western media," she said.

On June 4, 2009, President Obama went to Cairo, Egypt to deliver a much-anticipated address to the Muslim world. During the weeks prior to the speech, he made sure to invite Muslim Brotherhood leaders to attend. During the speech itself, the President stated that "anti-Semitism in Europe culminated in an unprecedented Holocaust." But he made no mention of the Arab anti-Semitism of the World War II era (and beyond), even though he was speaking in the very country that had made a national hero of Grand Mufti Haj Muhammed Amin al-Husseini, who spent the war years in Berlin as Hitler's guest, helping the Fuehrer facilitate the Final Solution. Nor did Obama once mention the word "terrorism."

Does everyone still think Obama is a Christian and that he has the best interest of this country at heart? It seems that the more damage that he does the most arrogant he becomes. Obama seems to have made it a priority to defend Islam at every opportunity.

"In 2011, the Arab Spring swept through the Middle East and North Africa, sparking revolutions that toppled several governments, including that of Egypt, which was subsequently replaced by the Muslim Brotherhood.

'However, Egyptians quickly realized their mistake in allowing the Muslim Brotherhood to seize power. Another uprising occurred, with the Egyptian military overthrowing the abusive theocratic regime of Mohamed Morsi, replacing him with the benevolently moderate Gen. Abdel Fattah el-Sisi.

'Egypt went on to declare the Muslim Brotherhood a terrorist organization, outlawing them from the country and locking up their leaders.

'Unfortunately for America's ally, the Obama administration doesn't see the Muslim Brotherhood the same way, and has reached out to support the radical Islamic group, even inviting them into the highest levels of our government, including the White House."

"Egyptian newspapers have long been critical of the Obama administration, even going so far as to accuse Obama of being an actual member of the Brotherhood. On top of that, both Obama and Hillary Clinton have been charged in Egyptian courts with providing aid to the terrorist group. Moderate Arabs and Muslims are now viewing

America as an ally to terrorist groups, instead of being an ally to the moderates working towards stability and reform." http://bit.ly/1lshbJt

"Perhaps the most serious charge against the two involves their attempted bribe to the tune of $8 billion which was an attempt to sway the Brotherhood to open up part of the Sinai Peninsula to Hamas groups to make it easier to attack Israel.

'While there are numerous reasons to impeach Obama at this point, news like this serves to strengthen the case further to do so. Obama continuously takes sides with terrorist groups and has managed to destroy America's reputation with his ridiculously idiotic foreign policy decisions." http://bit.ly/1Su8Obb

Shariah law is anything but free and is in complete opposition to American principles and the Constitution.

And do you wonder why people think Obama is a Muslim? Check it out: The White House has reportedly sent a top Department of Homeland Security (DHS) official to the Islamic Society of Greater Oklahoma City (ISGOC) to "present a special thank you to the Muslim congregation," Oklahoma's KFOR reports.

The beheader's mosque, the Islamic Society of Greater Oklahoma City, was founded by a sibling of a U.S.-designated Hamas terrorist, and in the past has welcomed an Imam who was a close confidant to al-Qaeda mastermind Anwar al-Awlaki.

David L. Myers, who serves as director of the DHS Center for Faith-based & Neighborhood Partnerships, was tasked with presenting a personal message from President Barack Obama. It read, "Your service is a powerful example of the powerful roots of the Abrahamic faiths and how our communities can come together with shared peace with dignity and a sense of justice."

Two days before proud ISGOC congregation member Alton Nolen (AKA Jahkeem Yisrael) ruthlessly beheaded an innocent woman while reportedly shouting Islamic slogans, ISGOC Imam Imad Enchassi made unproven claims about multiple death threats, specifically beheadings, against Muslims and their children in Oklahoma. Breitbart News investigated Oklahoma state hate crime databases and found no record of widespread anti-Muslim persecution in the state. Over the past five years, a total of seven anti-Islamic hate crimes has been documented in the State of Oklahoma. http://bit.ly/1Ti3lEd

Dearborn, Michigan's population is pretty much Arab Muslim and they make it plain that they do not want any whites or Christians living there and have pretty much caused all others to move out of the city. In June of 2010, a case arose from the annual Arab International Festival when Wayne County sheriff's deputies stood by while a Muslim mob threw rocks at Christians, bloodying them. The police officers then threatened the Christians with arrest if they did not leave the event.

"I have seen it with my own eyes, witnessed it in the backseat of a car and it is for real. No-go zones exist in the United States."

The Christians brought a lawsuit against Wayne County, and a three-judge panel dismissed it. However, a majority of the Sixth Circuit judges has agreed to rehear the matter. This is, of course, great news for religious freedom and freedom of speech. As AFLC co-founder, David Yerushalmi said the First Amendment "is under assault by both Muslim supremacists and Islamists on the one hand and progressives advocating 'hate-speech' crimes on the other."

This is not the first time that Muslim mob violence has caused problems at this Arab festival. In an earlier lawsuit, Christians were awarded $100,000 in damages because of attacks against them.

"AFLC said the rock-throwing incident left members of the evangelism team bloodied while deputies from the Wayne County sheriff's office stood by and watched. Then, when Ruben Israel, the leader of the evangelists, asked officers to enforce the law so that Christians could speak, he was told to either leave or be arrested.

"Whether you agree or disagree with the Christians' message, there is one issue to which there is no dispute: no citizen should be stoned in a city street in America for exercising his constitutional right to freedom of speech," Muise said when the case developed." http://bit.ly/1Qb0Xjq

How would you feel if you drove into a town here in the United States and found that many of the street signs were in Arabic only with no English wording? Then you look around and discover that many of the signs on businesses were also in Arabic. Not possible you say? Think again! Welcome to Dearborn, Michigan.

Steve Tarani, author and speaker recounts what he saw when he rode with a member of the Detroit Metro SWAT Police as they drove around Detroit and into Dearborn:

"The street signs suddenly went from English to Arabic. There wasn't a single English word on any shop or any street sign. And in fact, these little yellow signs were posted all along the edges. Jeremy said to me, 'this is it. We don't go past this line.' And I said to Jeremy, 'what do you mean? You guys are Detroit Metro. You're the SWAT team. You can go anywhere you want. What if you get a call over there?' He said 'This is it, it's hazardous for our team if we go past this line.'"

"Dearborn, Michigan is not the only place that these settlements exist. They are spread out over the country in various cities. There's an estimate of over 5,000 known terrorist cells in the United States. However, our most persistent and significant threat, right now, to us here today this morning, is the homegrown violent extremists."

Murfreesboro, Tennessee is fast becoming a second Muslim-controlled city like Dearborn and there are others on the way. Friends in the United Kingdom told me of how Muslims have taken over entire cities and areas in their country. What they tell me is that it all started with cities like Dearborn and Murfreesboro and just continues to spread. One of my friends compared Islam in England to a cancer that continues to spread and contaminate everything it encounters. In time it will spread to the point that the country dies from it and becomes the home of a religion that teaches hate, bloodshed and sharia law. Like a cancer, the only way to save the nation is to stop the spread of the religion of terrorism. Then he told me that in our modern sophisticated world full of freedoms and rights that it's impossible to stop the spread of Islam without igniting a worldwide religious war.

Maybe we should consider that the seat of our problem is in the White House.

"The Islamic supremacist movement's influence on Washington was reported in *Impeachable Offenses: The Case to Remove Barack Obama from Office* by *New York Times* bestselling authors Aaron Klein and Brenda J. Elliott. The book documents that Obama aided the rise to power of Islamic extremist groups in the Middle East as members served on important national security advisory boards.

The book confirms that the Obama Administration may have exposed national security information through Huma Abedin, Hillary Clinton's deputy chief of staff, who has deep personal and family associations with the Muslim Brotherhood. Abedin's parents are Muslim Brotherhood.

Apparently there are 10 to 15 members of the Muslim Brotherhood working in the government at this moment.

Islam Expert, Frank Gaffney, president of the Center for Security Policy, has created a publication called "The Muslim Brotherhood in the Obama Administration," which addresses the issue that was brought to the attention of Congress in July 2012 by Republican Reps. Michele Bachmann, Trent Franks, Louie Gohmert, Tom Rooney and Lynn Westmoreland.

"The lawmakers asked the inspector generals at the departments of Homeland Security, Justice and State to investigate, prompting Democrats and Republicans to rush to Abedin's defense.

"However, as WND reported, Abedin worked for an organization founded by her family that is effectively at the forefront of a grand Saudi plan to mobilize U.S. Muslim minorities to transform America into a strict Wahhabi-style Islamic state, according to an Arabic-language manifesto issued by the Saudi monarchy. Abedin also was a member of the executive board of the Muslim Student Association, which was identified as a Muslim Brotherhood front group in a 1991 document introduced into evidence during the terror-financing trial of the Texas-based Holy Land Foundation trial.

"The internal memo said Muslim Brotherhood members "must understand that their work in America is a kind of grand jihad in eliminating and destroying the Western civilization from within and 'sabotaging' its miserable house by their hands and by the hands of the believers so that it is eliminated and Allah's religion is made victorious over all other religions."

Claire Lopez, also an Islam expert, said the Brotherhood achieved "information dominance" during the George W. Bush administration that only intensified in the following years.

"Not only did figures associated and identified with the Muslim Brotherhood achieve broad penetration at senior levels of U.S. policy making, but voices that warned of their true agenda (such as Stephen Coughlin's) were actively excluded," she said.

'That information dominance has contributed to startling consequences, most evident in the U.S. policy toward the al-Qaida and Muslim Brotherhood-dominated revolutions that many call the 'Arab Spring,' but which in fact are more accurately termed an 'Islamic Awakening,'" she said.

'Under the Muslim Brotherhood-influenced Obama administration, U.S. policy has undergone such a drastic shift in the direction of outright support for these jihadist movements – from al-Qaida militias in Libya, to the Muslim Brotherhood in Egypt, and both al-Qaida and Muslim Brotherhood-linked rebels in Syria — that it is scarcely recognizable as American anymore."

"Impeachable Offenses" also reported that then-CIA director John Brennan announced the Obama administration was calibrating policies in the fight against terrorism to ensure Americans are never "profiled."

"His speech was arranged by a Muslim Brotherhood-tied group that has deep relations not only with other Brotherhood fronts but to the White House and national security agencies.

'Brennan's NYU session was organized by the Islamic Society of North America or ISNA. ISNA, whose members asked Brennan scores of questions during the event, stated the meeting was intended to initiate a "dialog between government officials and Muslim American leaders to explore issues of national security."

'ISNA was founded in 1981 by the Saudi-funded Muslim Students Association, which itself was founded by the Muslim Brotherhood. The two groups are still partners.

'ISNA is known for its promotion of strict Saudi-style Islam in mosques throughout the U.S.

'Islam scholar Stephen Schwartz describes ISNA as "one of the chief conduits through which the radical Saudi form of Islam passes into the United States." http://bit.ly/1RjdXEl

"In Muslim nations, both Christians and homosexuals are persecuted. That's Islam. Each is systemically jailed, tortured and even executed. Curiously, it's the same cowardly leftists who disingenuously accuse Christians of "anti-gay hate" at home who remain silent while homosexuals are, in point of fact, tortured to death by Muslims abroad.

'Islamic apologist and suspected Muslim Barack Hussein Obama is exhibit "A." If Islamists blew up the White House and the Pentagon (my bad, they already nailed the Pentagon), he'd blame it on the Christian Crusades, the Inquisition and "right-wing extremists."

'A few years back, homosexual columnist Andrew Sullivan declared Barack Obama to be "the first gay president." While this was intended to be a compliment, meaning that Obama had fully embraced and unilaterally implemented the political demands of "LGBT" pressure groups, it turned out to be a premature accolade. Consider the indisputable fact that our "gay president's" BFFs in Iran summarily execute those they suspect of practicing homosexuality. Whether they catch you cold in the bathhouse, or you simply walk with a wisp and speak with a lisp, if they even suspect you're a homosexual, the Iranian government will publicly hang you as a matter of official government policy. These are the evil tyrants with whom our own evil tyrant chooses to play footsie – the Islamic terrorists he intends to arm with nuclear weapons.

'Pick a side, Barry. Is it the "gays" or the Muslims? You can't swing both ways on this one." http://bit.ly/1Tr0f1y

According to Muslims, "Saying 'Merry Christmas' is worse than fornication and drinking alcohol and killing someone because you are approving of the biggest crime ever committed by the children of Adam's sin."

Apparently a large number of Muslim families live in Winooski, Vermont. One restaurant owner had a sign in the window advertising bacon and eggs, and the Muslims did not like the idea of their advertising bacon. I would think they would like that idea because they would know that particular restaurant served bacon and not halal foods. But Muslims can sometimes be bullies and let the restaurant owner know that if he did not remove the sign "there would be safety concerns against him." Perhaps if Muslims want to live in the United States, they should stop being bullies.

Alabama has passed a law banning the use of Islamic Sharia law. Islamic Sharia law is not compatible with Western society and the U.S. Constitution. CAIR has no interest in protecting religious liberty, other than that of Muslims and has made no bones about its desire to impose Sharia law on all Americans one day.

Naturally Muslims are angered and outraged and are pushing back.

Only in America can we have terrorists kill people in the name of Allah and have the media primarily react by fretting that the backlash might harm Muslims.

The United States Embassy celebrated July 4th on June 4th, 2015 in Jakarta, Indonesia. Why? We are being tolerant again and not offend anyone. The purpose was to avoid any conflict with the month-long Ramadan celebration in Jakarta.

Not counting ISIS, there are 57 Islamic countries. Does that number sound familiar? Do you think any one of those countries would move any of their embassy celebrations to accommodate our independence holiday?

The Ambassador said the theme of the event leaned toward "green" development and promoting a green economy.

He also praised Indonesia's performance as a fully functioning democracy, aiming for further collaboration between the two countries in the years to come.

"The United States will continue to support Indonesia in the future through its democratic achievements. Democracy is an American value that we have championed since [the country's birth in] 1776," Blake told the crowd during the festivities at his residence near Taman Suropati, Central Jakarta.

He added that moving the 4th of July celebrations to June 4 was one done out of respect for the upcoming Ramadhan month, which will last from June 17 to July 17. http://bit.ly/1BTKh6m

Since this President has been in office, the United States has constantly made concessions to the Muslims in one form or another, whether it be religious holidays, dress, or food. Recently the President hosted a Ramadan celebration at the White House. He never hosts any related Christian celebrations.

The President said, "The Quran teaches that God's children should tread gently upon the earth and when confronted by ignorance, reply "peace." In honoring these familiar values together–of peace and charity and forgiveness–we affirm that, whatever our faith, we're all one family."

He did not say anything about there is only one God, and his name was not Allah. He did not say anything about Sura 17:111, 10:68, and 43:72-81 denying Jesus is the Messiah. He did not say the Quran teaches that Christians and Jews who do not submit to Islam must be slaughtered.

Islam is a major worldwide player in illegal drugs, human trafficking, sex slavery, violating women's rights, and is the cause of death and destruction wherever it is allowed. To say otherwise is a lie. To say that we are all one family is a sorry attempt by a leader to bring an entire nation under submission to a death cult. www.dailyjot.com

The President continues to support the global Islamist militant group known as the Muslim Brotherhood even now in 2015. A White House strategy document regards the group as a moderate alternative to more violent Islamist groups like al Qaeda and the Islamic State.

The policy of backing the Muslim Brotherhood is outlined in a secret directive called Presidential Study Directive-11, or PSD-11. The directive was produced in 2011 and outlines administration support for political reform in the Middle East and North Africa, according to officials familiar with the classified study. Efforts to force the administration to release the directive or portions of it under the Freedom of Information Act have been unsuccessful.

The directive outlines why the administration has chosen the Muslim Brotherhood, which last year was labeled a terrorist organization by the governments of Saudi Arabia, Egypt and the United Arab Emirates as a key vehicle of U.S. backing for so-called political reform in the Middle East. Saudi Arabia in recent months appears to be moderating its opposition to the Brotherhood in a bid to gain more regional support against pro-Iran rebels in Yemen. http://bit.ly/1Su9xc9

On the close of Ramadan, 2015, and on the same day that a radical Muslim terrorist slaughtered four Marines, and now a Sailor in Chattanooga, Tennessee, President Obama issued the following statement:

"Michelle and I would like to extend our warmest wishes to Muslims in the United States and around the world celebrating Eid-ul-Fitr. As Muslims mark the end of the month, they are reminded that Ramadan is a time to reflect spiritually, build communally, and aid those in need. While Eid marks the end of Ramadan, it marks a new beginning for each individual – a reason to celebrate and express gratitude on this holiday.

'For millions of Muslims, the morning of Eid is marked with the call to prayer echoing through cities and towns across the globe. Millions of people head to local mosques for special Eid prayers followed by festive gatherings, gift exchanges, and feasts among friends, neighbors and families. The diversity of traditions paint the vibrant images we see from around the world capturing the spirit and excitement of Eid – colorful dresses or white garments decorating the masses of people standing in lines for prayer, lanterns and ornaments lighting up bazaars and neighborhoods, intricate henna designs painted on hands of young girls and women, and an abundance of delectable foods and aromatic cuisines.

'As Muslim Americans celebrate Eid across America, the holiday is a reminder to every American of the importance of respecting those of all faiths and beliefs. This past year New York City Public Schools announced adding Eid to their official school calendars alongside Christmas, Hanukkah and other holidays – an acknowledgement of the great diversity and inclusiveness that adds to the richness of our nation. During this year's White House Iftar, I had the opportunity to meet inspiring young Muslim Americans who are leading efforts for greater understanding and unity across diverse communities. Following the Iftar, one of the young attendees helped spearhead an effort that raised more than $75,000 for the churches burned in the wake of the shooting at Emanuel AME Church in Charleston, South Carolina. Americans of all faiths and beliefs must stand together to protect our democracy and strengthen our country as a whole.

'Michelle and I hope today brings joy to all of your homes, both here in the U.S. and around the world. From my family to yours, Eid Mubarak!"

Barack Obama, who claims to be a Christian, more than goes out of his way to appease the Muslim world. He has made a treaty with Iran that is very bad for the United States that has Iran laughing at the United States and has them still shouting death to arrogant Americans.

The Muslim Brotherhood and Common Core

"Should parents be penalized for demanding that their child be exempted from the required teaching of Islamic in Common Core curriculum? Should a teacher or public school administrator penalize parents and children for seeking exemption? Parents are finding out the answers to these questions first hand.

'Listen to learn more.

'To date, public school students are required to:

'Attend public school-sponsored trips to mosques, which also require non-Muslim girls to wear head scarves?

'Question if the Holocaust was "merely a political scheme created to influence public emotion and gain"?

'Learn Islamic indoctrination via vocabulary lessons, and world history (from an Islamic perspective), including the five pillars of Islam?

'Pledge allegiance to the flag in Arabic?

'Have school days off for "Muslim holy days"?

'Proselytize to younger school children by creating a pamphlet about Islam to "introduce Islam to 3rd graders" by describing Allah as the same God of Christians and Jews?

'Recite in class the Shahada ("There is No God but Allah") and kneel and learn to pray the Muslim call to prayer?

'Parents must first understand the origins of Common Core, and more importantly assert their First Amendment and Fourteenth Amendment rights– which protect their parental rights to make educational decisions for their children.

'Technically, Common Core originated from the National Governor's Association (NGA), Council of Chief State School Officers (CCSSO), Achieve Inc., ACT and the College Board. Its state standards are copyrighted by the NGA and CCSSO, a private company, which means they cannot be changed. (The Bill and Melinda Gates Foundation, the United Nations, and Pearson Education, an NGA donor and CCSSO's listed business and industry partner, were integral to creating these standards.)

'In 2009 the "Race to the Top" federal education initiative encouraged states to receive federal money to adopt new standards that would improve their public school children's test performance results. In order to participate, members of both state boards of education and state educational professional standards boards voted to adopt Common Core.

'However, Common Core really originated from the Connect All Schools program, which is part of the "One World Education" initiative orchestrated by Qatar Foundation International (QFI). The director of QFI's Research Center for Islamic Legislation and Ethics is Tariq Ramadan, grandson of Hassan al-Banna who was the founder of The Muslim Brotherhood.

'QFI enlisted Pearson Education to implement and assess Common Core. Pearson Education is listed on the London and New York Stock Exchange; the Libyan Investment Authority is its largest financial contributor, most recently holding 26 million shares.

'According to the Financial Times, the Libyan Investment Authority was founded by Muammar Gaddafi's son, Seif al-Islam. Along with Qatar, Turkey and Saudi Arabia also invested in the Libyan Investment Authority to fund Pearson Education's implementation of Common Core.

'According to the Guardian, Pearson Education claims it operates in a free market as a public company and has no control over its shareholders' alleged terrorist-related activities.

'Notably, in 2007, two years before the "Race to the Top" initiative, the FBI uncovered documents revealing the goals of the Muslim Brotherhood, which entailed indoctrinating American K-12 students by teaching Islam.

'The seized documents were part of a 2007 Holy Land Foundation trial, the largest terrorist-related funding trial in American history. The FBI uncovered an invaluable document, which exposed the Muslim Brotherhood's manifesto "on the General Strategic Goal for the Group in North America" (Exhibit 42945 and Exhibit 42946).

'In addition to creating Common Core curriculum and standards, Pearson Education also solely evaluates teachers in some states.

'In order for New York State, for example, to continue receiving "Race to the Top" federal funds, New York was required to implement "reforms." Pearson Education now solely administers the Teacher Performance Assessment (TPA).

'As a result, New York State no longer evaluates its teachers — a private company does — whose primary investors allegedly finance terrorism and propagate Islam.

'To date, no state or federal oversight exists for university programs (under Title VI of the Higher Education Act), which train K-12 teachers to develop lesson plans and seminars on "Middle East Studies."

'Essentially, a non-American public company largely owned by alleged terrorism financiers orchestrated the development and implementation of Common Core, defined and oversees its standards, and evaluates teacher and student performance– not state or federal agencies.

'As a result, the American government handed over public school education to foreign interests. Parents have the Constitutional right to reject both the indoctrination of Islamic teaching of their children by "unreasonable state interferences.'" http://bit.ly/1NkLkk5

VII

ISLAMIC TERRORISM

" Most Americans are unaware of the fact that over two hundred years ago, the United States had declared war on Islam, and Thomas Jefferson led the charge!

'At the height of the eighteenth century, Muslim pirates were the terror of the Mediterranean and a large area of the North Atlantic. They attacked every ship in sight and held the crews for exorbitant ransoms. Those taken hostage were subjected to barbaric treatment and wrote heart breaking letters home, begging their government and family members to pay whatever their Mohammedan captors demanded.

'These extortionists of the high seas represented the Islamic nations of Tripoli, Tunis, Morocco, and Algiers, collectively referred to as the Barbary Coast, and presented a dangerous and unprovoked threat to the new American Republic.

'Before the Revolutionary War, U.S. merchant ships had been under the protection of Great Britain. When the United States declared its independence and entered into war, the ships of the United States were protected by France. However, once the war was won, America had to protect its own fleets; thus the birth of the United States Navy.

'Beginning in 1784, seventeen years before he would become president, Thomas Jefferson became America's Minister to France. That same year, the U.S. Congress sought to appease its Muslim adversaries by following in the footsteps of European nations who paid bribes to the Barbary States, rather than engaging them in war.

'In July of 1785, Algerian pirates captured American ships, and the Dey of Algiers demanded an unheard-of ransom of $60,000. It was a plain and simple case of extortion, and Thomas Jefferson was vehemently opposed to any further payments. Instead, he proposed to Congress the formation of a coalition of allied nations who together could force the Islamic states into peace. A disinterested Congress decided to pay the ransom.

'In 1786, Thomas Jefferson and John Adams met with Tripoli's ambassador to Great Britain to ask by what right his nation attacked American ships and enslaved American citizens, and why Muslims held so much hostility towards America, a nation with which they had no previous contacts.

'The two future presidents reported that Ambassador Sidi Haji Abdul Rahman Adja had answered that Islam "was founded on the Laws of their Prophet, that it was written in their Quran, that all nations who should not have acknowledged their authority were sinners, that it was their right and duty to make war upon them wherever they could be found, and to make slaves of all they could take as prisoners, and that every Musselman (Muslim) who should be slain in battle was sure to go to paradise."

'Despite this stunning admission of premeditated violence on non-Muslim nations, as well as the objections of many notable American leaders, including George Washington, who warned that caving in was both wrong and would only further embolden the enemy, for the following fifteen years, the American government paid the Muslims millions of dollars for the safe passage of American ships or the return of American hostages. The payments in ransom and tribute amounted to over twenty percent of the United States government annual revenues in 1800.

'Jefferson was disgusted. Shortly after his being sworn in as the third President of the United States in 1801, the Pasha of Tripoli sent him a note demanding the immediate payment of $225,000 plus $25,000 a year for every year forthcoming. That changed everything.

'Jefferson let the Pasha know, in no uncertain terms, what he could do with his demand. The Pasha responded by cutting down the flagpole at the American consulate and declared war on the United States. Tunis, Morocco, and Algiers immediately followed suit. Jefferson, until now, had been against America raising a naval force for anything beyond coastal defense, but having watched his nation be cowed by Islamic thuggery for long enough, decided that it was finally time to meet force with force.

'He dispatched a squadron of frigates to the Mediterranean and taught the Muslim nations of the Barbary Coast a lesson he hoped they would never forget. Congress authorized Jefferson to empower U.S. ships to seize all vessels and goods of the Pasha of Tripoli and to "cause to be done all other acts of precaution or hostility as the state of war would justify."

'When Algiers and Tunis, who were both accustomed to American cowardice and acquiescence, saw the newly independent United States had both the will and the might to strike back, they quickly abandoned their allegiance to Tripoli. The war with Tripoli lasted for four more years, and raged up again in 1815. The bravery of the U.S. Marine Corps in these wars led to the line "to the shores of Tripoli" in the Marine Hymn, They would forever be known as "leathernecks" for the leather collars of their uniforms, designed to prevent their heads from being cut off by the Muslim scimitars when boarding enemy ships.

'Islam, and what its Barbary followers justified doing in the name of their prophet and their god, disturbed Jefferson quite deeply. America had a tradition of religious tolerance the fact that Jefferson, himself, had co-authored the Virginia Statute for Religious Freedom, but fundamentalist Islam was like no other religion the world had ever seen. A religion based on supremacism, whose holy book not only condoned but mandated violence against unbelievers was unacceptable to him. His greatest fear was that someday this brand of Islam would return and pose an even greater threat to the United States.

'This should bother every American. Islam's have brought about women-only classes and swimming times at taxpayer-funded universities and public pools; Christians, Jews, and Hindus have been banned from serving on juries where Muslim defendants are being judged, and piggy banks and Porky Pig tissue dispensers have been banned from workplaces because they offend Islamist sensibilities. Ice cream has been discontinued at certain Burger King locations because the picture on the wrapper looks similar to the Arabic script for Allah, public schools are pulling pork from their menus, on and on in the newspapers.

'It's death by a thousand cuts, or inch-by-inch as some refer to it, and most Americans have no idea that this battle is being waged every day across America. By not fighting back, by allowing groups to obfuscate what is really happening, and not insisting that the Islamists adapt to our culture, the United States is cutting its own throat with a politically correct knife and helping to further the Islamists' agenda. Sadly, it appears that today's America would rather be politically correct than victorious."

It seems to me that if you cannot label it by its real name; i.e., abortion = murder or infanticide; homosexuality = sodomy; you should be ashamed of it or embarrassed by it. We should take the term "politically correct" and shove it through a paper shredder. You know who decides what is politically correct, don't you? Liberals do. Now since when do liberals have the authorization – who gave them permission – to decide what is correct? This is important because whoever decides what is correct is the one that decides what the truth is and that has to do with the morality of our society. But liberals do not want the truth and they cannot handle the truth.

"Islam, not the Chinese nor the Russians, represent the greatest threat to the world and might be the fulfillment of the book of Revelation in the Holy Bible. This is very disturbing for a Christian to read, but read it and be educated." Adapted from Dr. Peter Hammond's book: *Slavery, Terrorism, and Islam: The Historical Roots and Contemporary Threat.* [anonymous]

It is a well-known fact that our current administration will not use the term "Islamic Terrorism." Since when has it been known as anything else? This administration is fond of coining new names in the hopes that America will forget how it used to be.

For instance, do you need food stamps? They are no longer called food stamps. You get a little plastic card that functions like a debit card, and it is now called the Supplemental Nutrition Assistance Program (SNAP). It is also called an EBT card.

And all of those illegal immigrants in this country! They are now supposed to be referred to as "undocumented workers."

Senior Citizens no longer receive Social Security checks. They receive Federal Benefit Payments.

Now we have the Islamic Terrorists who have been killing Americans since before 1968 and this administration will not use the word "Islamic," nor the word "Terrorist."

In my book, *The Lyin Kings*, I listed acts of terrorism of the Islamists from the time of killing Bobby Kennedy forward. Every major bombing, every assassination of an American, every airline bombing or cruise ship hijacking, was done by an Islamic terrorist. Islamic terrorists did every attack that was done on American soil. Still this administration cannot say the words "Islamic Terrorists?"

Is this administration part of the Terrorist organization? This administration entertains terrorist members in our nation's White House. This administration employs members of the terrorist's network in our Nation's Capital. Every day a few more of this administration's true colors are shown to the American people, and they are not red, white and blue.

When Islamist Terrorists murdered the Jews at a Jewish Deli in France, Obama referred to them as "random" and "folks."

Lt. Col. Allen West calls them "Islamapologist" in order to counter the phrase "Islamophobic" to describe anyone who criticizes radical Islam. West came up with his own term to describe those who constantly excuse or dismiss the brutal and murderous actions of radical Islamic jihadists. The term would apply to people like Secretary of State John Kerry, who go out of their way to perpetuate the false narrative that all Islam is a "religion of peace." ConservativeTribune.com

This Administration has a problem with the truth when it comes to who is responsible for all the terrorism in the world. This Administration sounds more like an apologist for radical terrorist groups that are a threat to this country.

And when ISIS killed the 21 Coptic Christians and this Administration still cannot call them ISIS, but refers to them as ISIL, Obama refused to comment about the Christians and went golfing instead.

Phil Robertson of Duck Dynasty was correct when "He compared radical Islam with four other ideologies: Communism, Shintoism, Nazism, and Atheism. He raised a valid point when he compared the five and listed one common denominator — they all lacked Jesus."

According to Ollie North, Obama is hindering the efforts of allies who are willing to take on the jihadists. North said that both Egypt and Jordan requested information from the United States regarding Islamic State group targets in Libya and Syria, but the Intel has been denied to them. The Kurds are begging for arms and ammo, and the United States has delivered nothing.

"Obama may still harbor resentment against the Egyptian president for his successful coup against the Obama-supported Muslim Brotherhood. Obama's reluctance to assist Jordan is more troubling. Perhaps he continues to hope that if he keeps his head buried in the sand long enough, other countries will deal with America's problems on the international stage. He can go back to his first love — destroying the American culture of lawful self-reliance from within.

'But whether or not Barack Obama chooses to go to war with them, at some point he needs to realize that the radical extremists of the Islamic State group are at war with us." http://bit.ly/1Otm9Bh

"During his remarks at the White House Summit on Countering Violent Extremism, President Barack Obama answered critics directly by laying out exactly why he and members of his administration do not use the word "Islamic" to describe extremist terrorist groups like Al Qaeda and ISIS.

"'Leading up to the summit has been a fair amount of debate in the press and among pundits about the words we use to describe and frame this challenge," Obama said. As he sees it, al Qaeda and ISIS are "desperate for legitimacy" and try to "portray themselves as religious leaders, holy warriors in defense of Islam."

'By calling itself the "Islamic State," the president said, ISIS "propagates the notion that America and the West generally, is at war with Islam."

"'We must never accept the premise that they put forward because it is a lie," Obama continued. "Nor should we grant these terrorists the legitimacy they seek. They are not religious leaders; they are terrorists," he said to applause. "We are not at war with Islam. We are at war with people who have perverted Islam."

'The president went on to say that Muslim communities have a "responsibility" to reject the terrorists' version of Islam. "They do depend upon the misperception around the world that they speak in some fashion for people of the Muslim faith, that Islam is somehow inherently violent," Obama said of extremists.

'"The terrorists do not speak for a billion Muslims that reject their ideology," he continued. "They no more represent Islam than any madman who kills innocents in the name of God represents Christianity or Judaism or Buddhism or Hinduism. No religion is responsible for terrorism; people are responsible for violence and terrorism."

'Of course, Obama did not mention that, at least in today's society, far more people are dying in the name of Islam than any of the other religions he mentioned. Despite consistent calls from the right for the Obama administration to label groups like ISIS "Islamic extremists," the president and his team are not budging from the stance that says those words would only "legitimize" their actions.

'Pundits like Bill O'Reilly may believe that the U.S. is in a "holy war" against radical Islamists, but President Obama is insisting "that we are not at war with Islam." http://bit.ly/1DBsJ3U

Recently, the Associated Press took a photograph of Obama as African dignitaries joined Obama in a State Department auditorium for a group photograph. The photograph was published in the Britain's Daily Mail.

In the photo, Obama displayed the one-finger Muslim gang sign where "the index finger points straight up while the thumb wraps underneath and presses against the digital phalange of the middle finger. The remaining fingers are squeezed against the palm in order to highlight the extended forefinger. The extended finger is symbolic of the one-God concept of Muhammad and is understood by all believers to be a symbolic shahada, the Muslim affirmation of faith: There is but one God and Muhammad is his messenger.

'Thus when believers stick their index finger in the air, they demonstrate they are partisans of Muhammad's God concept. And they also affirm their belief in Muhammad's claim he was the interface between God and man. They also demonstrate they are part of the umma, the exclusive transtribal super tribe of believers that Muhammad started 1,400 years ago.

'With his forefinger in the air, Obama affirmed his membership in this tribe.

'The reaction of Togo President Faure Gnassingbe, at the top row second to the left in the photograph, is less approving. Through his face, you can read the mind of this Sorbonne and George Washington University educated leader. His mind is screaming, "You gotta be kidding!"

'Gnassingbe's country is squeezed between Benin and the Ivory Coast and is not far from Nigeria and its Boko Haram plague. It is perhaps a two-hour flight in a slow Cessna from Togo's capital to the Nigerian capital, or less than an hour in something faster. At the time of the Washington Conference, Boko Haram's leader Abubakar Shekau had just declared Borno State in northeastern Nigeria as the seat of his caliphate. Massacres of entire villages were taking place; only a few months earlier nearly three hundred girls were abducted from a Borno secondary school.

'Togo has seven million people, 50 percent animists, 30 percent Christian. The remainder are Muslims, part of the Umma. Gnassingbe and all other non-Muslims of Togo have reason to worry about the radicalization of some of these members of the transtribal super tribe of Muhammad, who reside among them. And so his look of disdain. "You have got to be kidding."

'Maybe it was Obama's idea of a joke, but that is unlikely. The finger in the air was a position statement brazenly stated. His entire administration has been a promotion of Islam at home and abroad, and just cataloging the evidence would fill a book. He has made this country cozy for Islam, from ordering NASA to make Muslims feel good about themselves to calling ISIS beheading victim Peter Kassig by the Muslim name that he had adopted in the vain hope of saving his life.

'If only Obama's coziness were limited to such gestures, but from the very beginning of his administration, he labored to topple the strongman governments that had kept a lid on Islamic extremism: Tunisia, Egypt, Libya, Yemen. Overthrowing the Syrian government was also part of the program, not yet achieved but still possible. The methodology of each was a tactic from old-school radicalism: stir up domestic trouble that triggers a crackdown, then use the reaction to discredit the government and as a pretext for stirring up greater cycles of trouble until the targeted regime is replaced.

'Obama is comfortable with Islam's extreme. He arms such people throughout the Middle East. He has let them into our government. He supported the Muslim Brotherhood's Muhammad Morsi as the replacement for Hosni Mubarak, a staunch US ally and enemy of the Muslim Brotherhood, and threatened and bullied Egypt when a massive revolt replaced Morsi with a religious moderate.

In early 2011, as masses of Egyptian protesters forced their longtime president Hosni Mubarak to step down from power, Barack Obama declared that all opposition groups in Egypt should have some representation in the country's next government. He made no mention of the fact that such a development would essentially ensure that the Muslim Brotherhood – Egypt's largest opposition group – would be in a position to steer the new regime toward adopting Sharia Law and increasing its hostility toward the U.S. and Israel.

Throughout the weeks of Egyptian rioting, the Obama administration repeatedly shifted its posture, initially expressing confidence in Mubarak's government, later threatening to withhold U.S. aid to that regime, and finally pressing Mubarak to loosen his grip on power. "We want to see free, fair and credible elections," said State Department spokesman P.J. Crowley on February 2. "The sooner that can happen, the better."

Obama and his administration took the foregoing positions even though the Muslim Brotherhood had made it explicitly clear that it favored the dissolution of the 1979 peace treaty between Egypt and Israel; even though the Brotherhood's Supreme Guide, Muhammad Mahdi 'Akef, had stated that his organization would never recognize Israel's legitimate right to exist; and even though Muhammad Ghannem, a leading member of the Muslim Brotherhood in Egypt, had told the Iranian news network Al-Alam that "the people [of Egypt] should be prepared for war against Israel."

'The thread of all of these efforts was the reestablishment of the Islamic caliphate, the line of successors of Muhammad that ended nearly a century ago with the collapse of the Ottoman Empire. This has always been a Muslim Brotherhood objective. In their grandiose plans, the reestablished caliphate would stretch across the Middle East with Jerusalem as its capital. The glory of Islam resurrected! These people aspire to world domination, and the caliphate would serve as the base for an ever-expanding war on the world until domination is achieved. That was always the goal of their role model. Muhammad ordered his followers to make Islam the only religion — to create a universal umma. As with Obama, they are just following orders.

'The Caliphate was resurrected last year; only it is not in the hands of the Muslim Brotherhood — not yet anyway. However, it came about, the caliphate was Obama's creation, and he has only half-heartedly pushed back against it. Now he has asked the U.S. Congress for authorization for use of military force against what he created. What is Obama up to with this? In everything he does, mischief is the purpose. What mischief does he intend now?

'There is nothing in Obama's head that is American. He is an antithetical American, a polar opposite of its values that he is routinely undermining. He is an unabashed member of the transtribal super tribe that Muhammad created 1,400 years ago; he is of the Umma, not of America. His finger in the air at the African Leaders' Conference is unambiguous evidence." http://bit.ly/1Frv4Pn

If you have read any history, during 1911, General John J. "Black Jack" Pershing knew how to handle terrorists. General Pershing was in command of the Garrison in the Philippines, and there had been numerous Islamic terrorist's attacks.

Black Jack forced the terrorists to dig their own graves. Then the terrorists were tied to posts execution style. Then the United States soldiers brought in pigs and slaughtered them in front of the terrorists and rubbed bullets in the blood and fat from the pigs. The terrorists were terrorized by the thought that they would be contaminated with the pig's blood and could not enter Heaven even if they died as martyrs. All but one were shot and dumped into the grave, and the hogs guts were dumped on top of their bodies. The one survivor was allowed to escape and return to the terrorists' camp to tell his comrades what had happened to the other members. As a result, this ended all terrorism in the Philippines for the next 50 years.

What I do not understand is why the Obama administration would pay $5 Million to the Islamic terrorists in exchange for the release of accused Army deserter Sgt. Bowe Bergdahl in Afghanistan, along with five Taliban terrorists from Gitmo, yet he would not make a telephone call to the President of Mexico for the release of Sgt. Andrew Tahmooressi, who was held in a Mexican jail for 214 days for mistakenly taking a wrong turn at the border between the United States and Mexico. For that matter, he could have released one of the truly bad Mexican illegals from one of our prisons in exchange for Sgt. Tahmooressi.

Bergdahl was finally charged with Article 85 of the Uniform Code of Military Justice, "desertion with intent to shirk important or hazardous duty," and with Article 99, "misbehavior before the enemy by endangering the safety of a command, unit or place." He could be confined for life.

"Retired Gen. Barry McCaffrey recently appeared on MSNBC with bombshell claims that the White House was aware of Bergdahl's alleged desertion the entire time and had a one-word descriptor for the ceremony, saying, "It was incomprehensible to me that the president of the United States walked out into the Rose Garden with this guy's parents."

'He asked, "Who came up with that idea," and then expressed his disgust at National Security Adviser Susan Rice's comment at the time that Bergdahl "served with honor and distinction."

'The controversial, secretive swap that brought Bergdahl home from his Taliban captors was the release of five high-ranking Taliban commanders who'd been locked up at Guantanamo Bay, a prison that Obama has publicly stated he'd like to close.

'There have already been reports of some of the freed commanders attempting to get back into the terror game." http://bit.ly/1Rjf3jv

You might find this timeline interesting. In January of 2009, Obama called for Gitmo to be shut down within a year while his National Security Team is deciding five Taliban leaders are safe for release.

"In 2011, White House and State Department Officials begin secret talks with the Taliban in Germany and the Persian Gulf these five Taliban Leaders from Gitmo as part of "peace talks."

'January 3, 2012, the Taliban announces they are prepared to open a political office in Qatar to conduct peace negotiations in exchange for the release of the Taliban Commanders.

'April 2012, in working with the White House, Karzai sends a delegation of Afghan government officials to Gitmo to interview the Taliban prisoners and to secure their oath to cut ties with Al-Qaida.

'("On the issue of the release of the Taliban prisoners from Guantanamo, we are fully in support of that," Karzai says during a July 9, 2012, visit to Japan. "If they wish to go to Qatar, we want them rejoined with their families.")

'Karzai signed on to the deal because he thought it would buy peace and goodwill with the Taliban, which threatened to retake Afghanistan." http://bit.ly/1Do0lTN

Representative Duncan Hunter called for an investigation by the Pentagon's Inspector General into whether the Obama Administration paid a ransom to terrorists in exchange for the release of Bergdahl. He also requested that the Inspector General determine whether any such ransom payments violated laws prohibiting the support of terrorist organizations. http://bit.ly/1NnMPCt

Then we have 143 detainees left at the Guantanamo Bay facility, down from a high of close to 800 since the 9/11 terrorist attacks.

Obama promised in 2009 to close Gitmo, but the closure of the Guantánamo camp was delayed by opposition from Republicans and some Democrats in Congress, who argued that housing the detainees in prisons on U.S. soil would imperil national security. In 2013 more than half of the camp's 166 detainees, some of whom had been cleared for release or transfer, engaged in a hunger strike to draw attention to their situation.

President Obama, in his Bergdahl speech, stated there had been three former Presidents that had made prisoner swaps much like his. He said, "This is what happens at the end of wars…that was true for George Washington…That was true for Abraham Lincoln, and that was true for FDR. That's been true of every combat situation, that at some point, you make sure that you try to get your folks back. And that's the right thing to do."

According to ConservativePost.com, "The Obama White House is giving ISIS a 45 minute warning before bombing their oil tankers by dropping leaflets advising potential jihadists to flee before air strikes in Syria. "Get out of your trucks now, and run away from them. Warning: air strikes are coming. Oil trucks will be destroyed. Get away from your oil trucks immediately. Do not risk your life," the leaflet reads. This is Obama's idea on how to fight ISIS.

"The Revolutionary War ended in 1783 and George Washington wasn't president until 1789…six years later!

'Lincoln was assassinated in April of 1865. He never lived to see the end of the Civil War, which occurred the following month. Additionally, there were no deals made to free the prisoners taken on either side. Once the war ended, the prisoners were simply set free.

'FDR also was not around at the end of WWII. He had died of a stroke well before this. In fact, it was Harry S. Truman's decision to drop the two nuclear bombs on Japan that ultimately brought the war to a conclusion. Once again, we made no deals for prisoners. We simply went in and released them when it was necessary." http://bit.ly/1NnMWOx

None of these three presidents was alive at the end of the respective wards, let alone able to make prisoner swaps.

This speech alone brings up many questions. Has Obama surrounded himself with a staff that is just as clueless? Is Obama now writing his own speeches? Did he read the speech before he gave it? Did Obama have any American History classes in all his years of schooling? Does Obama think Americans are that fatuous? Has his audacity overcome any shred of decency and wisdom even to himself?

When interviewed on Super Bowl Sunday at the White House Kitchen, Obama said that George Washington drank beer in the White House when he was President. George Washington never lived in the White House.

VIII

DEFENCE OF MARRIAGE ACT

B arack Obama, a closet gay man and a champion of gay rights and sodomites, decided that the Defense of Marriage Act was unconstitutional, and ordered the Department of Justice to stop defending it.

One of the first events that ensued was that a letter was sent to Congress making it the Department of Justice's idea, and setting forth the reason the Defense of Marriage Act "DOMA" should be illegal and not enforced. That letter is as follows in its entirety:

"Dear Mr. Speaker:

After careful consideration, including a review of a recommendation from me, the President of the United States has made the determination that Section 3 of the Defense of Marriage Act ("DOMA"), 1 U.S.C. § 7, as applied to same-sex couples who are legally married under state law, violates the equal protection component of the Fifth Amendment. Pursuant to 28 U.S.C. § 530D, I am writing to advise you of the Executive Branch's determination and to inform you of the steps the Department will take in two pending DOMA cases to implement that determination.

While the Department has previously defended DOMA against legal challenges involving legally married same-sex couples, recent lawsuits that challenge the constitutionality of DOMA Section 3 have caused the President and the Department to conduct a new examination of the defense of this provision. In particular, in November 2011, plaintiffs filed two new lawsuits challenging the constitutionality of Section 3 of DOMA in jurisdictions without precedent on whether sexual-orientation classifications are subject to rational basis review or whether they must satisfy some form of heightened scrutiny. Windsor v. United States, No. 1:10-cv-8435 (S.D.N.Y.); Pedersen v. OPM, No. 3:10-cv-1750 (D. Conn.). Previously, the Administration has defended Section 3 in jurisdictions where circuit courts have already held that classifications based on sexual orientation are subject to rational basis review, and it has advanced arguments to defend DOMA Section 3 under the binding standard that has applied in those cases.

These new lawsuits, by contrast, will require the Department to take an affirmative position on the level of scrutiny that should be applied to DOMA Section 3 in a circuit without binding precedent on the issue. As described more fully below, the President and I have concluded that classifications based on sexual orientation warrant heightened scrutiny and that, as applied to same-sex couples legally married under state law, Section 3 of DOMA is unconstitutional.

Standard of Review

The Supreme Court has yet to rule on the appropriate level of scrutiny for classifications based on sexual orientation. It has, however, rendered a number of decisions that set forth the criteria that should inform this and any other judgment as to whether heightened scrutiny applies: (1) whether the group in question has suffered a history of discrimination; (2) whether individuals "exhibit obvious, immutable, or distinguishing characteristics that define them as a discrete group"; (3) whether the group is a minority or is politically powerless; and (4) whether the characteristics distinguishing the group have little relation to legitimate policy objectives or to an individual's "ability to perform or contribute to society." See *Bowen* v. *Gilliard*, 483 U.S. 587, 602-03 (1987); *City of Cleburne* v. *Cleburne Living Ctr.*, 473 U.S. 432, 441-42 (1985).

Each of these factors counsels in favor of being suspicious of classifications based on sexual orientation. First and most importantly, there is, regrettably, a significant history of purposeful discrimination against gay and lesbian people, by governmental as well as private entities, based on prejudice and stereotypes that continue to have ramifications today. Indeed, until very recently, states have "demean[ed] the existence" of gays and lesbians "by making their private sexual conduct a crime." *Lawrence* v. *Texas*, 539 U.S. 558, 578 (2003).

Second, while sexual orientation carries no visible badge, a growing scientific consensus accepts that sexual orientation is a characteristic that is immutable, see Richard A. Posner, Sex and Reason 101 (1992); it is undoubtedly unfair to require sexual orientation to be hidden from view to avoid discrimination, see Don't Ask, Don't Tell Repeal Act of 2010, Pub. L. No. 111-321, 124 Stat. 3515 (2010).

Third, the adoption of laws like those at issue in *Romer* v. *Evans*, 517 U.S. 620 (1996), and *Lawrence*, the longstanding ban on gays and lesbians in the military, and the absence of federal protection for employment discrimination on the basis of sexual orientation show the group to have limited political power and "ability to attract the [favorable] attention of the lawmakers." *Cleburne*, 473 U.S. at 445. And while the enactment of the Matthew Shepard Act and pending repeal of Don't Ask, Don't Tell indicate that the political process is not closed entirely to gay and lesbian people, that is not the standard by which the Court has judged "political powerlessness." Indeed, when the Court ruled that gender-based classifications were subject to heightened scrutiny, women already had won major political victories such as the Nineteenth Amendment (right to vote) and protection under Title VII (employment discrimination).

Finally, there is a growing acknowledgment that sexual orientation "bears no relation to ability to perform or contribute to society." *Frontiero* v. *Richardson*, 411 U.S. 677, 686 (1973) (plurality). Recent evolutions in legislation (including the pending repeal of Don't Ask, Don't Tell), in community practices and attitudes, in case law (including the Supreme Court's holdings in *Lawrence* and *Romer)*, and in social science regarding sexual orientation all make clear that sexual orientation is not a characteristic that generally bears on legitimate policy objectives. See, e.g., Statement by the President on the Don't Ask, Don't Tell Repeal Act of 2010 ("It is time to recognize that sacrifice, valor and integrity are no more defined by sexual orientation than they are by race or gender, religion or creed.")

To be sure, there is substantial circuit court authority applying rational basis review to sexual-orientation classifications. We have carefully examined each of those decisions. Many of them reason only that if consensual same-sex sodomy may be criminalized under *Bowers v.*

Hardwick, then it follows that no heightened review is appropriate – a line of reasoning that does not survive the overruling of *Bowers* in *Lawrence v. Texas*, 538 U.S. 558 (2003). Others rely on claims regarding "procreational responsibility" that the Department has disavowed already in litigation as unreasonable, or claims regarding the immutability of sexual orientation that we do not believe can be reconciled with more recent social science understandings. And none engages in an examination of all the factors that the Supreme Court has identified as relevant to a decision about the appropriate level of scrutiny. Finally, many of the more recent decisions have relied on the fact that the Supreme Court has not recognized that gays and lesbians constitute a suspect class or the fact that the Court has applied rational basis review in its most recent decisions addressing classifications based on sexual orientation, Lawrence and Romer. But neither of those decisions reached, let alone resolved, the level of scrutiny issue because in both the Court concluded that the laws could not even survive the more deferential rational basis standard.

Application to Section 3 of DOMA

In reviewing a legislative classification under heightened scrutiny, the government must establish that the classification is "substantially related to an important government objective." *Clark v. Jeter*, 486 U.S. 456, 461 (1988). Under heightened scrutiny, "a tenable justification must describe actual state purposes, not rationalizations for actions in fact differently grounded." *United States* v. *Virginia*, 518 U.S. 515, 535-36 (1996). "The justification must be genuine, not hypothesized or invented post hoc in response to litigation." Id. at 533.

In other words, under heightened scrutiny, the United States cannot defend Section 3 by advancing hypothetical rationales, independent of the legislative record, as it has done in circuits where precedent mandates application of rational basis review. Instead, the United States can defend Section 3 only by invoking Congress' actual justifications for the law.

Moreover, the legislative record underlying DOMA's passage contains discussion and debate that undermines any defense under heightened scrutiny. The record contains numerous expressions reflecting moral disapproval of gays and lesbians and their intimate and family relationships – precisely the kind of stereotype-based thinking and animus the Equal Protection Clause is designed to guard against. See *Cleburne*, 473 U.S. at 448 ("mere negative attitudes, or fear" are not permissible bases for discriminatory treatment); see also *Romer*, 517 U.S. at 635 (rejecting rationale that law was supported by "the liberties of landlords or employers who have personal or religious objections to homosexuality"); Palmore v. Sidotti, 466 U.S. 429, 433 (1984) ("Private biases may be outside the reach of the law, but the law cannot, directly or indirectly, give them effect.").

Application to Second Circuit Cases

After careful consideration, including a review of my recommendation, the President has concluded that given a number of factors, including a documented history of discrimination, classifications based on sexual orientation should be subject to a heightened standard of scrutiny. The President has also concluded that Section 3 of DOMA, as applied to legally married same-sex couples, fails to meet that standard and is, therefore, unconstitutional. Given that conclusion, the President has instructed the Department not to defend the statute in Windsor and Pedersen, now pending in the Southern District of New York and the District of Connecticut. I concur in this determination.

Notwithstanding this determination, the President, has informed me that Section 3 will continue to be enforced by the Executive Branch. To that end, the President has instructed Executive agencies to continue to comply with Section 3 of DOMA, consistent with the Executive's obligation to take care that the laws be faithfully executed, unless and until Congress repeals Section 3 or the judicial branch renders a definitive verdict against the law's constitutionality. This course of action respects the actions of the prior Congress that enacted DOMA, and it recognizes the judiciary as the final arbiter of the constitutional claims raised.

As you know, the Department has a longstanding practice of defending the constitutionality of duly-enacted statutes if reasonable arguments can be made in their defense, a practice that accords the respect appropriately due to a coequal branch of government. However, the Department in the past has declined to defend statutes despite the availability of professionally responsible arguments, in part because the Department does not consider every plausible argument to be a "reasonable" one. "[D]ifferent cases can raise very different issues with respect to statutes of doubtful constitutional validity," and thus there are "a variety of factors that bear on whether the Department will defend the constitutionality of a statute." Letter to Hon. Orrin G. Hatch from Assistant Attorney General Andrew Fois at 7 (Mar. 22, 1996). This is the rare case where the proper course is to forgo the defense of this statute. Moreover, the Department has declined to defend a statute "in cases in which it is manifest that the President has concluded that the statute is unconstitutional," as is the case here. Seth

P. Waxman, Defending Congress, 79 N.C. L.Rev. 1073, 1083 (2001). In light of the foregoing, I will instruct the Department's lawyers to immediately inform the district courts in Windsor and Pedersen of the Executive Branch's view that heightened scrutiny is the appropriate standard of review and that, consistent with that standard, Section 3 of DOMA may not be constitutionally applied to same-sex couples whose marriages are legally recognized under state law. If asked by the district courts in the Second Circuit for the position of the United States in the event those courts determine that the applicable standard is rational basis, the Department will state that, consistent with the position it has taken in prior cases, a reasonable argument for Section 3's constitutionality may be proffered under that permissive standard. Our attorneys will also notify the courts of our interest in providing Congress a full and fair opportunity to participate in the litigation in those cases. We will remain parties to the case and continue to represent the interests of the United States throughout the litigation.

Furthermore, pursuant to the President's instructions, and upon further notification to Congress, I will instruct Department attorneys to advise courts in other pending DOMA litigation of the President's and my conclusions that a heightened standard should apply, that Section 3 is unconstitutional under that standard and that the Department will cease defense of Section 3.

A motion to dismiss in the Windsor and Pedersen cases would be due on Ma152rch 11, 2011. Please do not hesitate to contact us if you have any questions.

Sincerely yours,
Eric H. Holder, Jr. Attorney General

The Defense of Marriage Act passed both Houses in May of 1996 and was signed into law by President William Clinton on September 21, 1996. It is a United States Federal law that allows states to refuse to recognize same-sex marriages granted under the laws of other states. In 2013, Section 3 of the Act was ruled unconstitutional.

The Defense of Marriage Act did not prevent individual states from allowing same-sex couples from marrying. It imposed constraints on the benefits received by all legally married same-sex couples and barred them from receiving Federal marriage benefits.

Section 3 codified non-recognition of same-sex marriages for all Federal purposes, including insurance benefits for government employees, social security survivors' benefits, immigration, bankruptcy, and the filing of joint tax returns, as well as excluding same-sex spouses from the scope of laws protecting families of federal officers (18 U. S. C. §115), laws evaluating financial aid eligibility, and federal ethics laws applicable to opposite-sex spouses.

In 2011, the Obama Administration announced that they concluded Section 3 was unconstitutional and that although they would continue to enforce it, they would not defend the law in Court. In *United States* v. *Windsor* (2013), the U.S. Supreme Court declared Section 3 of DOMA unconstitutional under the Due Process Clause of the Fifth Amendment.

In a separate letter to former Speaker of the House John Boehner, Holder noted that Congress could participate in these lawsuits in the Department's stead.

On September 15, 2009, three Democratic members of Congress, Jerrold Nadler of New York, Tammy Baldwin of Wisconsin, and Jared Polis of Colorado, introduced legislation to repeal DOMA called the Respect for Marriage Act. The bill had 91 original co-sponsors in the House of Representatives and was supported by Clinton, Barr, and several legislators who voted for DOMA. Congressman Barney Frank and John Berry, head of the Office of Personnel Management, did not support that effort, stating "the backbone is not there" in Congress. Frank and Berry suggested DOMA could be overturned more quickly through lawsuits such as Gill v. Office of Personnel Management filed by Gay & Lesbian Advocates & Defenders.

Nadler is a Representative from New York and a liberal Democrat with a liberal voting record in the House. He once described the impeachment process of Bill Clinton as a "partisan railroad job. He is pro-same-sex marriages.

Tammy Baldwin was a Representative from the State of Wisconsin and is now a Junior Senator. Baldwin is openly gay and one of the most liberal members of Congress. She is also a Democrat.

Jared Polis is a member of the House of Representatives from the State of Colorado and is the first gay parent in Congress. He is also a Democrat.

Barney Frank is probably the most prominent gay member of the House of Representatives and a Democrat from the State of Massachusetts.

John Berry, a Democrat, who is also openly gay, married to Curtis Ye, was made the director of the Office of Personnel Management by Barack Obama on March 4, 2009. The Senate confirmed him on March 26, 2009. Berry has been, according to the Human Rights Campaign, the highest-ranking openly gay official to serve in the executive branch in any U.S. administration. I guess they don't know about the President.

Following Holder's announcement that the Obama Administration would no longer defend DOMA Section 3 in court, on March 16, 2011, Democrat Senator Dianne Feinstein introduced the Respect for Marriage Act in the Senate again and Nadler introduced it in the House. The Senate Judiciary Committee voted 10–8 in favor of advancing the bill to the Senate floor, but observers believed it would not gain the 60 votes needed to end debate and bring it to a vote.

After the Supreme Court had stricken down DOMA Section 3 on June 26, 2013, Feinstein and Nadler reintroduced the Respect for Marriage Act as S. 1236 and H.R. 2523.

Obama is proud of his accomplishments as far as the LGBT Community and often speaks about how he has been able to alter the landscape of America. It is too bad the Media did not tell us we had a gay President before the election.

Obama is so proud of some of the quotes he brags about:

"So Pride Month is a time for celebration, and this year we've got a lot to celebrate. If you think about everything that's happened in the last 12 months, it is remarkable. In nine more states, you're now free to marry the person you love – that includes my two home states of Hawaii and Illinois.

'The NFL drafted its first openly gay player.

'The U.S. Postal Service made history by putting an openly gay person on a stamp – the late, great Harvey Milk smiling from ear to ear.

'When I took office, only two states had marriage equality. Today, 19 states and the District of Columbia do.

'But because of your help, we've been able to do more to protect the rights of lesbian and gay, and bisexual and transgender Americans than any administration in history.

'We repealed "don't ask, don't tell," because no one should have to hide who you love to serve the country we love... We stopped defending the so-called Defense of Marriage Act in the courts and argued alongside Edie and Robbie before the highest court in the land. http://bit.ly/1OC26P6

Now we have Hillary Clinton, another closet gay, flip-flopping on her position on gays and gay marriages in order to gain the gay vote for her run for the presidency.

"There has never been, and never will be, a marriage that is based on sodomy. It is an institution that belongs exclusively to the Church and not to the state. God-ordained marriage cannot be changed regardless of what the people or the judges may say or what the people want is contrary to God's moral law.

'As the Supreme Court looks at the issue of redefining marriage, the first "sodomite president" Barack Obama and his administration have already asked and gotten the Supreme Court to strike down the Federal law defining marriage as a union between only a man and a woman.

'Of course, to do that Obama had to set the stage. He repealed Don't Ask Don't Tell and place 225 homosexuals in key positions. Then he appointed a radical lesbian to the bench of the Supreme Court, Elena Kagan.

'Elena Kagan is the former dean of students at Harvard. Contrary to Harvard's founding mottos, "For Christ and the Church" and "For the glory of Christ," Kagan is known for "Queerifying Harvard." https://www.youtube.com/watch?v=5Yxsh3fJpmQ

'During her tenure, she did the following:

'Kagan hired former ACLU lawyer William Rubenstein to teach "queer" legal theory, in which he taught courses on taking up new identities such as bisexuality, transgender f**k, involving polygamy, sadomasochism, and the sexuality of minors.

'Kagan also hired other radicals (a lesbian and a transsexual) to teach transgender law courses, as well as Cass Sunstein, who has written in support of polygamy and free-for-all marriage relationships.

'Kagan viciously attacked our military in opposition to "Don't Ask, Don't Tell," even banning military recruiters from coming on campus. Kagan's attempt to ban the recruiters was unsuccessful, and even after losing her legal campaign, she encouraged students to continue protesting them.

'Kagan's radical activism on campus was so toxic that there was even a campaign to make the entire university trans-inclusive, using Harvard's "gender identity" non-discrimination policy to spew gender confusion among students on campus.

'Elena Kagan has never judged a case a day in her life. Yet, Obama, unqualified for office himself, has seen fit to "qualify" her for the Supreme Court." http://bit.ly/1PYjj8S

Obama has surprisingly remained silent on the matter of Bruce Jenner. As one reporter wrote:

"Take away the moral principles America was founded on and what you are left with is moral anarchy; the rules of the jungle written by those who have garnered the political power to control Congress. But one's sex is not something that can be voted on or changed by the will of the electorate. An individual's sex is not determined by a vote of Congress and it is not validated by a Supreme Court ruling. Nor is it determined by the surgeons' knife or hormones from a pharmicist. An individual's sex is determined by God. In fact, it is a gift from God. What God establishes, man cannot change and should not presume to try. For a man such as Bruce Jenner to think he has the right to "correct" any part of God's plan is presumptuous in the extreme.

'Jenner can grow his hair long, paint his nails, mainline female hormones, wear dresses, squeeze his man-sized feet into high heels, and even endure a so-called sex-change operation. He can do all of these things and in the end he will still be a man. No matter how Jenner feels, dresses, walks, talks, or presents himself, he will never be a woman—a fact established at the moment of his conception. He will never give birth to a child, never suffer through menstrual pain, and never feel the intense feelings of love a mother feels toward a baby she carried in her womb for nine months. Finally, the bottom line in all of this is that Bruce Jenner's DNA has not changed, will not change, and cannot change. It still contains the male chromosome no matter what name he chooses to go by.

For all those who are rushing to show how tolerant they are by jumping on the Bruce Jenner bandwagon, a note of caution is in order. If society accepts a man transforming himself into a woman, what is next? What happens when a man decides he wants to be a dog or a cat or a horse or a goat? Better yet, what happens when a liberal decides to transform himself into an intelligent being? Then again, never mind that last question. It will never happen. http://bit.ly/21rKf4I

Obama appointed seven gay Ambassadors that are over-stepping their authority. According to these seven gay Ambassadors, the International Free Trade Agreements like those being negotiated with countries in the Pacific and Europe should help to export American values such as human rights, including lesbian, gay, bisexual, transgender and intersex (LGBTI) people. Ambassador Randy Berry signed a joint letter published in The Advocate and reposted by the White House.

"Through the President's trade agenda, we will not only support more American jobs, but we can also promote greater justice beyond our borders," they wrote. "We are committed to working closely with the White House to ensure that any trade arrangement approved by Congress is a force for progress on human rights for everyone, including for LGBTI persons." "As the seven openly lesbian, gay, bisexual, transgender, and intersex U.S. Ambassadors and the Special Envoy for the Human Rights of LGBTI Persons, this approach is particularly important to us."

The seven joining Berry are Ambassadors to Dominican Republic James Brewster, Ambassador to Spain James Costos, Ambassador to Denmark Rufus Gifford, Ambassador to Australia John Berry, Ambassador to Vietnam Ted Osius, Ambassador to the Organization for Security and Cooperation in Europe Daniel Baer, and Deputy U.S. Trade Representative Robert Holleyman.

They did not name any countries, but of the TPP partners, Malaysia, Singapore and Brunei outlaw same-sex sexual acts, according to data compiled by the International Lesbian, Gay, Bisexual, Trans and Intersex Association (ILGA).

In Malaysia, anyone convicted of "carnal intercourse against the order of nature" can be imprisoned for up to 20 years, and also be flogged.

In Singapore, a male who commits "any act of gross indecency with another male person" can be jailed for up to two years.

Brunei punishes "carnal intercourse against the order of nature with any man, woman, or animal" with a prison term of up to 10 years, plus a fine.

Moreover, Brunei is scheduled to introduce the death penalty for certain same-sex activity by next year – as part of a roll-out of a controversial shari'a-based legal code – although ILGA said in a report last month that it "seems unlikely to be implemented in actuality."

(According to ILGA data, same-sex sexual acts are illegal in 76 countries. In five – Mauritania, Sudan, Iran, Saudi Arabia and Yemen – the death penalty is implemented for same-sex activity, along with some provinces in Somalia and Nigeria.) http://bit.ly/1l52nRa

The truth is that conservatives do not care what you do with your privates. We just do not want you legislating with your privates.

2015 – The United States Supreme Court ruled that same-sex couples have a right to marry nationwide, in a historic decision that invalidates gay marriage bans in more than a dozen states.

Gay and lesbian couples already can already have their fake marriages in 36 states and the District of Columbia. But in a 5-4 ruling, the court held that the 14th Amendment requires states to issue marriage licenses for same-sex couples and to recognize such marriages performed in other states.

This ruling will not take effect immediately because the court gives the losing side roughly three weeks to ask for reconsideration.

I was not going to address this matter in this book, but history keeps repeating itself, and it has been a large issue this year. The United States Supreme Court was asked to redefine the definition of marriage.

"Chief Justice John Roberts stated, "Every definition that I looked up, prior to about a dozen years ago, defined marriage as unity between a man and a woman as husband and wife." He went on to make the point that the justices were being asked to re-define what the institution of marriage is. He told the attorney representing same-sex marriage advocates, "The fundamental core of the institution is the opposite-sex relationship, and you want to introduce into it a same-sex relationship." Justice Scalia pointed out that there was no society in history that permitted same-sex marriage until the Netherlands did so in 2001.

'Justice Stephen Breyer, one of the most liberal justices on the court, made the point that the view that marriage was between a man and a woman "has been the law everywhere for thousands of years among people who were not discriminating even against gay people, and suddenly you want nine people outside the ballot box to require states that don't want to change to do it. Why cannot these states at least wait and see whether in fact doing so in the other states is not harmful to marriage?" Although Justice Breyer does not appear comfortable with the Supreme Court re-defining marriage, he does appear to be comfortable with voters changing the definition at the ballot box. This approach is just as wrong as re-defining marriage in the Courts. By what authority do voters change a definition that was given to them by a higher authority—the highest authority?"

In a full-page ad in the Washington Post a coalition of religious groups vowed they will not abide by the U.S. Supreme Court ruling if the majority of the nine justices decide that homosexuals have a constitutional right to marriage, stating "we must pledge obedience to our Creator," the ad stated. "While there are many things we can endure, any attempt to redefine marriage is a line we cannot and will not cross."

Where will it all stop? Will we ask to marry our beloved animals next?

We have come to a point in our lives where even the United States Supreme Court cannot be trusted. Have they become corrupt from bribes or morality? "America needs to come to terms and understand that no President, no administration, no Supreme Court, has a right to break God's laws." http://bit.ly/1PYjj8S

In July 2015, Obama gave a speech at the White House at an LGBT event in which he took credit for liberal LGBT progress since he took office six-and-a-half years ago.

Obama said, according to a White House transcript: "Together, we ended 'Don't Ask, Don't Tell.' We passed a historic hate crimes bill named in part after Matthew Shepard. We lifted the HIV entry ban, and this summer, we're going to be updating our national HIV/AIDS strategy which will focus on eliminating disparities that gay and bisexual men and transgender women face. We strengthened the Violence Against Women Act to protect LGBT victims. Hospitals that accept Medicare and Medicaid are now required to treat LGBT patients the same as everybody else. The pillar of the so-called Defense of Marriage Act was struck down by the Supreme Court as unconstitutional. Just yesterday, we announced that insurance companies that covers Federal workers will no longer be able to prohibit gender transition services."

He added, "When I became President, same-sex marriage was legal in only two states. Today, it's legal in 37 states – and the District of Columbia. A decade ago, politicians ran against LGBT rights. Today, they're running towards them. Because they've learned what the rest of the country knows – that marriage equality is about our civil rights, and our firm belief that every citizen should be treated equally under the law." http://www.weeklystandard.com/blogs/obama-who-opposed-gay-marriage-when-elected-takes-credit-lgbt-progress_977704.htm

The Supreme Court announced a constitutional right to same-sex marriage and states do not have the right to prevent same-sex sinners from legally marrying. Obama declared his gay independence by disgracing this country by setting up rainbow-colored lights to illuminate the real-life White House.

The first error in the high court's ruling is that they just violated the Tenth Amendment to the United States Constitution which reads:

"'The powers not delegated to the United States by the Constitution, nor prohibited by it to the States, are reserved to the States respectively, or to the people."

'There is not a single state that voted to give this power to the Federal government or the Federal courts. In fact, the Founding Fathers purposely wrote the Tenth Amendment to keep most of the power in the hands of the states and to keep the Federal government small. Over the past century, the Federal Court has steadily stripped the states of the constitutional power given to them by the Founding Fathers.

'The Supreme Court ruling also violates the First Amendment because no Christian business owner is allowed to run their business according to their faith. If any homosexual couple requests their services – photography, cake, flowers, venue, etc. – for their same-sex wedding, the Christian business owners will be forced by the Supreme Court ruling to violate their Christian faith. http://bit.ly/1l52BYC

"Critics worry that governance by social media will cheapen the power of the presidency by substituting hashtag activism for serious policymaking. And in these exceptionally partisan times, some see the president's prodigious use of social media as just another example of the cozy political relationship between the political left and Hollywood and Silicon Valley.

'However history judges Obama's role in transforming the office, this first American president of the social media age has already established a standard for how politicians connect with a digitally savvy electorate." http://bit.ly/1IiArSa

There are many that believe the people should fight back against the Supreme Court ruling. Time will tell.

Justice "Roberts wrote: "If you are among the many Americans – of whatever sexual orientation – who favor expanding same-sex marriage, by all means celebrate today's decision. ... But do not celebrate the Constitution. It had nothing to do with it."

"There are an estimated 390,000 married same-sex couples in the United States, according to UCLA's Williams Institute, which tracks the demographics of the gay and lesbian Americans. Another 70,000 couples living in states that do not currently permit them to wed would get married in the next three years, the institute says. Roughly 1 million same-sex couples, married and unmarried, live together in the United States, the institute says.

'The Obama administration backed the right of same-sex couples to marry. The Justice Department's decision to stop defending the Federal anti-marriage law in 2011 was an important moment for gay rights and Obama declared his support for same-sex marriage in 2012." http://fxn.ws/1dl6dAW

"As to violating the moral law, the Supreme Court simply ignored the fact that the framers of the Constitution were guided and informed by the words of Jefferson in the Declaration of Independence when he wrote that America is to be governed according to "the laws of nature and nature's God." The laws of nature's God clearly prohibit same-sex marriage—just compare the anatomies of men and women—and so do the laws of God. Marriage as a concept was not invented nor was it defined by man. It was defined by God when He created Adam and then gave him Eve as his wife. Consequently, to attempt to redefine marriage is to ignore the moral law upon which our nation was founded and our Constitution written.

'The Supreme Court also violated the concept of federalism established in the Constitution. Federalism is a concept in which government is limited, and most of the enumerated duties of government are assigned to the individual states as are any duties not specifically assigned to the federal government. With Federalism, the national government's powers are purposefully limited. In fact, the enumerated powers of the federal government described in the Constitution total only seventeen. There is nothing in the Constitution about marriage, much less an enumerated power concerning marriage given to the federal government. Consequently, the issue of same-sex marriage is a state issue—not a federal issue. In other words, the Supreme Court should never have agreed to hear Obergefell v. Hodges in the first place. By hearing the case, the Justices unlawfully impinged on the prerogatives of the states and, by doing so, violated the Constitution.

'Article IV, Section 4 of the Constitution reads in part: "The United States shall guarantee to every State in this Union, a republican form of government." This means that the states are empowered to elect public officials who, in turn, enact public policy for the state. For the Supreme Court to over-rule these state-level policies is a clear violation of a constitutional guarantee. Since 30 of the 50 states has already passed legislation verifying that marriage is the union of one man and one women, the Supreme Court violated the guarantee of federalism set forth in Article IV, Section 4 of the Constitution by ruling on Obergefell v. Hodges; a case the Court should have refused to even hear." http://bit.ly/1l52P20

Not so long ago an elected County Clerk in the State of Kentucky was jailed for refusing to issue gay marriage licenses for religious reasons. She was jailed for refusing to follow the law.

Why was Obama not jailed for refusing to follow the illegal immigration laws?

Why was not Attorney General Eric Holder jailed for refusing to prosecute New Black Panthers?

Why are Hillary Clinton and Barack Obama not being prosecuted for their role in Benghazi?

Why is Hillary Clinton not being prosecuted for having her emails on her personal server?

Why has Congress allowed Obama to remain in Office when America has put a majority in office so they could impeach him? In my first book *Soundoff* I listed fifty impeachable offenses by Obama and that was just in his first couple of years in office.

IX

BUDGET

Only in America could the people who believe in balancing the budget and sticking by the country's Constitution be thought of as "extremist."

If you lived to be 80 years old and saved $68 million a day, you would have a $2 trillion nest egg. (As reported on Breitbart.com)

"The fact that we are here today to debate raising America's debt limit is a sign of leadership failure. It is a sign that the US Government cannot pay its own bills. It is a sign that we now depend on ongoing financial assistance from foreign countries to finance our Government's reckless fiscal policies. Increasing America's debt weakens us domestically and internationally. Leadership means that 'the buck stops here.' Instead, Washington is shifting the burden of bad choices today onto the backs of our children and grandchildren. America has a debt problem and a failure of leadership. Americans deserve better." ~ Senator Barack H. Obama, March 2006. He was blaming Bush even then.

In 2014, House Budget Committee Chairman Paul Ryan submitted proposed budget cuts that promised a balanced Federal ledger within ten years and the termination of the Affordable Care Act. Twelve Republicans opposed it and not a single Democrat supported it. Republicans promised a balanced budget by 2024 but would do so at the expense of poor people and seniors on Medicaid, lower-income workers receiving "Obamacare" subsidies, and people receiving food stamps and Pell Grants. Democrats countered with a $1.5 Trillion tax hikes. The Ryan plan would cut $5 Trillion over the decade.

The Republicans say the tough cuts would strengthen the economy because less government borrowing would boost savings and investments. And it is unfair to saddle future generations with mountains of debts.

Senate Democrats have announced they won't bother with a budget this year.

Notice Social Security and the military are not on this list.

These are all the programs that the new Republican House has proposed cutting.

*Corporation for Public Broadcasting Subsidy – $445 million annual savings.
*Save America 's Treasures Program – $25 million annual savings.
*International Fund for Ireland – $17 million annual savings.
*Legal Services Corporation – $420 million annual savings.
*National Endowment for the Arts – $167.5 million annual savings.
*National Endowment for the Humanities – $167.5 million annual savings.
*Hope VI Program – $250 million annual savings.
*Amtrak Subsidies – $1.565 billion annual savings.
*Eliminate duplicating education programs – H.R. 2274 (in last Congress), authored by Rep. McKeon eliminates 68 at a savings of $1.3 billion annually.
*U.S. Trade Development Agency – $55 million annual savings.
*Woodrow Wilson Center Subsidy – $20 million annual savings.
*Cut in half funding for congressional printing and binding – $47 million annual savings.
*John C. Stennis Center Subsidy – $430,000 annual savings.
*Community Development Fund – $4.5 billion annual savings.
*Heritage Area Grants and Statutory Aid – $24 million annual savings.
*Cut Federal Travel Budget in Half – $7.5 billion annual savings.
*Trim Federal Vehicle Budget by 20% – $600 million annual savings.
*Essential Air Service – $150 million annual savings.
*Technology Innovation Program – $70 million annual savings.

*Manufacturing Extension Partnership (MEP) Program – $125 million annual savings.

*Department of Energy Grants to States for Weatherization – $530 million annual savings.

*Beach Replenishment – $95 million annual savings.

*New Starts Transit – $2 billion annual savings.

*Exchange Programs for Alaska Natives, Native Hawaiians, and Their Historical Trading Partners in Massachusetts – $9 million annual savings.

*Intercity and High-Speed Rail Grants – $2.5 billion annual savings.

*Title X Family Planning – $318 million annual savings.

*Appalachian Regional Commission – $76 million annual savings.

*Economic Development Administration – $293 million annual savings.

*Programs under the National and Community Services Act – $1.15 billion annual savings.

*Applied Research at Department of Energy – $1.27 billion annual savings.

*Freedom CAR and Fuel Partnership – $200 million annual savings.

*Energy Star Program – $52 million annual savings.

*Economic Assistance to Egypt – $250 million annually.

*U.S. Agency for International Development – $1.39 billion annual savings.

*General Assistance to District of Columbia – $210 million annual savings.

*Subsidy for Washington Metropolitan Area Transit Authority – $150 million annual savings.

*Presidential Campaign Fund – $775 million savings over ten years.

*No funding for federal office space acquisition – $864 million annual savings.

*End prohibitions on competitive sourcing of government services.

*Repeal the Davis-Bacon Act – More than $1 billion annually.

*IRS Direct Deposit: Require the IRS to deposit fees for some services it offers (such as processing payment plans for taxpayers) to the Treasury, instead of allowing it to remain as part of its budget – $1.8 billion savings over ten years.

*Require collection of unpaid taxes by federal employees – $1 billion total savings. WHAT'S THIS ABOUT?

*Prohibit taxpayer funded union activities by federal employees – $1.2 billion savings over ten years.

*Sell excess federal properties the government does not make use of – $15 billion total savings.

*Eliminate death gratuity for Members of Congress. WHAT???

*Eliminate Mohair Subsidies – $1 million annual savings.

*Eliminate taxpayer subsidies to the United Nations Intergovernmental Panel on Climate Change – $12.5 million annual savings.

*Eliminate Market Access Program – $200 million annual savings.

*USDA Sugar Program – $14 million annual savings.

*Subsidy to Organization for Economic Co-operation and Development (OECD) – $93 million annual savings.

*Eliminate the National Organic Certification Cost-Share Program – $56.2 million annual savings.

*Eliminate fund for Obamacare administrative costs – $900 million savings.

*Ready to Learn TV Program – $27 million savings.

*HUD Ph.D. Program.

*Deficit Reduction Check-Off Act.

*TOTAL SAVINGS: $2.5 Trillion over Ten Years

My question is what is all this doing in the budget in the first place? But not to worry. We continue funding it because although the House approved the Budget, the Senate did not. We have 435 House Members. Why do they approve so much crap and junk stuff?

Now for the budget submitted in 2015. For the first time since he took office in 2008, Barack Obama will be submitting a proposed budget for the year 2016. The average citizen is not supposed to understand the budget as it is told in "Washington speak" rather than the language of everyday American. In Washington, if something goes up less than expected, the politicians call it a "cut." Americans do not consider something a spending cut unless it goes down.

Congress even passed a law in 1974 to make this abuse of the English language official. At the time, Federal spending was starting to increase out of control and constituents wanted something done about it. Rather than deal with the basis of what voters wanted, Congress simply changed the definition of a word so that it meant one thing in Washington and another in America.

That let politicians campaign on claims of "cutting" government spending while spending continued to grow. Forty years of such deceit created the problems we face today.

And you thought you could trust your government! Our media is not any better. Federal spending in 2015 is projected to be $138 billion higher this year than it was in 2009 ($3,656 billion this year compared to $3,518 in 2009). Spending is higher than it was, but the media says spending cuts are the reason for declining deficits. It is the way the storyline comes from Washington that misleads everyone.

Recognizing that, when the 2015 Budget is reviewed you have to recognize that commitments already made insure that Federal spending will grow by $270 billion next year. That's a 7% jump from 2015. In just five years, annual Federal spending is expected to be another trillion dollars higher than it is today. Those figures don't include any new programs proposed by the president. Federal spending keeps on growing due to ever-expanding entitlement programs and military commitments along with other "mandatory" programs. Some might be justified due to inflation and/or population growth. But before these reasons can even be considered, voters need to understand the reality of ongoing Federal spending growth. http://bit.ly/1zwBPw5

The Obama budget proposes boosting funding for clean energy by seven percent and a new $4 billion fund to encourage U.S. states to make faster and deeper cuts to emissions from power plants.

He also calls for the permanent extension of the Production Tax Credit, used by the wind industry, and the Investment Tax Credit, used by the solar industry. Industries such as solar and wind companies are inundated with government grants and loans.

Overall, the Budget calls for $3.99 Trillion in spending for the fiscal year. This includes a 1.3% pay raise for all Federal workers and military personnel.

It also included a collection of tax measures and education initiatives meant to help middle-class families pay for childhood education and college tuition.

"The U.S. Chamber of Commerce called the budget proposal "more of a political document than an operational plan." And the

Business Roundtable said Mr. Obama's plan to levy a one-time 14% tax on companies' accumulated foreign earnings, along with a 19% minimum tax on overseas earnings, would harm the competitiveness of U.S. multinationals. But the group said it supported the goal of a long-term infrastructure spending bill and left the door open to supporting a tax-overhaul package that could pay for one."

Some Republicans want to boost military funding by making deeper cuts to domestic spending. Mr. Obama responded by saying any increases for the military would need equal increases on the nondefense side.

To quote former House Speaker John Boehner, "The president is advocating more spending, more taxes, and more debt. A proposal that never balances is not a serious plan for America's fiscal future." Boehner further said, "The budget they produce this spring will achieve balance within ten years, curb the explosive growth of government benefits programs and reform the loophole-cluttered tax code."

I cannot find anyone discussing any cuts.

"If our national debt were laid out in single-file dollar bills, the line would stretch all the way to the planet Uranus – and that doesn't count more than $120 trillion in unfunded liabilities and mandates we're still on the hook for. Every household in America would need to pay $540,000 to cover that shortfall, and only 1 percent of American households make that kind of money in the first place. If the interest alone on our debt were its own economy, it would be one of the 30 biggest in the world.

'There are currently 148 million Americans collecting entitlement checks of some sort from the U.S. government, but there are only 86 million taxpayers working in the private sector paying into the system. That means there is 70 percent more tax takers than tax payers. Ten states have a government as their biggest industry." http://patriotupdate.com/2015/03/why-2016-do-or-die-election-for-american-exceptionalism/

The Republicans and Democrats say that we are broke, yet they give Fourteen Billion Nine Hundred Thirty-Three Million Dollars each year in financial aid to foreign countries that vote against us before the United Nations.

Our Military is being cut, our Soldiers are having their benefits cut, our government has gone back on its promise of free medical care and denying disability to those torn physically and mentally apart in political wars.

The only citizens that receive aid are the ones that refuse to work and have babies for welfare payments.

Senior citizens and the working public get no breaks while our government and religious organizations pour hundreds of billions of dollars and tons of food into foreign countries and the illegals and the leeches within our own American borders.

Our own military soldiers and veterans wait in year-long lines to get an appointment for health care.

Our senior citizens that have HMO plans have to wait 4 or 5 months to get an appointment to see a care provider and another 2 or 3 months for proper treatment. They must go without medications because they are not affordable.

There are benefit shows for the people of Haiti on twelve TV stations with ships and planes lined up with food, water, tents, clothes, bedding, doctors and medical supplies.

What if America gave its own citizens the same support? How many floods and tornados do Americans go through where citizens get no support at all from this government?

So, who gets our money?

Hamas - $351 M
Libya - $1.45 Billion
Egypt - $397 M
Mexico - $622 M
Russia - $380 M
Haiti - $1.4 Billion
Jordan - $463 M
Kenya - $816 M
Sudan - $870 M
Nigeria - $456 M
Uganda - $451 M
Congo - $359 M
Ethiopia - $981 M
Pakistan - $2 Billion

South Africa - $566 M
Senegal - $698 M
Mozambique - $404 M
Zambia - $331 M
Kazakhstan - $304 M
Iraq - $1.08 Billion
Tanzania - $554 M

A total of $14,933,000,000

X

LOYALTY

O n May 28, 2014, Obama gave a speech in Brussels in which he said the following: "Ordinary men and women are too small-minded to govern their own affairs. And order and progress can only come when individuals surrender their rights to an all-powerful sovereign." http://bit.ly/1mfsEJe

Does anyone think this President has our best interests at heart? Right at the beginning of his term he complained that our Constitution was in the way of his getting done what he needs to do.

What happened to the Democrats in this Country? The party has turned Communist. And the ones that are not members of the Communist Party are members of the Socialist Party. Is there a difference? Democrats have become the most liberal, vile, and racist people on earth. You cannot carry on a conversation with them about any subject without them pulling out the race card. They still use the same Jim Crow tactics today that they used before the Civil Rights Act of 1964. Now the Democratic Party uses so-called Government Assistance to keep black Americans down. If he succeeds through individual initiative, the Democrats put him down. Nothing scares a Democrat more than a successful black man that does not want his help.

We have a Democrat Representative from the State of Minnesota, Keith Ellison. Mr. Ellison was elected to office in 2007, and when questioned about voting laws, Mr. Ellison said: "Why does anyone need to register to vote in the first place? … "Why should voting be so difficult? Tuesday? Who thought that up? I mean the fact is that there's wide variation in when people can vote. You can't necessarily register to vote on Election Day." He added: "I've often asked myself why you should have to register to vote. Why shouldn't it be automatic?"

Now, why didn't I think of that? I could just go and vote as many times as I wanted to, and maybe Obama would not be President if that were the case. Or maybe that is the reason he is the President. Some states do not require identification and many people voted several times. Someone always has to throw a clinker in the machine.

"On November 15, 2008, Sam Webb, National Chair of the Communist Party USA delivered an address to the Communist Party USA National Committee. During his address, he noted the following concerning the party's relationship with Obama, "The left can and should advance its views and disagree with the Obama administration without being disagreeable. Its tone should be respectful. We are speaking to a friend." http://keywiki.org/index.php/Barack_Obama_and_the_Communist_Party.

Manning Marable, a Marxist academic, said that Obama understands what socialism is. He said, "What makes Obama different is that he has also been a community organizer. He has read left literature, including my works, and he understands what socialism is. A lot of the people working with him are, indeed, socialists with backgrounds in the Communist Party or as independent Marxists. There are a lot of people like that in Chicago who has worked with him for years..."

Obama once said that Frank Marshall Davis was "a decisive influence in helping him find his present identity as an African-American, a people who have been the least anticommunist and the most left-leaning of any constituency in this nation." Davis was an active member of the Communist Party USA and tracked by the FBI. When he moved to Hawaii, he joined the Hawaii Communist Party, which moved underground. They were charged with agitating the U.S. Military bases every chance they got.

Davis met Obama, Jr. when he was about ten years old, and the relationship lasted until Obama left for college in Los Angeles in 1978.

Frank Marshall Davis and Stanley Dunham were great personal friends and played Scrabble often, drank together, smoked pot, and cracked jokes. Their children came and played together. Frank Marshall Davis was married to a white woman, and his children were half white. Stanley Dunham was a white man. His daughter, Stanley Anne Dunham was married to Barack Obama, Sr. She later married Lolo Soetoro and gave birth to Maya Soetoro.

The Rev. Addie Wyatt lived in Chicago and was a long-time member of the Chicago Communist Party. If you needed a place to hold an important meeting such as the Montgomery Bus Boycott, you go to Addie Wyatt's home. At her funeral, Barack and Michelle Obama read a letter that said she was a "champion of equality and a fierce advocate for working Americans." According to a Chicago Broadcaster, Addie was a mentor to Obama in his community organizing as a young man.

Vernon Jarrett, a prominent Chicago Journalist for the Chicago Sun-Times, worked in the communist controlled Packing House Workers Strike Committee with Frank Marshall Davis, and ran a radio show with Communist Party USA member Oscar Brown, Jr., who was also a fan of Barack Obama. When Obama worked for Project Vote, Jarrett wrote this: "Commenting on the 1992 race, Vernon Jarrett wrote in the Chicago Sun-Times of August 11th, 1992;

Good news! Good news! Project Vote, a collectivity of 10 church-based community organizations dedicated to black voter registration, is off and running. Project Vote is increasing its rolls at a 7,000-per-week clip. If Project Vote is to reach its goal of registering 150,000 out of an estimated 400,000 unregistered blacks statewide, "it must average 10,000 rather than 7,000 every week," says Barack Obama, the program's executive director..."

"In March 2008, Barack Obama sent a message of support to the Communist Party USA controlled Cesar E. Chavez National Holiday organization.

"April 1, 2008 Washington DC–Evelina Alarcon, Executive Director of Cesar E. Chavez National Holiday welcomed the backing for a Cesar Chavez national holiday from Presidential candidate Senator Barack Obama who issued a statement on Cesar Chavez's birthday

Monday, March 31, 2008. "We at Cesar E. Chavez National Holiday appreciate the backing of a national holiday for Cesar Chavez from presidential candidate Senator Barack Obama. That support is crucial because it takes the signature of a President to establish the holiday along with the Congress's approval," stated Evelina Alarcon. "It is also encouraging that Senator Hillary Clinton who is a great admirer of Cesar Chavez acknowledged him on his birthday. We hope that she too will soon state her support for a Cesar Chavez national holiday."

"Alarcon's remarks were part of a statement made at a press conference at our nation's Capitol on April 1st called by Chair of the Hispanic Congressional Caucus Rep. Joe Baca (D-CA) in support of HR 76, a resolution he authored with 62 Co-Sponsors that encourages the establishment of a Cesar Chavez national holiday by the Congress.

"Barack Obama's statement for a Cesar Chavez national holiday: "Chavez left a legacy as an educator, environmentalist, and a civil rights leader. And his cause lives on. As farmworkers and laborers across America continue to struggle for fair treatment and fair wages, we find strength in what Cesar Chavez accomplished so many years ago. And we should honor him for what he's taught us about making America a stronger, more just, and more prosperous nation. That's why I support the call to make Cesar Chavez's birthday a national holiday. It's time to recognize the contributions of this American icon to the ongoing efforts to perfect our union." Senator Barack Obama March 31, 2008.

"In June 2008, Communist Party USA leader and Executive Director of Cesar E. Chavez National Holiday, Evelina Alarcon presented an award from the organization to Barack Obama's younger sister Maya Soetoro-Ng at a gathering in East Los Angeles.

"Addressing a largely Latino audience in East Los Angeles yesterday, Dr. Maya Soetoro-Ng shared stories about her childhood with her older brother, Barack Obama, and the effect he has had on her life. Held in El Sereno's Hecho en Mexico restaurant, the event drew more than a hundred enthusiastic community activists, local elected officials, and regular citizens. Evelina Alarcon, a notable Obama supporter, and the sister of long-time Los Angeles politician Richard Alarcon, presented a poster to Obama's sister commemorating the life of Cesar Chavez. Alarcon recounted the accomplishments of the late Chicano leader and argued persuasively for honoring his accomplishments with a national holiday. Reminding those in attendance that Barack Obama supports the call to make Cesar Chavez's birthday a national holiday. Alarcon trusts that if Obama is elected president the holiday will become a reality. Obama has been quoted recently to say: "As farmworkers and laborers across America continue to struggle for fair treatment and fair wages, we find strength in what Cesar Chavez accomplished so many years ago and we should honor him for what he's taught us about making America a stronger, more just, and more prosperous nation. That's why I support the call to make Cesar Chavez's birthday a national holiday. It's time to recognize the contributions of this American icon to the ongoing efforts to perfect our union." http://bit.ly/1HO0kv1

From May 22-25, 2008, the Communist Party USA founded Coalition of Black Trade Unionists held their 37th International Convention in St. Louis, Missouri.

William Lucy, President, CBTU - Introduced Senator Barack Obama, who addressed the conference via phone.

"A report praising Barack Obama and the changes wrought by him, was delivered at the 14th International Meeting of Communist and Workers Parties, held in Beirut, Lebanon, November 22-25, by Erwin Marquit, member of the International Department, CPUSA.

'We express our gratitude to the Lebanese Communist Party for hosting this important meeting under the present difficult conditions. The Communist Party USA not only welcomes the reelection of President Barack Obama but actively engaged in the electoral campaign for his reelection and for the election of many Democratic Party congressional candidates. We regarded the 2012 election as the most important in the United States since 1932, an election held in the midst of the Great Depression.

'The election of President Franklin Roosevelt in 1932 led to the legalization of the right of workers to organize labor unions and to bargain collectively with employers. It led to the establishment of a compulsory employer-worker funded pension system for retired workers. It also introduced measures that enabled unemployed families to survive the Great Depression, among which were employment in the public sector for the unemployed, work camps for youth, and food provisions for the poverty stricken.

'Except for the youth camps, which ended with the onset of World War II, all of these are measures that the 2012 Republican Party agenda would have eliminated or greatly weakened. We believed that if the Republican candidate for President were elected and if both houses of the Congress fell under the control of the far right, racist sector (calling itself the "Tea Party") that now dominates the Republican Party, the nation's return to pre-1932 conditions would be a real danger. Because of this danger, we viewed our participation in mainstream electoral activity as obligatory, even though both major parties in the United States are dominated by capital, with no effective competition from a mass-scale social-democratic party. We are aware that some on the Left in the United States thought that the correct approach to the elections was either to boycott them, or as a protest, to run or support small-scale left-wing candidacies with no possible chance of winning.

'We Communists rejected this strategy because too much was at stake. The most important success of the Obama Administration since its election in 2008 was the introduction of a major expansion of the people's access to financing of their health care. As a result of this legislation, 25 million people now have access to health care that previously did not have it. The repeal of this health care law was one of the main points in the programs of the Republican Party presidential and Congressional candidates in the 2012 election.

'Even without a repeal, there is still the danger that it will be ruled unconstitutional by the present Supreme Court even though the lower courts have upheld it. Whatever the present Supreme Court might not rule, a Supreme Court loaded with right-wing justices appointed by a Republican president would still be able to do so. Obama has opposed Republican attempts to introduce austerity programs similar to those in the European Union.

'The Republicans have opposed his efforts to use government funds as economic stimuli to reduce unemployment, as well as his attempts to remove the special provisions of the income tax code that have allowed the rich to be taxed at a lower percentage of income than the average working person, and to eliminate of tax benefits that the corporations get when exporting of jobs abroad.

'The Occupy movement, with its slogan, "We are the 99%," that swept through the country in 2011, sharply drew attention to the power of the top 1%" of the population and stimulated support for Obama's efforts to require higher taxes for the wealthy. The Republicans have blocked all proposals to reduce global warming, environment destruction, industrial pollution, and other actions arising from corporate greed that threaten to destroy the biophysical basis of human existence. Republicans even want to privatize the FEMA, the Federal agency for disaster mitigation. Another important issue is that of justice for immigrant workers and their families.

'There are between ten and eleven million irregular immigrants in the United States, mostly from Mexico and other Latin American countries. Our Party supports the regularization of their status, with full rights in the workplace and in the community, and access to U.S. citizenship. The Obama administration has moved too slowly on this issue (and the CPUSA has been sharply critical of this), but it is now taking some modest but real steps. The Republicans, on the other hand, have whipped up a racist frenzy against immigrants that have led to vigilante action and in some cases the murder of immigrant workers.

'Romney had promised to make life so hard for undocumented immigrants that they would all "self" deport. Faced with a choice between the victory of either the Democratic Party or Republican Party, the Communist Party viewed a victory of the far-right Republican Party as an extreme disaster. In this situation, we saw the necessity of a policy of center-left alliances in order not to separate ourselves from the people's struggles for dealing with the far right onslaught, The basis of such an alliance now includes the labor movement, organizations of African Americans and Latinos, the women's movement, gay and lesbian civil rights groups, and organizations of the elderly and retirees.

'On some issues, these groups are joined by a few far-sighted elements of capital. What do we mean by "far-sighted" elements of capital? As in all capitalist countries, big capital is not a monolith of common interest. Not only are elements of capital in competition with one another, but differences in their investment policies giving rise to conflicting political interests. Corporations with investments in the oil, coal, and natural gas industries tend to have the most right-wing orientations.

'Corporations with heavy investments in China are somewhat wary of China bashing by the Republicans and even by Obama. Some corporations derive their super-profits by operations that do severe environmental damage and contribute heavily to global warming while others depend on a relatively healthy environment for their maximum profits. That is why some elements of big capital support the Republican Party while others support the Democratic Party because they can see a limited common interest some issues with the working-class base of support for the Democratic Party.

'Our present strategy is build alliances both inside and outside the Democratic Party to curtail the dominance of big capital over the lives of our people. We are well aware that mass political activity on issues of social justice domestically and anti-imperialist solidarity internationally will not spring from within the Democratic Party. The Communist Party must continue to work with other components of this alliance to generate mass activity independently of the two parties to pressure the president and the Congress to act on its demands. In our electoral policy, we seek to cooperate and strengthen our relationship with the more progressive elements in Democratic Party, such as the Progressive Caucus in the U.S. Congress, a group of seventy-six members of the Congress co-chaired by Raúl Grijalva, a Latino from Arizona, and Keith Ellison, an African American Muslim from Minnesota.

'We also will strengthen our relationship to the Congressional Black Caucus (formed by African Americans in the Congress), which has been the point of origin of innovative policies including an end to the U.S. economic blockade of Cuba, and with the Congressional Hispanic Caucus. In its domestic policy, for example, the Progressive Caucus has put forth a program for using the public sector to deal with unemployment. It has opposed the use of the so-called "war on terror" to incarcerate U.S. citizens indefinitely without criminal charges. In its foreign policy, the Progressive Caucus and the Black Caucus are outspoken in their opposition to U.S. imperialist policies abroad.

'The Progressive Caucus, now that Obama has been reelected, will be playing an important role in contributing to the mobilization of mass activity on critical issues to bring pressure on the Congress and administration to act on them. In this year's elections, the labor unions made vigorous efforts to involve their members and their retirees in phoning and door-to-door visits to campaign for Obama and the Democratic Party candidates for the Congress and state legislatures. In my state, our Party members preferentially participated in the election campaign through these labor-union channels.

'In our foreign policy, U.S. Communists consistently oppose all U.S. imperialist activities abroad. We participate in the Cuban solidarity movement and demand the end of the U.S. economic blockade against Cuba and the freeing of the Cuban Five. We opposed the NATO intervention in Libya and oppose U.S. intervention in Syria. We support immediate withdrawal of NATO troops from Afghanistan and oppose the use of drones for assassination and bombing. We call for the end of sanctions against Iran.

'We oppose the intrusion of the United States militarily and politically in the affairs of Southeast Asia. We oppose the China-bashing policies of the U.S. government. We welcome the election of several progressive, anti-imperialist governments in Latin America and oppose U.S. attempts to undermine them. This leftward shift in Latin American, opening a path to possible socialist development, is of tremendous importance in the worldwide anti-imperialist struggle.

'We call for the replacement of U.S. support of the apartheid regime in Israel by support for a two-state solution based on the 1967 borders with the right of return of Palestinians to their native cities and villages. The day before the elections, the New York Times, in discussing the prospects of a Palestinian/Israel agreement, wrote: "Whatever chance exists of a new American peace initiative after the election is likely to vanish if Mitt Romney wins; at private fund-raising event, he said that the Arab-Israeli conflict was 'going to remain an unsolved problem' and seemed unconcerned about it."

With the elections now over, there is a prospect that growing support in the United States for a just Middle East solution can induce President Obama once again to put pressure on the Israeli government to end the settlement expansion and resume negotiations leading to such a solution. An indication of such growing support is the letter on 19 October 2012 signed by fifteen leaders of the principal U.S. Christian churches calling upon the Congress to reconsider giving aid to Israel because of human rights violations. Reverend Gradye Parsons, the top official of the Presbyterian Church (U.S.A.) said,

"We asked Congress to treat Israel like it would any other country, to make sure our military aid is going to a country espousing the values we would as Americans—that it is not being used to continually violate the human rights of other people." The letter said that Israel had continued expanding settlements in the West Bank and East Jerusalem despite American calls to stop claiming territory that under international law and United States policy should belong to a future Palestinian state.

'This is a sharp contrast to the evangelical Christian churches, which have been part of the core of the far right support of the Republican candidates for president and the Congress. A Jewish-American organization called "J Street," first organized six years ago as a "pro-Israel pro-peace" organization, has been gaining growing support among Jewish Americans for its advocacy of an end to the settlement expansion and a two- state solution based on the 1967 borders. In the 2012 elections, it contributed 1.8 million dollars to support the election of 72 candidates for the U.S. Congress, of which 71 were elected,

'A key element of the Communist Party's strategy of alliances is to imbue the struggles of these alliances with enhancement of the democratic rights, and to promote the increasing use of the public sector to extend the acceptance of a socialist consciousness. Obviously the Communist Party needs far more growth than it has been able to achieve. We are, however, effectively using our participation in people's struggles and the Internet to recruit new members. We have an online daily news publication, People's World, www.peoplesworld.org, a monthly online theoretical journal Political Affairs, www.politicalaffairs. net, as well as national and district Websites.

'As a result of our online activities, we have been forming Party clubs in states in which we previously had very few or even no members. This influx of new members led us to have a national Party school earlier this year to acquaint new members with the Marxist-Leninist orientation of the Party. The reelection of Obama places before us the high-priority task of reversing the decline in labor-union membership by securing the enactment of the law requiring the recognition of labor unions when supported by the majority of workers of an enterprise and securing passage of other legislation that benefits the working people. The fact that the composition of the new Congress did not change ideologically enough to facilitate passage of this law still presents us with a difficult struggle.

'The fact that Republican Party still controls the lower house of the Congress and has enough votes in the upper house to block legislative changes of a highly progressive nature presents an obstacle that we will have to combat until it can be changed in the 2014 elections. We still have the task of strengthening the center-left alliance and enriching its anti-imperialist character. While the victory of Obama is a welcome aid for us in our domestic struggles, we still face the challenge of mobilizing mass pressure on his administration to reverse the imperialist character of U.S. foreign policy. The CPUSA will pursue this formidable task vigorously in alliance with domestic progressive forces and with our comrades in the Communist and Workers' Parties and their allies throughout the world." http://keywiki.org/index.php/ Barack_Obama_and_the_Communist_Party

In 1959, President Eisenhower and Congress made May 1st officially Loyalty Day. The Presidential Proclamation always calls on people to display the flag – that is our very own Stars and Stripes – not a red flag or the flag of Mexico or some other country. "Loyalty to the United States of America," Ike said, "is essential to the preservation of our freedoms in a world threatened by totalitarianism."

Obama's proclamation in 2013 said that on Loyalty Day we should reaffirm our commitment to "liberty, equality, and justice for all." That is pretty good considering in his book *Audacity of Hope* Obama said "I will stand with the Muslims should the political winds shift in an ugly direction."

Now for the kicker: At a press conference with hand-picked MSNBC Reporters, Obama announced reaching a deal between the United States and China which will allow the Chinese Special Operations, an elite military unit, to guard the interior vaults containing the gold in Fort Knox, the U.S. bullion depository.

"We as a nation owe China a whole lot of money," stated the President, "and I'm glad we finally found an amicable way to resolve issues with Chinese leaders who no longer trust us with our money. Placing our gold reserve under Chinese supervision will benefit both our nations and I'm confident it will flower into a beautiful friendship, let alone improve our financial well-being."

Fort Knox has the reputation of being the world's most secure vault; it is guarded by the U.S. First Armored Division, as well as by a nearby Air Force base. In addition to being the depository for the gold belonging to the United States, Fort Knox has also been a symbol of America's strength and impenetrability.

The changing of the guard will be marked with a private military ceremony as the People's Republic of China will hoist its flag alongside the U.S. flag over Fort Knox for the first time during the sunrise of June 6th 2015. U.S. Forces will continue to guard the exterior of the building for cosmetic purposes only, as they will not be permitted inside the depository itself.

Concerned citizens need not worry about Chinese soldiers parading around the local area because the agreement will not allow China any liberties on U.S. soil until after Barack Obama leaves office, which includes building a small military base by China in an undisclosed U.S. location by the year 2020. Even then China was placed under harsh restrictions with regards to choosing a name for their base; after exhausting hours of negotiations it was decided to name it symbolically after the current U.S. President, Barack Obama.

It sounds treasonous to me. http://bit.ly/1N47x9e

In 2015 while America was remembering September 11, what was our President doing? What would a national day of remembrance be without a photo of Barack Obama?

Barack Obama remembered the 9-11 attacks today by posting a photo of himself on Twitter.

The president did not attend the New York City memorial.

The president did not attend the Pennsylvania memorial.

The president did not even go across town to the Pentagon memorial.

But he did post a photo of himself on Twitter.

This is a man that learned early in life how to delegate. He was a community organizer and he still is a community organizer. The first thing he did when he became president was to appoint many czars to do all the work and now he does not have anything to do but ride around in Air Force One, play golf, take vacations, attend fundraisers, and stir up America.

Alaska, nor the rest of America, did not think it was necessary to have Mt. McKinley renamed. No one was asked if it was a good idea.

Obama just decided to go to Alaska and rename Mt. McKinley as Mt. Denali. Denali was the mountain's previous name. Obama thought Alaskans still called it Denali, which they did not. Alaskans and especially Ohioans, President McKinley's state, were enraged.

Some Alaskans said they cared more about other issues such as ISIS and our government sending billions of dollars to Iran in a horrible nuclear deal and our broken immigration system. But instead our government worries about renaming a mountain in Alaska.

XI

THE MEDIA

Not since the days of Bob Woodward and Carl Bernstein have I trusted the Media. Those were the days when if something big was happening, or you had a huge problem in the world, you knew you could go to the media for protection; they had your back. That was in the early 1970s.

Something happened after that. The Media started losing their morals, their values. They became more liberal, less trustworthy. There were scandals, fabrications, and there were plagiarisms. At one time I believed you could trust Fox News and perhaps CNN, but now not even them completely.

There was bias reporting and many stories that were not reported at all that should have been. Time was spent attacking those seeking the truth rather than not seeking the truth. At times, more energy was spent covering up than was spent on actual coverage of the news in order to protect the Power. The sad truth is they were just out for career-making stories.

Reporter Charyl Attkisson resigned from CBS after they gave her the assignment to check into Benghazi. When she reported back to the higher ups on her story, they told her they did not have air time for the story and to cease her investigation. The story exposed Obama and his lies and malfeasance.

How many years did we listen to Dan Rather on the CBS Evening News? In the end the conversation went something like this: "The dishonesty here is extraordinary. The documents Rather presented that fateful night in September 2004 were clearly forgeries. Not one person has come forward since proving they were not. Here he is nine years later saying on national television, "No question the story was true." And (Piers) Morgan didn't challenge him at all. Is this really what passes for journalism in our country today?" http://bit.ly/1NAWL7o

Jayson Blair resigned from the New York Times in 2003 when he was questioned about plagiarism and fabrication in some of his stories.

Now we have Brian Williams, known for his ten years as anchor of NBC's Nightly News, who recently resigned after a scandal of telling a whopper of a story about a military raid of all things. Do not toot your own horn at our troops' expense. And leftist, Dan Rather came to his defense. "That is like Jeffrey Dahmer defending Ted Bundy," said Kevin Jackson at Black Sphere, Inc.

Have you ever wondered if the Media was really in cahoots with the current administration? Why does the Media go so easy on Obama's many errors?

ABC News executive producer Ian Cameron is married to Susan Rice, National Security Adviser.

CBS President David Rhodes is the brother of Ben Rhodes, Obama's Deputy National Security Adviser for Strategic Communications.

ABC News correspondent Claire Shipman is married to former Whitehouse Press Secretary Jay Carney

ABC News and Univision reporter Matthew Jaffe is married to Katie Hogan, Obama's Deputy Press Secretary

ABC President Ben Sherwood is the brother of Obama's Special Adviser Elizabeth Sherwood

CNN President Virginia Moseley is married to former Hillary Clinton's Deputy Secretary Tom Nides.

If you want good press coverage, just appoint someone to a government office that is married to someone in the Media.

In my book *The Lyin Kings* I devote a chapter on abortion as being the perfect crime. On January 27, 2015, two hundred thousand (200,000)

people (I wish I could stress that number more clearly) marched in Washington, D.C. It was a March for Life. 200,000 people and it was dismissed by the Media as a non-event because it was a Pro-Life March. Fifty-Seven Million babies have been destroyed since the Roe v. Wade Supreme Court Decision in 1973. Only CBS mentioned the March and allotted just 15 seconds of time to the story. That is one second for every 3.8 million babies aborted in the last 42 years.

How about tyranny? A New Jersey family was homeschooling their son. They received a knock on their door from someone that said they were a caseworker for the state child protective services. The person started asking questions about vaccines and guns in the house.

The parents filed suit in the United States District Court alleging unlawful and unconstitutional home intrusion. The father said, "I won't forget that morning for a long, long time." He said the caseworker demanded to be let inside the house, now! He said, "when I asked the purpose of the visit, she refused to answer, saying only that his son was not getting a proper education."

Not knowing his rights, the father called the police. The police arrived and allowed the caseworker to enter the home and continue issuing threats to the family and inspecting the house, all without a warrant.

After two hours of intense interrogation, it became clear the matter would not be resolved. The caseworker started asking the boy questions like do your parents ever argue, are their guns in the house, do they use alcohol or drugs? She then demanded the keys to the safe and to see the guns and to see where the child slept. She asked the boy if he was ever suicidal. http://bit.ly/1N47qur

XII

CONGRESS

I don't know about the rest of you, but I was thrilled to hear about former Speaker John Boehner inviting Prime Minister Benjamin Netanyahu of Israel to speak before a joint session of Congress. If he keeps making moves like this, I am going to think better of him. Obama, with his nose out of joint, refused to grant Mr. Netanyahu a visit. The reason given was proximity to the Israeli election, but some of Obama's campaign staffers showed up in Israel in an attempt to defeat Netanyahu in his reelection bid.

A study by Reuters and the Brookings Institute shows that although Congress holds the purse strings and directs overall spending of Federal funds, the Obama Administration decides exactly where most of that money goes. A 2011 bill that banned earmarks placed even more control of Federal spending in the hands of the Obama Administration.

The Administration was quick to warn "elections have consequences" and Republican-leaning states were receiving less Federal aid and grant money than blue states. One Texas Republican Representative stated he had extraordinary trouble securing Federal funds to pay for border security, harbor dredging, or even basic aid after a chemical plant explosion in his district.

"The Obama administration approaches the Federal government the same way the Chicago machine politicians approach the Chicago public treasury: it's to be used for their own benefit." It works kind of like blackmail and that is how Obama manipulates Congress. http://bit.ly/1ljIgPn

I read somewhere, and I wish I had kept the url, that Obama had someone that dug up dirt on every Congressman every day; that he knew every check they wrote every day, who it was to and for how much it was for; every telephone call they made and received and what it was about, and every visitor they had or went to see. This is how Obama gets his votes from Congressmen – I believe it is called blackmail.

Senator Tom Cotton, a Republican from Arkansas gave his opinion on whether we should release the prisoners at Guantanamo Bay. He stated, "the drive to close the prison is simply a political one based on President Barack Obama's 2008 campaign promise." At the hearing, intelligence officials offered evidence of how the prison is being used as "propaganda" in terrorist recruitment videos. Cotton dismissed those claims as a "pretext to justify a political decision."

Senator Cotton continued, "In my opinion, the only problem with Guantanamo Bay is there are too many empty beds and cells there right now. We should be sending more terrorists there for further interrogation to keep this country safe. As far as I'm concerned, every last one of them can rot in Hell. But as long as they don't do that, then they can rot in Guantanamo Bay." http://bit.ly/1OaO9Fp

Only 122 prisoners remain and Obama continues to find ways to trade prisoners. Senator McCain, who has been with Obama, has finally proposed a bill on Jan. 13 that would restrict detainee transfers from the detention facility at Guantanamo Bay, Cuba. The bill would prohibit the transfer of high or medium-risk detainees and any transfers to Yemen, as well as increase transparency about detainees' risk assessments, among other measures. McCain said, "Too many detainees released from Guantanamo are re-engaging in terrorism."

Total detainees held since 2002: more than 750; Detainees Released: 620; Former detainees confirmed of re-engaging: 107 (17.3 percent); Former detainees suspected of re-engaging: 77 (12.4 percent). http://bit.ly/1IDBUk5

Isn't the real problem the fact that all of the detainees are Muslims?

Do you think Congress isn't sexist? Only 44 women have ever served in the Senate. As a freshman Senator in 2008, Kay Hagan, a Republican from North Carolina was told by other male Senators that the Senate swimming pool was males-only, "because some of the male senators liked to swim naked." It took an intervention by Senator Chuck Schumer, head of the Rules Committee, to put a stop to the practice, and even then there was a fight.

Apparently sexism is pretty rampant as Sen. Kirsten Gillibrand (D-NY) once recounted how a colleague once told her to stop losing weight, as he liked "chubby" women, but it is reported that the story extended far beyond her telling of it.

Utah Republican Orrin Hatch will become chairman of the Senate Finance Committee — and he is a proponent, along with incoming House Ways and Means Committee Chairman Paul Ryan, of revising the tax code.

It is important that Congress investigate efforts by our enemies to buy influence in the American political and governmental system.

There is evidence that our political and intellectual communities have been infiltrated by cash from foreign regimes in ways that are very dangerous to the future of our free society.

Congress has an obligation to establish how extensive the problem is and how these foreigners are buying their way into positions of influence.

"The amount of money the Clintons have collected from dictatorships in the Middle East through their foundation raises profound questions. Americans deserve to know about the process by which a potential future president accepts money from people who, at best, have values totally unacceptable to most Americans. Also, at worst, those who are funding the very terrorists who want to kill us and destroy our civilization.

'As the Wall Street Journal reported this month, the Clinton Foundation recently resumed accepting money from foreign governments, a practice it had stopped in 2009 when Hillary Clinton became Secretary of State. Now among the Foundation's recent donors, according to the report, are the United Arab Emirates, Saudi Arabia, Oman, and Qatar.

'The amount of money is as startling as the sources. According to the Journal analysis, the UAE gave the Clinton Foundation between $1 and $5 million last year. Saudi Arabia has given between $10 million and $25 million since 1999. Qatar, widely known also to fund Hamas (a designated terrorist group), has given the Clinton Foundation up to $5 million. Oman has given a similar amount.

'Countries better-aligned with American values, including Germany and Australia, have given millions more but still pose important conflicts of interest.

'Yet to be fair to the Clintons, the purchase of influence by foreign countries through donations to American institutions is widespread." Newt Gingrich Productions.

Al Gore received an estimated $100 Million when he sold his television network to Al Jazeera, which is owned by the ruling family of Qatar.

The New York Times investigations have suggested that some arrangements between American organizations and overseas governments may already be violating existing laws. More aggressive laws are necessary about elected officials and government officials.

Senator Hillary Clinton recently said in a speech at Georgetown University "that America must have empathy for its enemies."

Additionally, Clinton said, "smart power" is using every possible tool and partner to advance peace and security.

Can you put that in the context of someone having empathy for ISIS beheading James Foley?

In December 2014, the House passed a Bill to block President Obama's Executive actions on illegal immigration policies. The Bill declares Obama's actions as "null and void and without legal effect." The bill, which has little chance of getting past the still Harry Reid-controlled Senate, and which was called "nonsensical" by the White House, would likely be vetoed by Obama. Speaker Nancy Pelosi has reportedly offered a "hand of friendship" to Boehner and is extending Democrat support for a funding bill, provided they get something out of it.

House Republican leaders are close to sealing a deal with Democrats over objections from Tea Party lawmakers to fund most of the U.S. government through September 2015 and avoid a repeat of last year's partial shutdown.

"Let us supply the votes to keep the government open but we can't do that unless we have a bill worthy of our support," Pelosi, of California, told reporters today. That is Washington "speak" for "what is in it for me."

Congress knows the American people want to have the border fixed before any immigration reform is enacted. Congress knows America would prefer to have Obamacare repealed.

Congress knows America has voted in a Republican Congress so that America's choices could be made. I hope this Congress is aware that America can still make new choices in the next election if this Congress does not carry out the wishes of the American people.

Congress has many choices, and one of those is impeachment in order to get America back on the right track.

When Israel's leader, Benjamin Netanyahu spoke of his concern about Iran's nuclear ambitions and the great risk they could impose upon Israel, he said "My responsibility is to worry not only about the state of Israel but also the future of the Jewish people, and for that reason, we are strongly opposed to the agreement being formulated between the world powers and Iran that could endanger Israel's very existence."

Senator Dianne Feinstein became outraged and said he did not speak for her and that it was an arrogant statement. She further commented, "I think the Jewish community is like any other community," said Feinstein. "There are different points of view. I think that arrogance does not befit Israel, candidly." (H/T: Breitbart News)

It apparently has not occurred to Feinstein that Israel is 800 miles from Iran and is about the size of Feinstein's own state of California.

In 2016, the Republicans have to defend twenty-four seats in the Senate while the Democrats only have to defend ten. If the Republicans do not start doing some work, they may find they have to defend more than twenty-four seats.

My respect for Congress keeps getting lower. The Trans-Pacific Partnership Agreement is so secret that "If you're a member who wants to read the text, you've got to go to a room in the basement of the Capitol Visitor Center and be handed it one section at a time, watched over as you read, and forced to hand over any notes you make before leaving. And no matter what, you can't discuss the details of what you've read." Only two Senate Republicans from the entire conference of 54 members have admitted they read the details. They expect to listen to Obama's logic and then vote on it.

Did you ever wonder how Congressmen get so rich? And do not believe that there will ever be a cap on Congressional terms limits. Don't you believe it.

Recently there was a vote taken on Trans-Pacific Partnership Agreement (TPP). It began as a secret agreement in a room where a Senator had to make an appointment one at a time to go into the room to read it. How many Senators went in to read it? I read of two that did. I do not know if they then reported to the other Senators, or what happened from there. Perhaps it was like the Obamacare bill where Pelosi said "you have to pass it to find out what is in it." But I did find out the following and perhaps that will give you more input on whether or not it was read: "An average of $17,676.48 was donated to each of the 65 "yea" votes. The average Republican member received $19,673.28 from corporate TPP supporters. The average Democrat received $9,689.23 from those same donors. The amounts given rises dramatically when looking at how much each Senator running for re-election received."

'Two days before the fast-track vote, Obama was a few votes shy of having the filibuster-proof majority he needed. Ron Wyden and seven other Senate Democrats announced they were on the fence on 12 May, distinguishing themselves from the Senate's 54 Republicans and handful of Democrats as the votes to sway.

'In just 24 hours, Wyden and five of those Democratic holdouts – Michael Bennet of Colorado, Dianne Feinstein of California, Claire McCaskill of Missouri, Patty Murray of Washington, and Bill Nelson of Florida – caved and voted for fast-track.

'Bennet, Murray, and Wyden – all running for re-election in 2016 – received $105,900 between the three of them. Bennet, who comes from the more purple state of Colorado, got $53,700 in corporate campaign donations between January and March 2015, according to Channing's research.

'Almost 100% of the Republicans in the U.S. Senate voted for fast-track – the only two non-votes on TPA were a Republican from Louisiana and a Republican from Alaska.

'Senator Rob Portman of Ohio, who is the former U.S. trade representative, has been one of the loudest proponents of the TPP. (In a comment to the Guardian Portman's office said: "Senator Portman is not a vocal proponent of TPP - he has said it's still being negotiated, and if and when an agreement is reached he will review it carefully.") He received $119,700 from 14 different corporations between January and March, most of which comes from donations from Goldman Sachs ($70,600), Pfizer ($15,700), and Procter & Gamble ($12,900). Portman is expected to run against former Ohio governor Ted Strickland in 2016 in one of the most politically competitive states in the country.

'Seven Republicans who voted "yea" to fast-track and are also running for re-election next year cleaned up between January and March. Senator Johnny Isakson of Georgia received $102,500 in corporate contributions. Senator Roy Blunt of Missouri, best known for proposing a Monsanto-written bill in 2013 that became known as the Monsanto Protection Act, received $77,900 – $13,500 of which came from Monsanto.

'Arizona Senator and former presidential candidate John McCain received $51,700 in the first quarter of 2015. Senator Richard Burr of North Carolina received $60,000 in corporate donations. Eighty-one-year-old Senator Chuck Grassley of Iowa, who is running for his seventh Senate term, received $35,000. Senator Tim Scott of South Carolina, who will be running for his first full six-year term in 2016, received $67,500 from pro-TPP corporations.

'"It's a rare thing for members of Congress to go against the money these days," said Mansur Gidfar, spokesman for the anti-corruption group Represent. us. "They know exactly which special interests they need to keep happy if they want to fund their reelection campaigns or secure a future job as a lobbyist." http://bit.ly/1ljHTob

Donations Made By Business Coalition For TPP Members Between Jan. and Mar. 2015

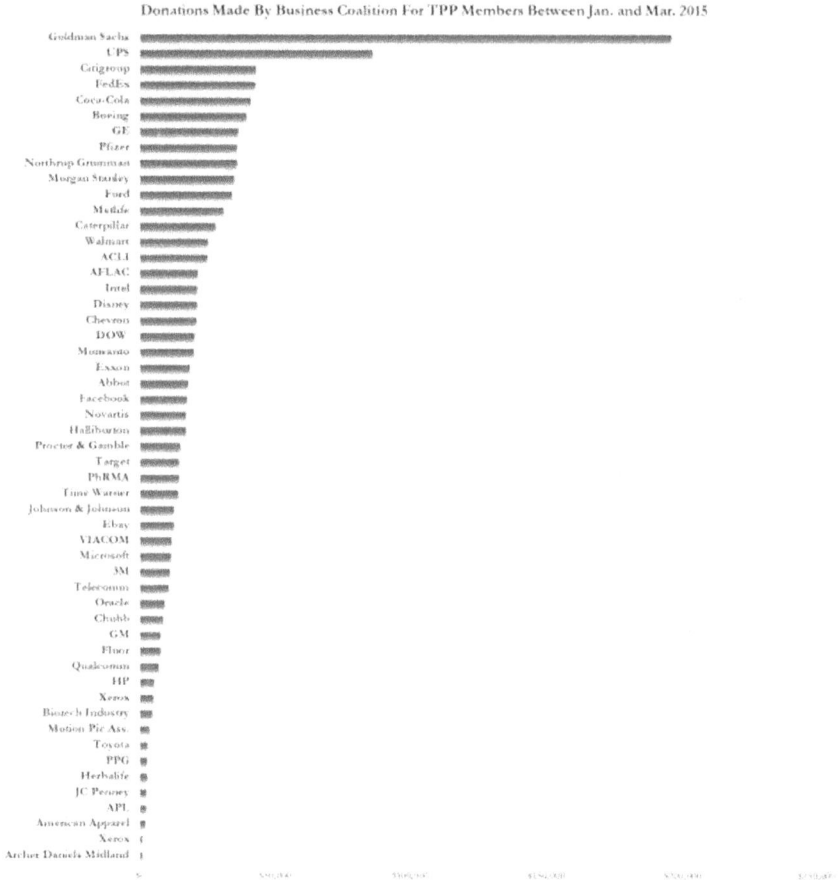

These are the Senators that we elect to make fair and impartial decisions on our behalf and on behalf of this country. How can they make fair and impartial decisions when they are more interested in campaign funds, lucrative job offers, and extravagant gifts?

We have a Congress that is more loyal to Big Donors, Lobbyists, Corporate Welfare, Cronyism, and corrupt deal making.

Robert Menendez, a U.S. Senator from New Jersey, was indicted in connection with a bribery scheme in which he allegedly accepted gifts from in exchange for using the power of his Senate office to benefit a friend's financial and personal interests." said a Justice Department spokesman, in a statement. Menendez was indicted for one count of conspiracy, one count of violating the travel act, eight counts of bribery and three counts of honest services fraud; he was also charged with one count of making false statements.

New York Senate Majority Leader Dean Skelos was arrested on charges that he used his power over real-estate laws to enrich his son. "Within days of taking over as New York Senate majority leader in January, prosecutors say, Dean Skelos was basking in his newfound power, announcing to his son Adam: "I'm going to control everything.""

"I'm going to control who gets on what committees, what legislation goes to the floor, what legislation comes through committees, the budget, everything," Skelos allegedly said on a phone call with Adam, not knowing the Federal Bureau of Investigation was listening.

'Father and son, both of Rockville Centre in New York's Long Island, were arrested and charged with running a scheme dating back to 2010 in which Skelos, 67, used his position first as a co-leader of the Senate and then as majority leader to obtain more than $200,000 in payments for his 32-year-old son in exchange for favorable treatment in the Legislature." Christopher Conniff, Adam Skelos's lawyer, said his client "is not guilty of these charges and looks forward to fighting them in the courtroom."

The following might sound a bit familiar to you.

The Affordable Plumbing Act

Only weeks after leaving office on January 20, 2017, former President Barack Obama discovers a leak under his sink, so he calls Troy the Plumber to come out and fix it.

Troy drives to President Obama's new house, which is located in a very exclusive, gated community near Chicago where all the residents have a net income of way more than $250,000 per year.

Troy arrives and takes his tools into the house. He is led to the guest bathroom that contains the leaky pipe under the sink. Troy assesses the problem and tells President Obama that it's an easy repair that will take less than 10 minutes. President Obama asks Troy how much it will cost. Troy checks his rate chart and says, "$9,500."

"What? $9,500?" Obama asks, stunned, "But you said it's an easy repair. Michelle will whip me if I pay a plumber that much!"

Troy says, "Yes, but what I do is charge those who make more than $250,000 per year a much higher amount so I can fix the plumbing of poorer people for free. This has always been my philosophy. As a matter of fact, I lobbied the Democrat Congress, who passed this philosophy into law. Now all plumbers must do business this way. It's known as the 'Affordable Plumbing Act of 2014'. I'm surprised you haven't heard of it."

In spite of that, Obama tells Troy there's no way he's paying that much for a small plumbing repair, so Troy leaves. Obama spends the next hour flipping through the phone book calling for another plumber, but he finds that all other plumbing businesses in the area have gone out of business. Not wanting to pay Troy's price, Obama does nothing and the leak goes un-repaired for several more days. A week later the leak is so bad President Obama has had to put a bucket under the sink.

Michelle is not happy as she has Oprah and guests arriving the next morning. The bucket fills up quickly and has to be emptied every hour, and there's a risk the room will flood, so Obama calls Troy and pleads with him to return.

Troy goes back to President Obama's house, looks at the leaky pipe, checks his new rate chart and says, "Let's see, this will now cost you $21,000."

President Obama quickly fires back, "What? A few days ago you told me it would cost $9,500!"

Troy explains, "Well, because of the 'Affordable Plumbing Act,' a lot of wealthier people are learning how to maintain and take care of their own plumbing, so there are fewer payers in the plumbing exchanges. As a result, the price I have to charge wealthy people, like you, keeps rising. Not only that, for some reason the demand for plumbing work by those who get it for free has skyrocketed! There's a long waiting list of those who need repairs, but the amount we get doesn't cover our costs, especially paperwork and record-keeping. This unfortunately has put a lot of my fellow plumbers out of business, they're not being replaced, and nobody is going into the plumbing business because they know they can't make any money at it. I'm hurting too, all thanks to greedy rich people like you who won't pay their 'fair share.' On the other hand, why didn't you buy plumbing insurance last December? If you had bought plumbing insurance available under the 'Affordable Plumbing Act,' all this would have been covered by your policy."

"You mean I wouldn't have to pay anything to have you fix my plumbing problem?" asks Obama.

"Well, not exactly," replies Troy. "You would have had to buy the insurance before the deadline, which has passed now. And, because you're rich, you would have had to pay $34,000 in premiums, which would have given you a 'silver' plan, and then, since this would have been your first repair, you would have to pay up to the $21,000 deductible, and anything over that would have a $7,500 co-pay, and then there's the mandatory maintenance program, which is covered up to 17.5%, so there are some costs involved. Nothing is for free."

"WHAT?!" exclaims Obama. "Why so much for a puny sink leak?"

With a bland look, Troy replies, "Well, paperwork, mostly, like I said. And the internal cost of the program itself. You don't think a program of this complexity and scope can run itself, do you? Besides, there are millions of folks with lower incomes than you, even many in the 'middle class', who qualify for subsidies that people like you must support. That's why they call it the 'Affordable Plumbing Act'! Only people who don't make much money can afford it. If you want affordable plumbing, you'll have to give away most of what you have accumulated and cut your and Michelle's income by about 90%. Then you can qualify to get your 'Fair Share' instead of giving it."

"But who would pass a crazy act like the 'Affordable Plumbing Act'?!" exclaims the exasperated Obama.

After a sigh, Troy replies, "Congress... because they didn't read it."

XIII

FIRST AMENDMENT RIGHTS

O n December 19, 2014, Brandon Raub, a veteran of the United States Marine Corps, made a post about Barack Obama that caused such a stir that the FBI, Secret Service Agents, and local police swarmed his home and arrested him.

"The First Amendment is the cornerstone of the Bill of Rights. It guarantees every American the right to express their political opinions, no matter how unpopular they are.

'However, in this day and age, the First Amendment is under assault. And it's under assault by the very people who claim to stand for the freedom of speech — liberals.

'Brandon Raub is a veteran of the United States Marine Corps, who decided to post critical opinions about Barack Obama on Facebook. What happened to him then will strike fear into the hearts of any good American and make them wonder what country they're living in.

'According to the Rutherford Institute, Raub was arrested by "a swarm of FBI, Secret Service agents, and local police," and detained without charges for "mental evaluation."

'The detention, it's alleged, was done under a Federal program codenamed "Operation Vigilant Eagle." The program is intended to surveil former veterans who publicly express opinions critical of the government.

'After ten days of detention, Raub was released, with the presiding judge noting that the government's case for detention was "so devoid of any factual allegations that it could not be reasonably expected to give rise to a case or controversy."

'Nevertheless, Raub's lawsuit against the government was dismissed, with the judge finding that censorship concerns were "far-fetched."

'John W. Whitehead, president of the Rutherford Institute, disagrees.

"What may sound far-fetched to the courts is a grim reality to Americans who are daily being targeted for daring to exercise their constitutional rights to speak their minds, worship as they please, criticize the government, defend themselves and their families against over-reaching government surveillance and heavy-handed police tactics," Whitehead said.

"Ultimately, Brandon Raub's case tests our tolerance for free speech and those dissidents who keep the First Amendment relevant, because if we cannot proclaim our feelings about the government, no matter how controversial — on our clothing, or to passersby, or to the users of the world wide web — then the First Amendment really has become an exercise in futility," he added.

'Below is one of Brandon Raub's posts. While not exactly in the mainstream of political thought, it certainly doesn't seem to represent someone who represents a danger to the community (H/T Teaparty.org).

"The Truth

'by Brandon J Raub on Friday, November 11, 2011, at 10:00 am

'America has lost itself. We have lost who we truly are. This is the land of the free and the home of the brave.

'This is the land of Thomas Jefferson.

'This is the land of Benjamin Franklin.

'This is the land of Fredrick Douglas.

'This is the land of Smedley Butler.

'This is the land John F. Kennedy.

'This is the land of Martin Luther King.

'This is the land where the cowboy wins. This is the land where you can start from the bottom and get to the top. This is the land where regardless of you race and ethnicity you can succeed and build a better life for you and your family. This is the land where every race coexists peacefully. This is the land where justice wins. This is the land where liberty dwells. This is the land where freedom reigns. This is the land where we help the poor, and people help each other. This is land where people beat racism.

'The Federal Reserve is wrong. They have designed a system based off of greed and fear. They designed a system to crush the middle class between taxes and inflation. This is wrong, and it is unjust. It is wrong.

'We have allowed ourselves to be deceived and seduced by the powers of the printing press. It is not a good system. It discourages saving: the foundation for all stable economic activity. The Federal Reserve is artificially manipulating interest rates and creating phony economic data.

'This thing has deceived our entire nation.

'They created it in 1913. They also created the income tax in 1913. They encouraged the growth of debt so they can tax you on it. There is interest on the debt. Your government is in bed with these people. They want to enslave you to the government so that they can control every aspect of your lives. It is an empire based on lies. They operate on greed and fear.

'There is a better way. It's called freedom. Freedom is called a lot of things. But there is a true meaning. It means very simply that you have the right to do whatever you want as long as you are not infringing on the freedoms of other people.

'I firmly believe that God set America apart from the other nations of the world. He saved a place where people could come to escape bad systems of government. This system we have created works. It really works.

'There is evil going on all around the world. The United States was meant to lead the charge against injustice, but through our example, not our force. People do not respond to having liberty, and freedom forced on them.

'Men and Women follow courage. They follow leadership and courage. Our example has paved the way for people all around the world to change their forms of government.

'Force is not the way because liberty is a powerful concept. The idea that men can govern themselves is the basis for every just form of government.

'We can govern ourselves. We do not need to be governed by men who want to install a one world banking system. These men have machine hearts. Machine and unnatural hearts.

'They have blocked out the possibility of a better world. They fear human progress. They have monopolies on everything.

'This life can be free and beautiful. There are enough resources on this earth to support the world's population. There are enough resources on this earth to feed everyone. There is enough land for everyone to own their own land and farm, and produce their own energy.

'These people have been hiding technology. There are ways to create power easily. There is technology that can provide free cheap power for everyone. There are farming techniques that can feed the entire world.

'The Bill of Rights is being systematically dismantled. Men have spilled their blood for those rights.

'Your sons and daughters, your brothers and sisters, and Americas best young men and women are losing their limbs. They are losing their lives. They are losing the hearts. They do not know why they are fighting. They are killing. And they do not know why.

'They have done some extraordinary acts. Their deeds go before them. But these wars are lies. They are lies. They deceived our entire nation with terrorism. They have gotten us to hand them our rights. Our Rights! Men died for those rights!

'September Eleventh was an inside job. They blew up a third building in broad daylight. Building 7.

'Your leaders betrayed you.

'You elected an aristocracy. They are beholden to special interests. They were brainwashed through the Council on Foreign Relations. Your leaders are planning to merge the United States into a one world banking system. They want to put computer chips in you.

'These men have evil hearts. They have tricked you into supporting corporate fascism. We gave them the keys to our country. We were not vigilant with our republic.

'There is hope. BUT WE MUST TAKE OUR REPUBLIC BACK."
http://bit.ly/1NbemUe

Obama will punish anyone that dares to tell what his true agenda is. Even the daughter of his friend. A senior special agent with Immigration and Customs Enforcement told the Senate Committee on Homeland Security and Governmental Affairs that she faced massive retribution after revealing irregularities in the EB-5 visa program. The agent told the Committee she found corruption and mismanagement that posed national security risks.

"Some of the violations investigated surrounding the project included bank and wire fraud, and I discovered ties to organized crime and high-ranking politicians and they received promotions that appeared to facilitate the program," she said.

After she had blown the whistle on the EB-5 program, the retaliation was swift and severe. The agent was escorted from her desk and denied access to her case files. The government then informed adoption social workers that the agent had lost her job due to criminal activity.

"When an adoption social worker tried to contact and verify employment, she was told that I had been terminated for a criminal offense," she said, on the verge of tears. "I almost lost my 1-year-old child."

In addition, Johnson was not permitted to carry a firearm.

"I was told I couldn't even carry or own a personal weapon which is a constitutional rights violation," she testified. http://bit.ly/1PKAVVM

XIV

CUBA

On January 3, 1961, President Dwight D. Eisenhower severed relations between the United States and Cuba following the Cuban Revolution of the 1950s. Relations were subsequently restored by Cuban President Raul Castro and President Barack Obama on July 20, 2015. Since 1965, Cuba has been under the rule of Fidel Castro and the Communist Party. It is the largest island in the Caribbean with over 11 million inhabitants.

The Cuban missile crisis occurred in October 1962 and by 1963, Cuba was on their way to being a full-fledged communist country patterned after Russia.

By the 1970s the standard of living was sparse, and Castro admitted the failures of the economic policies in a 1970 speech. Cuba faced a severe economic depression following the withdrawal of Soviet subsidies worth $4 to $6 Billion annually resulting in losses such as food and fuel shortages. The Cuban would not accept food, medicine, or cash from the United States until 1993.

Now Cuba has found new friends and new sources of aid and support. His new friends are the People's Republic of China, Hugo Chávez, former President of Venezuela, and Juan Evo Morales, President of Bolivia.

In February 2008, Fidel Castro announced his resignation as President of Cuba and his brother Raúl Castro was declared the new President. In his inauguration speech, Raúl promised that some of the restrictions on freedom in Cuba would be removed. Some of his brother's appointees were removed.

As of December, 2014, talks with Cuban officials and American officials including President Barack Obama, have resulted in the exchange of releasing Alan Gross, fifty-two political prisoners, and an unnamed non-citizen agent of the United States, in return for the release of three Cuban agents currently imprisoned in the United States. Additionally, while the embargo between the United States and Cuba will not be lifted, it will be relaxed to allow import, export, and certain commerce within a limit between the two.

As is his practice, President Obama made the statement that it was his intention to normalize relations with the United States and the communist regime in Cuba. Never mind that he does not have the Constitutional authority to do anything about making changes to international policy.

According to Fox News, Obama's deal was called "another concession to tyranny" and was heavily criticized in both the media and Congress, from both sides of the aisle.

"These changes will lead to legitimacy for a government that shamelessly continuously abuses human rights, but it will not lead to assistance for those whose rights are being abused," Florida Senator and Cuban-American Marco Rubio said, adding "It's absurd and its part of a long record of coddling dictators and tyrants."

'Rubio reminded that the administration is "constantly giving away unilateral concessions … in exchange for nothing." He also said that Obama is the "worst negotiator" he has seen in his lifetime and intimated that Congress would not support a lifting of the trade embargo.

'Incoming Senate Majority Leader Mitch McConnell joined Rubio in criticizing Obama's plan, saying he would defer to Rubio on the matter.

'They were also joined by Senators Lindsey Graham and John McCain, who released a joint statement saying that the move was damaging to American values.

"Unfortunately, we fear the most damaging chapter to America's national security is still being written. We dread the day President

Obama takes to the podium to announce a nuclear deal with the Iranian ayatollahs which does little, if anything, to deter their nuclear ambitions, placing our nation and our closest allies in even deeper peril," the joint statement read.

'But it wasn't just Republicans who were critical of the move, with New Jersey Senator Bob Menendez, who is also Cuban-American, expressing concern over yet another swap of convicted prisoners for a captured American.

"President Obama's actions have vindicated the brutal behavior of the Cuban government," he said in a statement. "Trading Mr. Gross for three convicted criminals sets an extremely dangerous precedent. It invites dictatorial and rogue regimes to use Americans serving overseas as bargaining chips."

'Thankfully some members of Congress are speaking up about this deal. Once again, Obama has done something on his own that normally falls within Congressional purview.

'Article 1, Section 8 of the Constitution grants Congress the sole power of regulating commerce with foreign nations. Some supporters of Obama's executive action on Cuba may point to Article 2, Section 2 of the Constitution, which grants the executive the power to make treaties, but they conveniently ignore the very next clause of that section, which requires the advice and consent of Congress, something Obama didn't have.

'To be sure, the relationship between the United States and Cuba should be normalized. Free trade is the most effective way at spreading the message of liberty and freedom. History has shown that embargoes and sanctions don't always work, and more than 50 years of isolation for Cuba has not succeeded in effectively weakening or destroying the oppressive Castro regime.

'It is time for the trade embargo and sanctions on Cuba to be eased, but it must be done the right way, through legislative action, and it must be a free and fair trade, with the communist regime in Cuba making just as many concessions as the U.S. is making."

The policy change will open both countries to some commerce and transportation though it will not end a long-standing trade embargo. That needs congressional approval — and some travel restrictions will gradually be eased

President Obama is expected to speak with Cuban President Raúl Castro at the Summit of the Americas, the White House said.

Deputy National Security Adviser Ben Rhodes told reporters there will not be a formal meeting between the two leaders, but they will likely have a chance to meet. "I'm sure that President Obama will be interacting with President Castro at the summit events as leaders gather on the margins of those events," Rhodes said on a conference call. http://bit.ly/1QnFiok

U.S. officials revealed last week that Obama and Castro would interact at the gathering of leaders from the Western Hemisphere in Panama City, which runs April 10-11. But the format of the encounter had not been clear.

The informal meeting will be the first between Obama and Castro since the U.S. president announced in December he would begin normalizing relations with Cuba.

Some members of Congress and business leaders applauded the move to re-establish ties with Cuba, saying it ended a failed policy of isolation and will expand trade and travel with Cuba

But many Republicans and some Democrats have dismissed it as a giveaway to the Castro regime, saying it does nothing to address human rights abuses and restrictions on free speech on the island.

U.S. and Cuban officials have held three rounds of talks since December to form new diplomatic ties. A sticking point in the process is Cuba's demand that the U.S. remove it from its list of state sponsors of terrorism. Obama said the State Department would review Cuba's status on the list in December.

Rhodes said that review was nearing its conclusion.

Obama and Castro last met in person in 2013 in South Africa, when they shook hands at the funeral of Nelson Mandela. http://bit.ly/1PKAGdg

"Ros-Lehtinen, the daughter of Cuban exiles living in the United States, chaired the House Foreign Affairs Committee for two years.

"We did not help the Cuban people get freer today by this deal," she said.

"This policy change is a gift for the Cuban government that has done nothing to provide basic, fundamental human rights to the Cuban people," said Iowa Sen. Chuck Grassley, a member of the Senate

Budget Committee. "This decision rewards a brutal regime without any significant commitment toward change for the oppressed Cuban people." http://nws.mx/1HNZa2K

"Cuban President Raul Castro went off on U.S. policy towards Cuba in his Summit of the Americas speech today, before apologizing to President Obama and absolving him of any blame in the matter.

'According to reports from the summit, Castro went on and on about grievances Cuba has had with the United States for decades, bringing up military invasions, occupations, the Bay of Pigs, et cetera.

'And then, for some reason, Castro ended up apologizing to Obama. He said, "I apologize to Obama for expressing myself so emotionally. President Obama has no responsibility for this. There were ten presidents before him; all have a debt to us, but not President Obama."

'He even pointed out that Obama was born after the conflict originally began, a point Obama himself made when he spoke.

'Castro also took some time to personally praise Obama and call him an honest man." You can watch part of what he said below, via CNN: http://bit.ly/1ljHoKw

WASHINGTON - President Barack Obama told Congress that he plans to remove Cuba from the U.S. list of state sponsors of terrorism, clearing away the main obstacle to restoring diplomatic relations and reopening embassies after more than half a century of enmity.

Obama's decision comes on the heels of a Western Hemisphere summit in Panama where Obama and Cuban President Raul Castro sat down for the first meeting of its kind between U.S. and Cuban leaders in nearly 60 years.

Cuba's communist government had demanded removal from the U.S. blacklist to move forward on efforts to normalize relations between the two former Cold War foes. Obama ordered a review of Cuba's presence on the list after he and Castro announced a diplomatic breakthrough on Dec. 17.

"After a careful review of Cuba's record, which was informed by the intelligence community, as well as assurances provided by the Cuban government, the Secretary of State concluded that Cuba met the conditions for rescinding its designation as a State Sponsor of Terrorism," the White House said in a statement.

Congress has 45 days to consider Obama's decision before it takes effect, and lawmakers are extremely unlikely to block the move.

There had been some expectations that Obama would announce his intention to remove the terrorism designation and move forward on restoring diplomatic relations at the summit.

But U.S. officials held off and privately made clear that they sought to time the move as leverage in broader normalization negotiations.

Cuba's removal from the list will remove certain economic sanctions on the island, but the broader U.S. embargo on Cuba will remain in place because only Congress can end it.

"We will continue to have differences with the Cuban government, but our concerns over a wide range of Cuba's policies and actions fall outside the criteria that is relevant to whether to rescind Cuba's designation as a State Sponsor of Terrorism," the White House said.

Washington placed Cuba on the list in 1982, citing then-President Fidel Castro's training and arming of communist rebels in Africa and Latin America. But Cuba's presence on the list has been questioned in recent years.

In his report to Congress, Obama certified that "the government of Cuba has not provided any support for international terrorism during the preceding six-month period," and "has provided assurances that it will not support acts of international terrorism in the future."

Secretary of State John Kerry said, "circumstances have changed since 1982," when Cuba was listed "because of its efforts to promote armed revolution by forces in Latin America. Our hemisphere and the world look very different today than they did 33 years ago." (Reporting by Matt Spetalnick and Julia Edwards; Editing by Doina Chiacu and Jonathan Oatis) http://bit.ly/1IwZaUQ

In a stunning move, President Barack Obama has said that he will remove Cuba from the list of state sponsors of terrorism.

In a message to Congress, Obama said that Cuba "has not provided any support for international terrorism" for the past six months, which apparently qualifies them to be removed.

The Obama administration has been very careful to not call Cuba a state sponsor of terrorism amid a diplomatic thaw between the two countries.

In December of 2014, when Obama and Castro announced the beginning of a thaw in diplomatic relations, Obama expressed his willingness to remove Cuba from the list.

Presumably, Cuba and the U.S. have solved some of the problems that were preventing him from removing the nation from the list, mainly restrictions on U.S. diplomats in Havana.

This move could pave the way for a U.S. embassy in Cuba in the future and other steps that would bring the two countries closer together.

There has been no word yet on whether or not Cuba will send all the criminals and terrorists hiding there back to the U.S. to face punishment for their crimes.

There has also been no word on whether or not Cubans will no longer have to flee a tyrannical and oppressive government.

White House press secretary Josh Earnest stated that taking Cuba off the terror list does not change the fact that the U.S. has its differences with the Cuban government (H/T Breitbart).

"Our concerns over a wide range of Cuba's policies and actions fall outside the criteria that is relevant to whether to rescind Cuba's designation as a state sponsor of terrorism."

When Cuba is removed from the list, there will only be three countries left: Iran (with whom Obama is negotiating), Sudan and Syria.

Obama's discussions with Cuba have angered a number of Cuban refugees in America, who see these relations like essentially caving into the Cuban government.

Presidential candidate Marco Rubio, whose parents fled to the U.S. from Cuba, has taken a very firm stance against stronger U.S. relations with Cuba under Castro. He has not released a statement yet on this move by the Obama administration.

This act continues Obama's foreign policy of catering to dictators and terrorists. http://bit.ly/1lFwQoM

XV

WELFARE

No longer will the taxpayers fund drug users in the State of Michigan. The State Legislators recently passed a bill allowing the State to drug test recipients of state welfare programs.

The Bill had a strong conservative backing and, of course, the Liberals were very unhappy about it. The program is to be conducted on a trial basis in several Michigan counties. It's a "suspicion-based" program that allows state officials to drug test those that they suspect are using their EBT cards for drugs instead of food.

If a person fails a drug test, their benefits will be immediately revoked, and restrictions will be placed on any future eligibility. If anyone declines to take the test, they are automatically ineligible for benefits for six months.

A bonus for the addict is that if they test dirty, the state will offer treatment that gives the addict a chance for a new start.

Michigan is not the only state to do drug testing. Several other states have been doing it for some time. Arizona, Kansas, Mississippi, Missouri, Oklahoma, Tennessee, and Utah are spending hundreds of thousands of dollars to search for drug users. And the statistics have shown that the applicants tested at a lower rate than the drug use of the general population.

In 2011, Missouri tested 38,970 applicants, and only 48 of them tested positively for drugs. The cost of testing was $336,297.

Oklahoma was looking a little better. In 2012, they tested 3,342 applicants of which 297 tested positive. They are saying it cost them $395,872 for testing.

In 2012, Utah tested 9,552 and 29 tested positive. Testing costs were $64,566.

In 2013, the State of Kansas tested 2,783 applicants and 11 tested positive. The cost of testing was $40,000.

In 2014, the State of Mississippi tested 3,656 applicants for drugs and 2 tested positive. The cost of testing was $5,290+.

In 2012, the State of Tennessee tested 16,017 applicants for drugs and 37 tested positive. The cost of testing was $5,295. Tennessee does testing on recipients of Medicaid, food stamps and Temporary Assistance for Needy Families, or TANF, benefits.

In 2009, the State of Arizona tested 142,424 applicants for drugs and three tested positive. The cost of testing was $499.

In 2011, the State of Florida passed a law that every applicant must pass a urine test at his or her own expense. The State would reimburse applicants who tested negative.

A Federal court stopped the requirement as a violation of the Fourth Amendment's "unreasonable search and seizures" clause in 2013 — a ruling upheld in December by the U.S. Circuit Court of Appeals for the 11th Circuit. The three-judge panel noted that Florida had "not demonstrated a more prevalent, unique or different drug problem among TANF applicants than in the general population."

Legislators in 12 other states will deliberate bills that would require applicants for state assistance, including unemployment insurance and food stamps, to pass a drug screening before receiving benefits. Connecticut, Hawaii, Iowa, Kentucky, Minnesota, Mississippi, Montana, New York, Oregon, South Carolina, Texas and West Virginia seek to join 12 other states that have passed similar procedures recently.

Let's go back to the old system of welfare and community service.

According to the Washington Times, because the amnestied illegals are exempt from Obamacare, employers who decide to hire them will not have to pay the $3,000 annual penalty for each employee who goes on the Obamacare exchange and receives a subsidy. Now who do you supposed is paying for those subsidies?

"If it is true that the president's actions give employers a $3,000 incentive to hire those who came here illegally, he has added insult to injury," Smith told the Washington Times. "The president's actions would have just moved those who came here illegally to the front of the line, ahead of unemployed and underemployed Americans." http://bit.ly/1NymXEc

In 2014, President Obama signed the SNAP Fairness Act of 2014 Into Law. Starting on January 1, 2015, anyone who has a SNAP card, previously known as food stamps, can now purchase alcohol, beer, wine, tobacco and cigarettes using their EBT card.

Hakeem Jeffries of New York's 8th Congressional District stated, "There is no reason my constituents should be barred from purchasing a 6-pack of Coors Light with their EBT card to go along with their steak dinner, also purchased with their EBT card. To expect low-income hardworking Americans to go out of pocket for essentials such as cigarettes and beer is not only racist but cruel. I am proud to stand with my president today in this historical signing for food stamp fairness."

It has been my experience that anyone with an EBT card is not working, let alone hardworking. And what does race have to do with it?

The SNAP Fairness Act also increased the annual budget for SNAP for the 2015 fiscal year. Those who have been on food stamps for over two years will receive a 50% increase in their monthly food stamp earnings.

Making it easy to get freebees from the government does not give the receiver an incentive to get out and look for a job. Instead, it rewards the recipient for being on the program. How are we ever going to get people off of the welfare system if our government continues supporting them with raises and more incentives to stay on assistance programs instead of pursuing goals?

There is still a ton of welfare abusers out there – people perfectly capable of finding jobs, but choosing instead to live on the welfare system because they can make more money working the system. Some leeches live in luxury high-rise apartments that offer such amenities as rooftop pools, manicure services, and world-class workout centers.

You know, the things you treat yourself to when you go on vacation, not the things you can afford every day because you are a working class middle American.

What happens is a real estate developer makes a deal with the Federal Government to set aside a number of "affordable" units, ones that can be rented by welfare voucher abusers, and the developer receives incredibly attractive tax incentives. He gives welfare abusers who pay their rent with housing vouchers, formerly known as Section 8, the ability to reside in some of the most luxurious dwellings available on the market. Naturally, the abuser will never find a job – why should he even look, so he will never have to move out of such luxury and no one else will ever have the opportunity to occupy his luxury abode.

And the Low-Income Housing Tax Credit that developers receive in exchange for voucher-eligible units allows them to pay a dollar less in taxes for every dollar they spend on building the units — which as you can imagine, adds up to billions. http://bit.ly/1m4AqJC

Take the case of Kiara. She has four children. Kiara is 30 years old and has been on welfare for over 12 years. She feels the welfare is owed to her, and she has no intention of looking for a job.

"I get $780 in food stamps, $500 in tenant," she explained, "and I get Medicaid and WIC." That is the Special Supplemental Nutrition Program for Women, Infants, and Children.

According to the U.S. Census Bureau, over 100 million Americans receive some form of government assistance. That's around 34% of the population. The elderly and disabled, for example, may be truly unable to work. However, the number of people on welfare has gone up dramatically in recent years. For many able-bodied people like Kiara, it has become a crutch that is abused — at the expense of hard workers who actually pay the taxes. http://bit.ly/1m4AqJC

It is not only the welfare recipients that abuse the system. In 2013, a father and son were involved in a welfare fraud scheme concerning their convenience store. They would purchase the buying power of cash-strapped EBT recipients at around 20 to 30 cents on the dollar and use them to buy inventory for their business. It was reported that more than 1,400 stores were involved in this type of fraud.

Kansas and Missouri are changing their laws so that recipients cannot use their cards for liquor stores, fortune tellers, cruise ships and strip clubs. They will also limit the length of time the benefits are offered to needy families. Missouri will disallow the purchase of cookies, candy, energy drinks, soft drinks, seafood or steaks.

Now we are getting some place. I think we are all in favor of a treat now and then even for the needy, but when the taxpayers are the ones footing the bill for the hand up, the needy should not be eating better than the taxpayer.

How to work the system:

How to get $75k in benefits for you and your girlfriend.

Follow these proven steps.

1. Don't get married to her.
2. Use your mom's address to get your mail sent to.
3. The guy buys the house.
4. Guy rents out house to his girlfriend who has two of his kids.
5. Section 8 will pay $900 a month for a three-bedroom home.
6. Girlfriend signs up for ObamaCare so the guy doesn't have to pay out the butt for family insurance.
7. Girlfriend gets to go to college for free being a single mother.
8. Girlfriend gets $600 a month for food stamps.
9. Girlfriend gets free cell phone.
10. Girlfriend get free utilities.
11. Guy moves into the home but uses mom's house to get mail sent to.
12. The girlfriend claims one kid and guy claims one kid on taxes. Now you both get to claim head of household at $1800 credit.
13. Girlfriend gets disability for being "crazy" or having a "bad back" at $1800 a month and never has to work again.

This plan is perfectly legal and is being executed now by millions of people. A married couple with a stay at home mom yields $0. An unmarried couple with stay at home mom nets:

21,600 disability +
10,800 free housing +
6,000 free ObamaCare +
6,000 free food +

4,800 free utilities +
6,000 Pell grant money to spend +
12,000 a year in college tuition-free from Pell grant +
8,800 tax benefit for being a single mother: Total =
————
$75,000 a year in benefits!

Any idea why the country is $18 + trillion in debt? Keep it up, your children and grandchildren will pay the debt.

To all of you welfare recipients and people on food stamps: you do not have the right to a big screen television, new car, or new truck unless you can "legally" acquire them on your own. They are not guaranteed you because of your government status.

You do not have the right to free food and housing. Get off the couch and find a job. Americans are very generous and charitable, but after a while they will get tired of subsidizing you.

Seems we constantly hear about how Social Security is going to run out of money. How come we never hear about welfare or food stamps running out of money? What's interesting is the Social Security worked for their money, but the welfare and food stamp recipients didn't.

This country is based on freedom. If you are offended by something, you may leave the room, change the channel, or express a different opinion.

If you hit your finger with a hammer, be more careful. Do not expect the manufacture of the hammer to make you and your family independently wealthy.

You do not have the right to free health care. Get a job, so you can afford to pay for health care.

If you kidnap, rape, intentionally maim, or kill someone, do not be surprised if everyone wants to see you go to jail.

If you rob, cheat, or coerce away the goods or services of other citizens, do not be surprised if we lock you away.

If you shoot a cop, you will get locked up.

All of us sure want you to have a job, and will gladly help you along in hard times, but we expect you to take advantage of the opportunities of education and vocational training laid before you to make yourself useful.

This is an English speaking country. We don't care where you came from, English is our language. Learn it!

You do not have the right to change our country's history or heritage. This country was founded on the belief in one true God. And yet, you are given the freedom to believe in any religion, any faith, or no faith at all; with no fear of persecution. The phrase IN GOD WE TRUST is part of our heritage and history. [Lewis Napper, Jackson, Mississippi]

"The Center for Immigration Studies released a report using numbers from the Census Bureau. The study found that 51% of immigrant households were using some form of welfare. This is far higher than the native-born rate, which stands at 30%, and it includes Medicaid benefits, food stamps, reduced-price school lunches, and housing assistance. For immigrant households with children, that figure goes up to a stunning 76%. What it represents is a system that allows a lot of less-educated immigrants to settle in the country, who then earn modest wages and are eligible for a very generous welfare system. The real issue is about what happens when the moochers outnumber the producers. One, Democrats hope that this issue will help them turn Hispanics into consistent, reliable Democrat voters. Two, they hope the welfare state will grow to the point where government dependency becomes a way of life for the majority of Americans." http://bit.ly/1R29Du4

XVI

WHO DO YOU OWE?

S ince Hillary Clinton is running for President of the United States, let's review just a few of the debts she owes.

We know when Bill Clinton ran for President that the Clintons made a list of every single person that gave them money and how much. They carefully recorded who endorsed who and who stayed on the sidelines. They wanted to know who went the extra mile.

For Hillary, the spreadsheet was what you would call a "favor file." It meant that when asks rolled in, she and Bill would have at their fingertips all the information needed to make a quick decision—including extenuating, mitigating, and amplifying factors—so that friends could be rewarded and enemies punished.

Hillary said her speaking fees were donated to charity. Her charity is "The Clinton Foundation." Last year the Clinton Foundation racked up $8.448 million in travel expenses according to The Blacksphere.net.

Then the New York Times reported that Saudi Arabia donated between $10 and $25 Million to the foundation as did other government agencies in Australia, the Dominican Republic. Brunei, Kuwait, Norway, Oman, Qatar and Taiwan, with each giving more than $1 million; as did the ruling family of Abu Dhabi and the Dubai

Foundation, both based in the United Arab Emirates, and the friends of Saudi Arabia, founded by a Saudi prince.

Among the largest donors were a businessman who was close to the onetime military ruler of Nigeria, a Ukrainian tycoon who was son-in-law of that former Soviet republic's authoritarian president, and a Canadian mining executive who took [Bill] Clinton to Kazakhstan while trying to win lucrative uranium contracts.

All of these entities are owed favors in the event Hillary becomes President. And these are just the ones known. How many more debts were accumulated while she was Secretary of State?

When Bill Clinton made speeches during the time Hillary Clinton was Secretary of State, all speaking engagements had to be reviewed and approved by the State Department in order that there would be no conflict of interest. Perhaps this was done on the honor system because the records show that the State Department lawyers acted on scant information about business requests and were under pressure to approve the proposals immediately. There were no regulations to limit how much Bill Clinton could charge for those profitable speeches.

On the one hand the Clintons tell us the funds went to the Clinton Foundation, but on the other hand when Bill Clinton ended his term as President and Hillary was lamenting that they were very poor, the truth is that both Clintons had written best-selling books that had made them millions, both were making six-figure speaking engagements, and Mr. Clinton made more than $200,000 a year over the eight years he was President. That is over a million dollars alone. When Mrs. Clinton talked about being "dead broke" when they came out of the White House, they were not putting the money they earned from their speaking engagements into the Clinton Foundation. If they were, then they were living out of the Clinton Foundation. Hillary said, "We had no money when we got there, and we struggled to, you know; piece together the resources for mortgages, for houses, for Chelsea's education. You know, it was not easy." When asked about the reported $5 million she has earned and over $100 million that Bill Clinton has earned from speeches, the former Secretary of State said the former president has worked "very hard."

"It's been amazing to me — he's worked very hard. First of all, we had to pay off all our debts, which was, you know, he had to make double the money because of obviously taxes and then pay off the debts and get us houses and take care of family members," Clinton said. [*The Lyin Kings* www.author.ispetteice.com]

The locations of some of Bill Clinton's speeches are also raising questions. Significant money from foreign governments has been provided by China, Saudi Arabia, and the United Arab Emirates either through speaking fees or to the "Clinton Foundation."

Hillary Clinton announced her run for the Presidency for 2016 and when I wrote *The Lyin Kings*, I felt fairly certain she would run. However, I do not believe she is presidential material, and even she is finding that out. The media are doing a better job of vetting Clinton than they did when Obama was running in 2008 and again in 2012. I expect her to bow out of the race before the actual 2016 election.

When Hillary Clinton had a speaking engagement in Las Vegas at the University of Nevada, Las Vegas in 2014, she agreed to discount her speaking fees from $300,000 to $225,000, but she had other stipulations. (1) She insisted on staying in the presidential suite of a luxury hotel of her staff's choice with up to 5 additional rooms for her staff and aides; and (2) a $39 Million Gulf Stream G450 16-passenger or larger jet must be provided. They also had to agree that she was the only person on stage during her remarks, and she got final approval for the contract and any remarks of the moderator or introducer.

Her standard speaking contract also provides that she does not have to stay at the event any longer than ninety minutes, she does not have to pose for more than 50 photos, or with more than 100 people. The only record allowed to be made of the event is by a stenographer whose $1,250 bill will be paid by UNLV.

Barack Obama never forgot the people he owed when he became President. Decisions have been made according to the wishes of George Soros.

Paybacks were made to big unions. Immediately after taking office, Obama said "We need to level the playing field for workers and the unions that represent their interests, because we know that you cannot have a strong middle class without a strong labor movement."

Obama had a political debt to pay to Hillary Clinton. He made her Secretary of State.

He promised to give mortgages to people who could not afford to give them back and caused the housing market to crash.

Obama promised the young people that he would pay for their education or he would get rid of their student loans. Obama proposes to do that by continuing to increase the number of students eligible for Pell Grants, which give students up to $5,550 for college costs per year. (The number of students eligible for Pell Grants has increased from 6 million in 2008 to 9 million today.) "The president also wants to create a $1 billion grant competition, along the lines of Race for the Top . . . to reward states that take action to keep college costs down, and a separate $55 million competition for individual colleges to increase their value and efficiency."

Obama won his election by four constituencies that were essential to his successful bid for re-election—Hispanics, women, young people, and African-Americans. His push for immigration reform brought out the Latino vote in both the 2008 and 2012 elections.

This does not touch the surface.

XVII

UNDERSTANDING THE OBAMAS

A Jew will tell you that they suspect that Obama's mother's father, Stanley Dunham, was Jewish. It was said Obama's mother, Stanley Anne Dunham, looked and acted like a Communist Jew. Obama said: "And I speak with some experience on this matter. I was not raised in a particularly religious household, as undoubtedly many of the audience were. My father, who returned to Kenya when I was just two, was born a Muslim but as an adult became an atheist. My mother, whose parents were non-practicing Baptists and Methodists, was probably one of the most spiritual and kindest people I've ever known, but grew up with a healthy skepticism of organized religion herself. As a consequence, so did I."

"To call Barrack Obama 'America's First Jewish President' is disingenuous. Many other presidents are rumored to have had Jewish blood: Theodore Roosevelt, FDR, Truman, Eisenhower, Johnson and the Bushes to name a few. So it's not surprising to read in Wikipedia that, Stanley Dunham, a lowly furniture salesman from Kansas was related to six US Presidents.

"'Stanley Armour Dunham's distant cousins include six US presidents: James Madison, Harry Truman, Lyndon Johnson, Jimmy Carter, George H. W. Bush and George W. Bush. Through a common ancestor, Mareen Duvall, Stanley Dunham is related to former Vice-President Dick Cheney (an eighth cousin once removed). Through another common ancestor, Hans Gutknecht, Stanley Dunham is President Harry S. Truman's fourth cousin, twice removed.

"Obama's mother, Stanley Anne, became a Communist and fought the 'Establishment,' not realizing the Communists are the Establishment.

"Stanley Anne was an 'idealistic' part-Jewish woman who got her Ph.D. and worked for Timothy Geithner's father in Indonesia at the elite Ford Foundation. Some suspect she did double time for the CIA." ("Obama's Jewish Grandfather")."

It seems that Michelle Obama's cousin is a Jewish rabbi:

Michelle Obama's cousin is Rabbi Capers C. Funnye, spiritual leader of a mostly black synagogue on Chicago's South Side. Funnye's mother, Verdelle Robinson Funnye (born Verdelle Robinson) and Michelle Obama's paternal grandfather, Frasier Robinson Jr., were brother and sister.

"Funnye is chief rabbi at the Beth Shalom B'nai Zaken Ethiopian Hebrew Congregation. He also serves on the Chicago Board of Rabbis.

"The rabbi is known for his efforts to bring together the mainstream Jewish population and smaller black Jewish congregations – commonly referred to as Hebrews or Israelites. He has repeatedly called on the larger Jewish community to accept more non-white Jews.

"Much analysis of Obama's relationship with the Jewish community has been made during the presidential campaign. On the one hand, wealthy Jewish families played a major role in Obama's rise to power in Chicago. On the other hand, the presidential nominee has not been a success breaking skepticism by the Jewish community over Israel. http://bit.ly/1NOIg6g

"According to an INS agent memo, the agents believed Barrack Obama Sr. might have engaged in a sham marriage to Ann Dunham so he could gain U.S. citizenship and they even questioned whether Barrack Obama senior was Obama's biological father.

'The INS had every reason to be concerned. Ann Dunham was not the angel that was portrayed by a host of Obama supporters. According to Barrack Obama's book, *Dreams from My Father* his maternal Grandfather sought out the communist activist Frank Davis Marshall as a mentor for the younger Barack Obama.

"'I was intrigued by old Frank, with his books and whiskey breath and the hint of hard-earned knowledge behind the hooded eyes."

'Frank Marshall Davis also seemed to influence young Ann Dunham. Recently discovered nude photos of Ann Dunham were found in Frank Davis' house. It was also discovered that she posed nude in vintage bondage magazines.

'Frank Davis published a pornographic novel titled "Sex Rebel Black: Memoires of a Gash Gourmet," where he described a swinging lifestyle in which he and his wife had sex numerous times with an underage girl named "Anne."

Neighbors of Davis said Obama and his mother visited Davis every week at his home from the time Obama was 10 years old.

When Obama was growing up in Indonesia he had a nanny named Evie who was a man, but believed she was a woman. ""Evie says she chose her current name because she thought it sounded sweet. But she adds, as she pulls out her national identification card, her official name is Turdi and gender male. Several longtime residents of Obama's old Menteng neighborhood confirmed that Turdi had worked there as his nanny for two years, also caring for his baby sister Maya. When asked about the nanny, the White House had no comment." She insisted Obama never saw her in a dress. "He was so young," says Evie. "And I never let him see me wearing women's clothes. But he did see me trying on his mother's lipstick, sometimes. That used to really crack him up."

"During an interview with WND, a former radical activist from Occidental College recalls an encounter with Obama and his Pakastani roommate who accompanied him. They both left an impression they were homosexual lovers." John Drew, founder of the Marxist-socialist club at Occidental met the future President in December of 1980. Obama was 19 years old and a sophomore at the time and was with his Pakistan roommate Mohammed Hasan Chandoo.

"I really had the feeling that Obama was Chandoo's 'boy toy." "The first time I saw Barack Obama and Hassan Chandoo together, I thought they were a wealthy gay couple."

"In fact, they looked so gay that my girlfriend, Caroline Boss, whispered to me, 'They're not gay.' So, that confirmed to me I wasn't the only one who thought Barack Obama and Hassan Chandoo looked like they were in a very close, intimate relationship.

While in college, Barrack Obama wrote a poem called "Pop's" in which Frank Marshall Davis was identified as Pop. The poem describes "amber stains" on both Obama and "Pop's" shorts. A psychotherapist who writes under the pseudonym of Robin of Berkeley said Obama's poem "evoked images of sexual abuse" and notes the parental abandonment Obama suffered in his childhood.

"It is common knowledge in the Chicago gay community that Obama actively visited the gay bars and bathhouses in Chicago while he was an Illinois state senator."

Reggie Love, a former Duke University basketball and football star has been Obama's constant companion for the past two years. He was known as Obama's bodyman, but hired under the auspices of "Deputy Political Director." He resigned last November, 2014. Apparently there were some photos of Love on the internet heavily inebriated and engaged in homosexual acts at a party.

Chris Duhon, a former Duke teammate said of Love, "To me, he's just Reggie, my teammate for three years at Duke whom I still speak to every day. Through Reggie, I met President Obama and played pickup basketball games with him this past April, May and June – 5 on 5 – in Chicago's East Bank Club. Reggie invited me to yesterday's inauguration – an offer I had to decline." http://bit.ly/1XRUISl

Back in February, President Barack Obama was decidedly un-presidential during an interview with Buzzfeed that was actually little more than a promotion for Obamacare.

The video featured the president clowning around in front of a mirror, purportedly doing the things that everybody does, but nobody talks about.

One of the things that Obama did was pose with his sunglasses on while making a finger gun gesture with his hand like he was some sort of secret agent or something.

The National Rifle Association seized upon this seemingly insignificant picture to prove a broader point, that if school children did the exact same thing as the president, they would be suspended because of the "zero tolerance" regulations in most schools regarding guns.

The NRA points out that many kids across the country have been suspended for making similar hand gestures, making a gun shape out of a Pop-Tart, drawing a picture of a gun or wearing a shirt with a picture of a gun.

According to BizPac Review, the NRA has released a statement making note of the absurdity of such "zero tolerance" rules, using the president's picture to prove their point to school administrators.

"Attention overbearing public school administrators: you might want to remove any portraits of the 44th U.S. president hanging on your walls," the statement began.

"In a recent Affordable Care Act promotional video produced for the website Buzzfeed, President Barack Obama uses his index finger and thumb to form a finger gun and aim it at the viewer. Apparently, the commander-in-chief has not been briefed on the supposedly anti-social, threatening, and disruptive nature of this gesture, so we are here to help."

The statement goes on to list many examples of students doing similar things and getting in trouble for it, most notably a young preschool student named Hunter, who is deaf and must make a gun symbol with his hand in order to say his own name in sign language.

They also talk about the efforts they are making around the country to roll back some of these ridiculous "zero tolerance" policies and encourage schools to allow kids to be kids, so long as they aren't really hurting anyone.

Summing up, the NRA concludes that "imaginary gun gestures made in good fun or during imaginative play are perfectly normal and acceptable behavior, even for the leader of the free world."

This is simply fantastic, and the use of Obama's own "clowning around" pictures helps the NRA prove its point to the overwhelmingly progressive school administrators across the country who no doubt worship all things Obama.

Hopefully, this episode will help at least some schools realize the absurdity of their "zero tolerance" anti-gun policies, which makes everyone less safe and hurts kids who are simply playing around. These policies should be relaxed to reflect some semblance of rationality. http://bit.ly/1NymJNm

I remember many years of fun when I was a child of playing "cops and robbers" and "cowboys and Indians" and having a cap pistol. My friend and I shot at each other behind trees and rocks. But not once did it enter our minds that we would ever do it for real. We knew it was a game and every once in a while we would pretend to fall over dead. That was part of the game and we would giggle about it. It was a kid's game.

When my father thought I was old enough, he taught me to shoot a rifle. He took me hunting. He was very particular about how I was to shoot a duck or a squirrel. It had to be in the eye.

XVIII

OBAMA AND ISRAEL

On June 4, 2009, Barack Obama gave a speech in Cairo, Egypt, in which he said, "America's strong bonds with Israel are well known. This bond is unbreakable. It is based upon cultural and historical ties, and the recognition that the aspiration for a Jewish homeland is rooted in a tragic history that cannot be denied."

"On the other hand, it is also undeniable that the Palestinian people – Muslims and Christians – have suffered in pursuit of a homeland. For more than sixty years, they have endured the pain of dislocation. Many wait in refugee camps in the West Bank, Gaza and neighboring lands for a life of peace and security that they have never been able to lead. They endure the daily humiliations – large and small – that come with occupation. So let there be no doubt: the situation for the Palestinian people is intolerable. America will not turn our backs on the legitimate Palestinian aspiration for dignity, opportunity, and a state of their own."

Never has anyone ever put so much strain on a foreign relationship as Barack Obama has on the United States' relationship with Israel.

The author and economist Thomas Sowell alleged that Obama's relationship with Israel had been consistent with the president's pattern of "selling out our allies to curry favor with our adversaries."

According to a 2010 poll commissioned by The Jerusalem Post, only 9 percent of Jewish Israelis believe that the Obama administration is more pro-Israel than pro-Palestinian.

For nearly two decades, Barack Obama was a member of Rev. Jeremiah Wright's Trinity United Church of Christ in Chicago. Obama described Wright as his "spiritual advisor," his "mentor," and "one of the greatest preachers in America." Moreover, Obama contributed large sums of money to Wright's church, and he chose Wright to perform his wedding ceremony and to baptize his two young daughters.

Wright has long been a vocal critic of Israel and Zionism, which he has blamed for inflicting "injustice and … racism" on the Palestinian people. According to Wright, Zionism contains an element of "white racism." Likening Israel's treatment of the Palestinians to South Africa's treatment of blacks during the apartheid era, Wright advocates divestment campaigns targeting companies that conduct any business in, or with, Israel. He has referred to Israel as a "dirty word," asserting that "ethnic cleansing [by] the Zionist is a sin and a crime against humanity."

On December 4, 2007, Wright was named as a member of the Obama presidential campaign's newly created African American Religious Leadership Committee. But Wright was compelled to step down from the Committee three months later, after videotapes of his many hate-filled sermons ignited fierce public debate and criticism.

Obama first visited Israel in 2008 when he was a candidate for President. During the debates with Governor Romney, Obama could only relate his visit to the Yad Vashem Holocaust memorial during his 2008 trip, and his visit then to the rocket-battered town of Sderot on the Gaza border. Whenever he was questioned further about visiting Israel, he would say he wanted to go when he was sure "they were moving something forward."

Back in 2009, President Obama made the following statement: "The United States does not accept the legitimacy of continued Israeli settlements. This construction violates previous agreements and undermines efforts to achieve peace. It is time for these settlements to stop." Obama has always felt that there should be two settlements, Israel and Palestine, and he is not in agreement that the two should live together peacefully as some of them do.

That statement did not go over very well with Israel and later that month Obama refused to be photographed with Prime Minister Netanyahu and walked out of a dinner.

Obama then made a speech stating that he believed that the Israel and Palestine borders should be based on the 1967 lines. This was after the United States had always said we would never take that position.

In response to Obama's speech, Prime Minister Netanyahu said that a Palestinian state based on the borders of 1967 would leave the Jewish state "indefensible." "The viability of a Palestinian state cannot come at the expense of Israel's existence," the Israeli leader said.

Obama and Netanyahu met behind closed doors for over ninety minutes.

But Obama could not keep his disgust to himself. He was caught on an open mike moment speaking to French President Nicholas Sarkozy about Israel. Sarkozy was quoted as saying, "I cannot bear Netanyahu. He's a liar." Obama's response, "You're fed up with him, I have to deal with him even more than you." http://fxn.ws/21G2iUF

Two days after his inauguration, President Obama placed his first phone call to a foreign leader – Palestinian Authority President Mahmoud Abbas. Abbas had repeatedly emphasized the importance of "implementing the principles of Yasser Arafat," the most prolific Jew-killer since Adolf Hitler; he had praised the terrorist group Hezbollah as a shining example of "Arab resistance" against alleged Israeli oppression; he had lauded Palestinian terrorists as "strugglers" and "martyrs" whom "Allah loves"; he had steadfastly refused to acknowledge Israel's right to exist; he was the head of the Fatah Party, a movement whose Charter continued to advocate terrorism against, and the annihilation of Israel; he had authorized lump-sum payments of $2,200 apiece to the surviving family members of Palestinian shahids (martyrs) – including suicide bombers; and he had exhorted Palestinians to "unite the Hamas and Fatah blood in the struggle against Israel as we did at the beginning of the Intifada."

Obama does not play well with people that do not agree with him, and he cannot run the United States, let alone run the State of Israel. Obama has always wanted to push the Israelis and the Palestinians into peace negotiations at his control, of course. He also has Iran's nuclear program and Syria's civil war as an agenda. He has his own "do it my way" of doing things and kicks the door on the way out if he does not get his way. Obama and Netanyahu frequently sparred over the Palestinian peace process during his first term as President.

Upon Obama's first visit to Israel after becoming president of the United States, he joked that he was "getting away from Congress." This occurred in March of 2013. Obama did not visit Israel during his first term.

The Obama Administration went so far as to send funds to Netanyahu's Opposition prior to Israel's last election in the hopes that Mr. Netanyahu would lose the election. But the rest of America, being Israeli fans, was rooting for Mr. Netanyahu to win the election.

After the election, the Prime Minister set out the differences between Israel and America and said, ""The president of the United States, I believe, is always concerned about the security of the United States, "but the prime minister of Israel, and I can speak personally of the nine years that I've been in office, that there's not been a day — a day — that I haven't thought about the things I have to do to protect the survival of Israel and that's the difference."

When Obama did finally contact the Prime Minister, what he said was that the U.S. would be "reassessing" its relationship with Israel, especially as it relates to the formation of a Palestinian state (H/T Western Journalism).

In July 2009, President Obama hosted American Jewish leaders at the White House and informed them that he sought to put "daylight" between America and Israel. "For eight years [i.e., during the Bush administration], there was no light between the United States and Israel, and nothing got accomplished," Obama said. In that same meeting, the President told those in attendance that Israel would need "to engage in serious self-reflection."

Obama says he will "absolutely not" give permission for Israel to attack Iranian nuclear facilities: In July 2009, Obama told CNN that he would "absolutely not" give Israel permission to strike Iran's nuclear facilities.

It sound like Obama intends to continue widening the gap between America and Israel and handing America over to Iran who yells death to America instead of holding hands with our mid-eastern ally who has been with us since 1948 and who Americans hold dear. This would be a tragedy.

Obama is a child and holds grudges. He did not like it that Netanyahu won the election. He does not like losing. Obama put his money on Netanyahu's opposition and lost. So what does Obama do? He releases documents from the Pentagon that the United States were supposed to remain silent on declassifying details of Israel's nuclear program. The timing of this story has revenge written all over it.

The document goes into detail on how Israel is developing codes that detail fission and fusion processes on a microscopic and macroscopic level. "It acknowledged that some of the technology" is more advanced than in the U.S.

During one of his stump speeches just days prior to the Israeli elections, Prime Minister Benjamin Netanyahu made a startling claim that may have the Obama administration in serious legal hot water.

In his speech, Netanyahu cited a large amount of foreign funding provided to opponents of his Likud party to remove him from his leadership position though he declined to give specifics.

It makes the Obama administration's claim that they didn't meet with Netanyahu during his trip to Capitol Hill because they have a "long-standing policy" of not meeting with heads of state prior to their elections potentially quite ironic.

In February 2008, then-U.S. Senator (and presidential candidate) Barack Obama told an audience in Cleveland: "There is a strain within the pro-Israel community that says unless you adopt an unwavering pro-Likud approach to Israel, that you're anti-Israel." When Obama made that assertion, Likud had already been out of power for two years, and the country was being led by the centrist Kadima government (of Ehud Olmert, Tzipi Livni, and Shimon Peres) which had been pursuing territorial compromise of unprecedented magnitude. Moreover, as the Wall Street Journal points out: "It was under Likud that Israel made its largest territorial compromises—withdrawals from Sinai and Gaza."

Fox News reported that a bipartisan group of senators were conducting an investigation into whether political operatives linked directly to Obama attempted to influence the Israeli election in favor of the Zionist Union party.

"A powerful U.S. Senate investigatory committee has launched a bipartisan probe into an American nonprofit's funding of efforts to oust Israeli Prime Minister Benjamin Netanyahu after the Obama administration's State Department gave the nonprofit taxpayer-funded grants," Fox said.

They're also looking into a group called OneVoice, which received $350,000 in State Department grants and potentially used that money to influence Israeli elections — and not in Netanyahu's favor.

Though the efforts to investigate foul play concerning illegally influencing the elections have officially begun, the damage may have already been done as Israelis took to the polls.

Reports from the Washington Free Beacon are saying that another U.S.-based non-profit called the PeaceWorks Network Foundation also may have assisted in efforts to unseat Netanyahu (H/T Western Journalism).

Netanyahu's Likud Party has taken a hard line stance against negotiating with Palestinians over land concessions as well as Iran's nuclear program, while the Zionist Union party would likely give in to both, positions much more in agreement with the Obama administration.

This could be a long year for Obama should Senate investigations reveal that his people and organizations linked to the Democrat Party had any influence on Israel's election process. http://bit.ly/1NymBxi

Drawing a moral equivalence between the historical experiences of the Jews and Middle Eastern Arabs, Obama said: "The Jewish people were persecuted.... [A]nti-Semitism ... culminated in an unprecedented Holocaust... Six million Jews were killed.... On the other hand, it is also undeniable that the Palestinian people — Muslims and Christians — have suffered in pursuit of a homeland."

Obama also made reference to the "pain" of the "dislocation" experienced by some 600,000 Arabs during the 1948 war – a war that began when five Arab armies united to attack Israel in an effort to destroy the nascent Jewish state on the very day of its birth. But he said nothing of the 900,000 Jewish refugees who were forcibly expelled from regions all over the Arab Middle East, where they and their ancestors had lived for hundreds, even thousands, of years.

"There has been a stalemate," Obama elaborated. "Two peoples with legitimate aspirations, each with a painful history.... It's easy to point fingers — for Palestinians to point to the displacement brought about by Israel's founding, and for Israelis to point to the constant hostility and attacks."

Obama said of the Palestinians: "They endure the daily humiliations – large and small – that come with occupation. So let there be no doubt: the situation for the Palestinian people is intolerable. America will not turn our backs on the legitimate Palestinian aspiration for dignity, opportunity, and a state of their own."

Professor and Hudson Institute fellow Anne Bayefsky observed: "Calling the Israeli-Arab conflict a 'stalemate' represents an abysmal failure to acknowledge historical reality. The modern state of Israel emerged after an internationally approved partition plan of November 1947 that would have created two states, one Jewish and one Arab; this plan was accepted by Jews and rejected by Arabs. One people has always been prepared to live in peace, and the other has chosen war in 1948 and 1956 and 1967 and 1973 and 1982 and renewed terrorism after its every loss."

In 2009, Obama wanted to show his displeasure over Israel's plan to build 900 new homes in Gilo, a settlement of 40,000 situated in the West Bank that Israel had captured in 1967. Obama said he did not think the settlement contributed to Israel's security and felt it made it harder to make peace with their neighbors. Obama said, "I think it embitters the Palestinians in a way that could end up being very dangerous."

During Biden's visit to Israel in 2010, Israel announced plans to build 1,600 housing units, and Biden told the Prime Minister that "This is starting to get dangerous for us. What you're doing here undermines the security of our troops who are fighting in Iraq, Afghanistan and Pakistan. That endangers us, and it endangers regional peace."

What happened next was "the president launched an unprecedented weeks-long offensive against Israel. Mr. Biden very publicly departed Israel."

Then "Secretary of State Hillary Clinton berated Prime Minister Benjamin Netanyahu on a now-infamous 45-minute phone call, telling him that Israel had 'harmed the bilateral relationship.' (The State

Department triumphantly shared details of the call with the press.) The Israeli ambassador was dressed-down at the State Department, Mr. Obama's Middle East envoy canceled his trip to Israel, and the U.S. joined the European condemnation of Israel.

"Moments after Mr. Biden concluded his visit to the West Bank, the Palestinian Authority held a ceremony to honor Dalal Mughrabi, who led one of the deadliest Palestinian terror attacks in history: the so-called Coastal Road Massacre that killed 38, including 13 children and an American. The Obama administration was silent. But that same day, on ABC, [Obama adviser David] Axelrod called Israel's planned construction of apartments in its own capital an 'insult' and an 'affront' to the United States. Press Secretary Robert Gibbs went on Fox News to accuse Mr. Netanyahu of 'weakening trust' between the two countries.

"Ten days later, Mr. Netanyahu traveled to Washington to mend fences but was snubbed at a White House meeting with President Obama—no photo op, no joint statement, and he was sent out through a side door."

Washington Post columnist and the Middle East expert Jackson Diehl wrote that "Netanyahu is being treated [by Obama] as if he were an unsavory Third World dictator."

It should be noted that contrary to the Obama administration's insistence that Israel was jeopardizing peace by encroaching on negotiable terrain, the construction site in Jerusalem was anything but disputed territory. Jerusalem is Israel's capital, and the construction site was in Ramat Shlomo, a Jewish neighborhood where housing construction had been underway since the early 1990s. By its insistence that Israel cease all building in East Jerusalem, it was the Obama administration and not Israel, that was breaking with precedent.

On November 9, 2010, The New York Times issued the following report regarding the increasingly strained relations between the U.S. and Israel:

"President Obama's criticism of new Israeli housing plans for East Jerusalem, and Prime Minister Benjamin Netanyahu's even sharper retort, have thrown the Middle East peace talks into jeopardy, with the dispute over Jewish settlements looming as a seemingly insuperable hurdle.... [T]he brusque exchange between Mr. Obama and Mr.

Netanyahu reflected again the gulf between Israel and the United States over settlements — an issue Mr. Obama initially made the centerpiece of his Middle East diplomacy....

"When asked about Israel's plans for 1,000 housing units [in] a contested part of East Jerusalem, Mr. Obama said, 'This kind of activity is never helpful when it comes to peace negotiations.' ... A few hours later, Mr. Netanyahu's office responded with a statement, saying that 'Jerusalem is not a settlement; Jerusalem is the capital of the State of Israel.'"

In May 2010, when President Obama signed the Daniel Pearl Press Freedom Act, he did not mention that Pearl, the late Wall Street Journal reporter, had been beheaded by Islamist terrorists because he was a Jew. Nor did the President mention that Pearl, in the video recorded of his gruesome murder, had been forced to state specifically that he was an American Jew. Instead, Obama euphemistically referred only to Pearl's "loss."

In April 2010, Israeli Prime Minister Netanyahu withdrew from an Obama-sponsored Washington summit on nuclear proliferation after it became apparent that Turkey and Egypt intended to use the occasion to denounce Israel's nuclear program; Obama chose not to intervene in this dispute.

The Obama administration's response to Israel's interception of a terrorist-laden flotilla headed for Gaza:

In early 2010, a Turkish organization known as the IHH – which has known ties to Hamas, al Qaeda, and the Muslim Brotherhood – collaborated with the Free Gaza Movement (FGM) to organize a six-ship flotilla of Muslim and anti-Israel activists who would sail (from various points in the Mediterranean region) to Gaza for the purpose of breaking Israel's naval blockade (which had been established to prevent Hamas from importing weaponry from Iran and other allies abroad).

IHH owned and operated the Mavi Marmara, the flotilla's lead ship. The flotilla embarked on its journey toward Gaza in late May of 2010. For several days, Israel issued warnings that the ships would not be permitted to dock in Gaza without first submitting to an inspection of their cargoes. But the crews of the vessels refused to comply; thus Israeli commandos intercepted the flotilla in the early morning hours of May 31. The IHH-affiliated activists responded violently, attacking the commandos with knives, clubs, and pistol fire. In the melee that ensued, nine activists were killed and seven Israeli soldiers were wounded.

In the wake of the flotilla incident, MSNBC reported that the Obama administration "wants to see a new approach that would allow more supplies into the impoverished Palestinian area while guaranteeing Israel's security"; that there was "a growing consensus within the administration that U.S. and Israeli policy toward Gaza must change"; that "White House officials said they had warned Israeli Prime Minister Benjamin Netanyahu's government to use 'caution and restraint' before the raid on the aid convoy"; that Vice President Joe Biden was in favor of putting "as much pressure and as much cajoling on Israel as we can to allow [the Palestinians] to get building materials and other designated humanitarian aid into Gaza"; and that Secretary of State Hillary Clinton supported a Security Council statement condemning the "acts" that had cost the lives of the activists aboard the Mavi Marmara.

$400 Million in Aid for Palestinians:

In an effort to contain the political fallout from the Mavi Marmara incident (see above), in June 2010 President Obama offered to send an extra $400 million in "humanitarian aid" to the Palestinians of the West Bank and Gaza Strip. (This was to be above and beyond the $600+ million in aid which the U.S. was already sending to the Palestinian Authority each year.) In remarks he made during a meeting with Palestinian President Mahmoud Abbas, Obama urged Israel to put a stop to its settlement activity and called on the Palestinians to avoid inciting further confrontation. He also called on Israel to reassess its blockade on Gaza, while conceding that "[t]here should be means by which we will be able to stop flow of arms that endanger Israel's security." Added Obama: "If we can get a new conceptual framework, we should be able to take what is a tragedy [the recent flotilla incident] and create an opportunity, so the lives of people of Gaza are improved. But in the long run, the way to solve this problem is the creation of the Palestinian state and ensuring Israel's security."

The Obama administration allows the Palestinian flag to fly at the PLO office in DC:

On July 25, 2010, JTA News reported that "[t]he Obama administration will allow the PLO office in Washington to fly the Palestinian flag and assume the title of 'delegation'"; that this decision had "symbolic value" but had "no meaning under the Vienna Convention on Diplomatic Relations"; and that the White House "suggested the [measure] would help spur the Palestinians toward direct peace talks with Israel."

A stark contrast between Obama's holiday messages to Jews and to Muslims:

In his Rosh Hashanah message in 2010, President Obama only once referred to "Jews"; made no reference at all to "Judaism'; promoted the creation of a Palestinian state; and never mentioned the monumental contributions Jews had made to the United States.

By contrast, in his August 2010 Ramadan Message, Obama referred to "Muslims" six times and to "Islam" twice; he stated that "American Muslims have made extraordinary contributions to our country"; and he praised "Islam's role in advancing justice, progress, tolerance, and the dignity of all human beings ... a faith known for great diversity and racial equality." Moreover, the President made no reference to what Muslims might need to do differently in order to achieve peace with Israel.

Three decades earlier, President Jimmy Carter had urged another staunch American ally – the Shah of Iran – to loosen his own grip on power, only to see the Shah's autocratic regime replaced by Ayatollah Khomeini's Islamic Republic. More recently, U.S.-supported elections had strengthened such groups as Hezbollah in Lebanon, Hamas in the Palestinian territories, and anti-American radicals in Iran. "Jimmy Carter will go down in American history as 'the president who lost Iran,'" analyst Aluf Benn wrote in the Israeli daily Haaretz. "Barack Obama will be remembered as the president who 'lost' Turkey, Lebanon, and Egypt, and during whose tenure America's alliances in the Middle East crumbled."

"Iran is not building these ballistic missiles, these ICBMs, to hit Israel. They already have missiles that can hit Israel everywhere. They're building these ICBMs to hit you. To hit the United States. You're the great Satan, we are just the small Satan," says Netanyahu.

XIX

OBAMA AND IRAN

An Iranian military observation jet was reported as intentionally flying within fifty yards of an armed U.S. Navy helicopter over the Persian Gulf. Under any other President, this type of bullying would not be tolerated by any other country. But apparently Iran is allowed to get away with it, and Obama does nothing. http://bit.ly/1ljGs93, http://bit.ly/1jGJX7U

On March 5, 2015, Arkansas Senator, Tom Cotton, wrote and sent a letter to the government of Iran. The letter was signed and supported by 46 other United States Senators.

"In this letter, which was less than a page, Senator Cotton stated that the nuclear deal between Iran and the United States that was currently being negotiated would not stand as the current Senate would not ratify it. He also stated if the President of the United States chooses to ignore the Senate, the next President would likely negate the deal anyway in 2017. For this, Senator Cotton and the others who signed the letter are now being called "traitors" by the Obama Administration and told they should be prosecuted under the Logan Act. The Logan Act states citizens "without authority of the United States" shall not influence conduct with foreign governments."

Well, that dog doesn't hunt, because the Senate does have the authority to engage in foreign relations. What Obama really has to worry about is selling his deal to Congress and getting it passed. And if he chooses to ignore the Senate, will the next President negate the deal? http://bit.ly/1NbduPC

Representative Michael McCaul, a Republican from Texas, said that the Islamic State in Iraq and Syria (ISIS) has a greater influence worldwide than President Obama realizes. He said that "ISIS is not just regionalized, like the administration says, in only Iraq and Syria." "This is a global threat," the House Homeland Security chairman said. "This is a new generation of terrorists."

ISIS is claiming responsibility for a beheading in France, a mosque bombing in Kuwait and a mass shooting in Tunisia. McCaul said that "any debate over whether ISIS inspired or managed the violent acts is mere "semantics." "I think in all three instances that ISIS was the driving force," he said. "There were very significant attacks."http://bit.ly/1RwOQ1c

In July of 2015, President Obama announced that an Iran deal had been reached where every path to a nuclear weapon will be cut off from Iran under a historic agreement. He warned Congress that it would be irresponsible to block the treaty. He claimed the deal was not based on trust, but rather verification.

Congress has 60 days to assess the accord and decide whether to pursue legislation imposing new sanctions on Iran or prevent Obama from suspending existing ones. The President warned he would veto any such legislation and urged lawmakers to consider the repercussions of their actions. http://bit.ly/1jGJGSn

National Security Advisor, Susan Rice, said that Iran would not get all of the money from the Treaty until "they take out two-thirds of their centrifuges. They have to get rid of 98% of their uranium stockpile. They have to render inoperative their plutonium facility. They have to let the IAEA do the inspections and the interviews that are necessary to answer the questions that remain about Iran's past nuclear activities. Among — they have to let the IAEA in and establish this 24/7 monitoring that I described. All of those steps have to be taken."

She thinks some of the money will go to the Iranian military and could potentially be used for the kinds of bad behavior that we have seen in the region up until now. Our goal was not to stop their bad behavior. Our goal was to stop a nuclear weapon.

Secretary of State announced that Iran may try to kill us. That should have stopped the Nuclear deal, but no one in Washington seems to listen.

United States Senate
WASHINGTON DC 20510

March 9, 2015

An Open Letter to the Leaders of the Islamic Republic of Iran:

It has come to our attention while observing your nuclear negotiations with our government that you may not fully understand our constitutional system. Thus, we are writing to bring to your attention two features of our Constitution—the power to make binding international agreements and the different character of federal offices—which you should seriously consider as negotiations progress.

First, under our Constitution, while the president negotiates international agreements, Congress plays the significant role of ratifying them. In the case of a treaty, the Senate must ratify it by a two-thirds vote. A so-called congressional-executive agreement requires a majority vote in both the House and the Senate (which, because of procedural rules, effectively means a three-fifths vote in the Senate). Anything not approved by Congress is a mere executive agreement.

Second, the offices of our Constitution have different characteristics. For example, the president may serve only two 4-year terms, whereas senators may serve an unlimited number of 6-year terms. As applied today, for instance, President Obama will leave office in January 2017, while most of us will remain in office well beyond then—perhaps decades.

What these two constitutional provisions mean is that we will consider any agreement regarding your nuclear-weapons program that is not approved by the Congress as nothing more than an executive agreement between President Obama and Ayatollah Khamenei. The next president could revoke such an executive agreement with the stroke of a pen and future Congresses could modify the terms of the agreement at any time.

We hope this letter enriches your knowledge of our constitutional system and promotes mutual understanding and clarity as nuclear negotiations progress.

Sincerely,

Tom Cotton

David Perdue

The above letter was signed by forty-six out of one hundred Senators. Yet Vice President Biden felt the need to chastise Senator Cotton for initiating the letter and embarrassing the President of the United States, stating the letter was "expressly designed to undercut a sitting President in the midst of sensitive international negotiations, is beneath the dignity of an institution I revere."

Biden further stated, "This letter, in the guise of a constitutional lesson, ignores two centuries of precedent and threatens to undermine the ability of any future American President, whether Democrat or Republican, to negotiate with other nations on behalf of the United States. Honorable people can disagree over policy. But this is no way to make America safer or stronger.

'In thirty-six years in the United States Senate, I cannot recall another instance in which Senators wrote directly to advise another country— much less a longtime foreign adversary— that the President does not have the constitutional authority to reach a meaningful understanding with them. This letter sends a highly misleading signal to friend and foe alike that that our Commander-in-Chief cannot deliver on America's commitments—a message that is as false as it is dangerous.

'The decision to undercut our President and circumvent our constitutional system offends me as a matter of principle. As a matter of policy, the letter and its authors have also offered no viable alternative to the diplomatic resolution with Iran that their letter seeks to undermine."

According to the New York Times, the White House yielded and said President Obama would sign a compromise bill giving Congress a voice on the proposed nuclear accord with Iran as the Senate Foreign Relations Committee, in rare unanimous agreement, moved the legislation to the full Senate for a vote. http://nyti.ms/1CFqFTu

According to the Washington Free Beacon, Secretary of State, John Kerry reportedly assured his Iranian counterparts that he wouldn't mind if the president was more like Ayatollah Ali Hosseini Khamenei.

"Ayatollah Alam al-Hoda claimed during prayer services in Iran that in negotiations over Tehran's contested nuclear program, Kerry told the country's foreign minister that he "wished the U.S. had a leader like Iran's supreme leader," according to a Persian-language report on the remarks published by the Asriran news site.

"In the negotiations Kerry told [Iranian Foreign Minister Javad] Zarif that he [Kerry] wished U.S. had a leader like Iran's supreme leader," according to Alam al-Hoda, who is a senior member of the Iran's powerful Assembly of Experts."

"Keep in mind that the talks began with the U.S. and its European partners demanding that Iran dismantle its nuclear program. But to persuade the Ayatollah to accept the recent "framework" accord, Mr. Obama has already conceded that Iran can keep enriching uranium, that it can maintain 5,060 centrifuges to do the enriching, that its enriched-uranium stockpiles can stay inside Iran, that the once-concealed facilities at Fordow and Arak can stay open (albeit in altered form), and that Iran can continue doing research on advanced centrifuges.

'All of these concessions are contrary to previous U.S. positions, and we're no doubt missing a few. But none of that was enough for the Ayatollah, who quickly asserted two new deal-breaking objections: immediate sanctions relief, and no inspections under any circumstances of Iran's military sites." http://bit.ly/1QnDNXg

Iran, Obama, and John Kerry are the only ones that have championed the nuclear deal. We are not just giving Iran a fortune that they really do not need. Obama thinks nothing of spending taxpayer monies and I have always maintained that he is attempting to bankrupt this country. The Ayatollah is amused by Obama and has no respect for him or the United States. In his speech to the Iranians, he told the Iranians that nothing has changed for them, and they continue with their "Death to Arrogant America" chant.

Critics are condemning the deal as a historic and catastrophic agreement that will strengthen Iran and endanger national security for America and its allies. According to http://bit.ly/1XRTRkB

"1. U.S. Nuclear Inspectors Are Banned from Inspecting Iran's Nuclear Sites. Obama National Security Adviser Susan Rice admitted to CNN's Wolf Blitzer that "no Americans will be part of the IAEA [International Atomic Energy Agency] inspection teams." The administration's claim that the deal provides inspections "anytime, anywhere" is also false. Obama's deal allows Iran to block inspector access to any undeclared nuclear site. As Charles Krauthammer notes, "The denial is then adjudicated by a committee—on which

Iran sits. It then goes through several other bodies, on all of which Iran sits" and the whole process may take up to 24 days.

'2.	Obama's Iran Nuclear Deal Lifts Economic Sanctions that Could Boost Iran's Economy with $150 Billion in Revenue. As the Washington Post reports, "Yet another worry is that the lifting of tough economic sanctions on Iran would provide it with as much as $150 billion in revenue. Some of that money would be spent on infrastructure and the Iranian people. Some of it, critics say, would go to the likes of Hezbollah, Syrian Bashar al-Assad and Iraqi militias that not long ago were killing Americans."

'3.	The Obama Administration Admits That 'We Should Expect' Iran Will Spend Some of the $150 Billion in Revenues Obama's Deal Gives Them On Their Military and Possibly Terrorism. In the same interview with Wolf Blitzer, Obama National Security Adviser Susan Rice conceded the following: "Yes, it is real, it is possible, and, in fact, we should expect that some portion of that money would go to the Iranian military and could potentially be used for the kinds of bad behavior that we have seen in the region up until now."

'4.	On the Very Week Obama Brokered His Iran Nuclear Deal, Large Crowds Across Iran Could Be Heard Chanting "Death to America"—And Iran's Ayatollah Ali Khamenei Declared 'Death to America' Just Months Ago. As even the Huffington Post noted under a headline titled, "'DEATH TO AMERICA'": "Hatred towards the United States remains a basic tenet of Iran's ruling system, on display just last week during an annual protest day that saw large crowds across Iran chanting 'Death to America' and 'Death to Israel.'" Similarly, as CNN reported, Iran's Supreme Leaders Ayatollah Ali Khamenei called for "death to America" as recently as late March of 2015. John Kerry said, "the Iranian government's cries of "Death to America" "not helpful" and suggested that the Supreme Leader might not really mean it….." Kerry said at no time was he made aware of an Iranian plan to destroy America.

When Kerry appeared before the House Foreign Affairs Committee to defend the Iran nuclear agreement, Rep. Ted Poe (R-Texas) asked him about Tehran's policy in the light of the "death to

America" chants common at events presided over by supreme leader Ayatollah Ali Khamenei and President Hasan Rouhani. "It is the policy of the ayatollah – if you can answer for him – that Iran wants to destroy the United States?" Poe asked Kerry. "Is that still their policy, as far as you know?" [Kerry:] "I don't believe they've said that. I think they've said 'Death to America' in their chants, but I have not seen this specific." "Well, I kind of take that to mean that they want us dead," Poe said. "That would seem like that would be their policy. He said that. That – you don't think that's their policy?" … "I think they have a policy of opposition to us and of great enmity, but I have no specific knowledge of a plan by Iran to actually destroy us," Kerry replied.

'5. Obama's Iran Nuclear Deal Does Not Require Iran to Release Any American Prisoners. Obama's proposed deal with Iran does not require the Iranians to release American prisoners like Iranian-American Christian missionary Saeed Abedini, Iranian-American Washington Post journalist, Jason Rezaian, or U.S. Marine Amir Hekmati.

'6. Obama's Deal Allows Russia and China to Supply Iran with Weapons. Russian Foreign Minister Sergey Lavrov confirmed that "weapons supplies will be possible" under the new deal. As the International Business Times reports, "Russia and China will continue to make weapons deals with Iran under U.N. procedures." Krauthammer argues that "the net effect of this capitulation will be not only to endanger our Middle East allies now under threat from Iran and its proxies but to endanger our own naval forces in the Persian Gulf." He added, "Imagine how Iran's acquisition of the most advanced anti-ship missiles would threaten our control over the Gulf and the Strait of Hormuz, waterways we have kept open for international commerce for a half century."

'7. 77 Percent of Americans Oppose Obama's Lifting of Sanctions Against Iran. According to the latest Associated Press-GfK poll, 77 percent of Americans believe U.S. sanctions against Iran should be kept the same or increased, not lifted as Obama's deal calls for. Prior to the announcement of Obama's controversial Iran nuclear deal, 60 percent of Americans disapproved of his handling of U.S.

relations with Iran. Obama embarked on a 60-day campaign to build support for his controversial Iran nuclear deal."

Israel's Prime Minister Benjamin Netanyahu has publicly condemned the emerging deal as a historic mistake. Obama is reportedly refusing to meet with Netanyahu before the June 30 deadline. http://bit.ly/1IwXWsN

Why is it that the Obama Administration supports terrorism and turns its back on more moderate Arab and Muslim groups?

Qatar provides weapons and ammunition to members of the Islamic state of Libya. Thirty-Five Qatari aircraft were involved in transferring munitions. Qatar is one of the biggest funders of Hamas, whose leader, Khaled Mashaal, is based in Qatar's capital, Doha. During the past few years, Qatar has provided Hamas with hundreds of millions of dollars – money used to purchase and develop weapons to attack Israel.

"The Egyptians are furious with U.S. President Barack Obama for meeting at the White House with the emir of Qatar, Sheikh Tamim bin Hamad al-Thani. They say that the Obama Administration has once again turned its back on moderate Arabs and Muslims by endorsing those who support and fund Islamic terror groups.

'The meeting between Obama and the emir of Qatar came shortly after Egypt accused the emirate of supporting terrorism.

'Obama was quoted as saying that "Qatar is a strong partner in our coalition to degrade and ultimately defeat ISIL. We are both committed to making sure that ISIL [ISIS/Islamic State] is defeated, to making sure that in Iraq there is an opportunity for all people to live together in peace."

'Obama's decision to host the emir of Qatar and his ensuing statements in praise of the emirate's role in "combating" the Islamic State have drawn sharp criticism from the Egyptians and other Arabs and Muslims."

Arab political analysts are also concerned about Obama's ongoing attempts to appease Iran, which continues to expand its presence in Arab countries such as Yemen, Iraq and Lebanon – as well as in Syria, where it is deeply involved in backing Hezbollah and operating along the border with Israel. Iran also has hundreds of advisors in Iraq.

The Egyptian president is hoping that the Saudis will use their influence to convince Obama to stop supporting a country that openly backs terror groups.

The Egyptian condemnations of Qatar are also directed at the Obama Administration, which seems to be losing one Arab ally after the other because of its perceived support for Qatar and its proxy, the Muslim Brotherhood. http://bit.ly/1ljFAS0

What Michelle Obama just did proves she should not be our First Lady

Michelle Obama, the first lady of the United States, has proven through her actions and statements numerous times that she simply doesn't live up to the level of class of others who have held the same position.

The first lady hosted a celebration in the White House, honoring Iran by celebrating the Persian holiday of Nowruz, which represents their new year.

Cynics may claim that this was done solely to garner good will and support from Iranians, as President Barack Obama is desperately trying to reach an agreement with the Islamic Republic over their nuclear enrichment program.

Regardless of her motives, she hosted the celebration nonetheless, entertaining her guests with a Persian dance group and a lavish dinner, no doubt of higher quality than the stuff she is forcing schoolchildren across America to eat for lunch.

"I think it's so fitting we're holding this celebration here today," she said, welcoming her guests to the White House.

"One of the things I love about the White House is how it truly is the people's house. It is a house that reflects the diversity of culture and traditions that make us who we are as a country. Nowruz is one of those traditions," she continued, according to BizPac Review.

We would be remiss if we didn't point out that this isn't the first time an Islamic holiday has been celebrated in the Obama White House, as they have hosted celebrations in the past for Eid al-Fitr, a massive feast that marks the end of Ramadan.

It should also be noted that, just six short (or long, depending on your point of view) years ago, Michelle Obama claimed to be proud of her country, and its traditions, for the very first time.

But perhaps most importantly, let's not forget that "who we are as a country" generally brings about chants of "Death to America" from much of Iran and not cheers of celebration or gratitude for our "diversity of culture and traditions." http://bit.ly/1N44Fco

One teacher in Washington, D.C. was told he would possibly have a monetary fine for giving wrapped candy to students as a reward for their hard work and good behavior because the practice was an alleged violation of the Federal rules championed by first lady Michelle Obama.

If the rules are not strictly followed, schools can be required to return Federal school lunch money, be penalized for state and Federal food service programs, or make all schools in the county vulnerable to similar punishment. http://bit.ly/1Nbd7Ew

A school in Wisconsin takes a different view. They decided not to take Federal funds as they believe food nutrition and food portion should be decided at a local level. This means they can serve whatever meals they want in their schools.

It is true that a lot of children are obese, but schools have found that when they are not presented with edible food they do not eat. If they do not eat, they do not learn. And the schools are throwing away the uneaten food. Liberals are pointing their fingers in the wrong place. http://www.fixthisnation.com/conservative-breaking-news/michelle-obama-faces-school-board-fury-food-nutrition-best-decided-at-local-level/#sthash.hQXsQX91.dpuf

While being a guest on the Letterman show, the first lady hinted that she might run for the Presidency in 2016.

China is taking steps to lower the chances of a radical islamist terrorist attack. All female Muslims are banned from head coverings. Chinese legislators state that burqas "are not a national dress of Muslims," and indeed, there is nothing in the Koran that mandates this.

Men with long beards are banned from riding public buses. Islamic restaurants must sell cigarettes and alcohol and display them prominently. If they do not follow this order, they will lose their business.

XX

FREEDOM AND SOCIALISM

This is America. I like it the way it is and even more so the way it was. Stop trying to change it into France, Italy, Russia or China, or some other socialist country. If you were, or were not born here and do not like it, you are free to move to any Socialist country that will have you. I believe it is time to really clean house, starting with the White House, the seat of our biggest problems at the moment.

Only in America could the rich people (who pay 86% of all income taxes) be accused of not paying their "fair share" by people who don't pay any income taxes at all.

A student looked at his professor and asked a strange question, "Do you know how to catch wild pigs?"

The professor thought it was a joke and asked for the punch line. The young man assured the professor that his question was no joke and went on to say.

"You catch wild pigs by finding a suitable place in the woods and put corn on the ground. The pigs find it and begin to come every day to eat the free corn.

'When they are used to coming every day, you put a fence down one side of the place where they are used to coming. When they get used to the fence, they begin to eat the corn again, and you put up another side of the fence.

'They get used to that and start to eat again. You continue until you have all four sides of the fence up with a gate in the last side.

'The pigs, which are now used to and want the free corn, eventually begin to come through the gate to get to the free corn.

'When all the pigs get inside, you slam the gate and catch the whole herd.

'Suddenly the wild pigs have lost their freedom. They are confused and run around inside the fence, but soon they go back to eating the free corn. They are so used to it that they have forgotten how to forage in the woods for themselves, so they accept their captivity."

The young man then told the professor that is exactly what he sees happening in America.

The government keeps pushing us toward Communism/Socialism and keeps spreading the free corn out in the form of programs such as supplemental income, tax credit for unearned income, tax exemptions, tobacco subsidies, welfare entitlements, medicine, drugs, etc., while we continually lose our freedoms, just a little at a time.

God help us all when the gate slams shut!

Marx once said, "Remove one freedom per generation and soon you will have no freedom, and no one would have noticed."

I grew up believing a man was to be left alone to live his own life. But I remember hearing about the Feds arresting Communists. I wonder when it was they stopped doing that. I guess they figured they were not a threat to our country any longer. Communists used to be associated with Russia. Now they are associated with a way of life. But when they are working for us, in our government, I think they should be impeached, or forced to resign their position, or the people of their state should vote them out of office.

Senator Barbara Boxer is a member of the Communist Party of United States of America which works closely with several Marxist groups but is particularly close to the Democratic Socialists of America. She served in the House of Representatives from 1983 to 1993 when she became a Senator. In 2015, she announced she would not be seeking re-election in 2016.

Senator Dick Durbin is another member of the Communist Party of the United States of America. Durbin is the senior United States Senator from Illinois, in office since 1997. He has been the Senate Minority Whip, the second highest position in the Democratic Party leadership in the Senate, since 2005 and for a period of eight years (2007-2015) became the Majority Whip.

Senator Tom Harkin, another Democrat from Iowa, served as a Representative from 1975 to 1985. He became a Senator in 1984. On January 26, 2013, he announced his intention to retire from the Senate after completing his fifth term in 2015.

Senator Barbara Mikulski, a Democrat from Maryland. She also served in the House of Representatives from 1977 to 1987. She was originally a social worker and community organizer. She is the ranking Minority Member. After five terms in office, on March 2, 2015, Mikulski announced that she would retire at the end of the 114th Congress in 2017.

Senator Elizabeth Warren, also a Democrat from the State of Massachusetts. "Warren has been described as a leading figure in the Democratic Party and among American progressives, and has frequently been mentioned by political pundits as a potential 2016 presidential candidate. However, Warren has repeatedly denied her intent to run." http://bit.ly/1PlWIQc

Senator Ed Markey, a Junior Democratic Senator from Massachusetts since 2013. He served in the House of Representatives from 1976 to 2013. Wikipedia describes him as a "Liberal."

Senator Debbie Stabenow, a member of the Democratic Party was a member of the House of Representatives from 1997 to 2001. She is serving her third term as a Senator.

Senator Al Franken, Junior Democratic Senator from Minnesota. He ran for the Senate in 2008 and was elected to a second term in 2014.

Sherrod Brown is the Senior Democratic Senator from Ohio. He served in the House of Representatives from 1993 to 2007. He was elected to the Senate in 2006. He is a member of the Socialist Progressive Caucus. He is tight with George Soros. He is known as the Senate's most liberal member. He is a champion of ACORN. He was named in an ACORN Corruption Congressional Report stating the promotion of a partisan political agenda in violation of many tax and election laws. Brown supports such programs as universal healthcare, expanded animal welfare laws, support of healthy, organic foods and vegetarianism, a minimum wage, progressive taxation, and tight gun control. "Brown's first wife had placed a restraining order on him, citing in divorce records that Brown was guilty of extreme cruelty toward her, on several occasions, Larke alleged, her husband had "intimidated, pushed, shoved, and bullied her." http://bit.ly/1RwOhV3

Senator Ron Wyden, a Democrat from Oregon, served in the House of Representatives from 1981 to 1996. He has served as a Senator since 1996. Wyden is for abortion, LGBT, and is an advocate of gun control. He also voted against re-authorization of the Patriot Act.

Senator Jeff Merkley, another Democrat from Oregon, has been a Senator since 2008.

Senator Patty Murray, Democrat, was elected to the Senate in 1992 from Washington state. Murray has served as the Senate Majority Conference Secretary since 2007, making her the fourth-highest-ranking Democrat and the highest-ranking woman in the Senate.

Senator Bernie Sanders, an admitted Socialist, presently running for President on the Democratic ticket. He is a Junior United States Senator

That leaves Senator Tammy Baldwin from Wisconsin. Baldwin is also a member of the Democratic Party. She previously served in the House of Representatives from 1999 to 2013. She was elected to the Senate in 2012. Her record makes her one of the most liberal members of Congress. She is openly gay. On August 1, 2007, Baldwin cosponsored H. Res. 333, a bill proposing articles of impeachment against Vice President Dick Cheney, and H Res. 589, a bill proposing the impeachment of Attorney General Alberto Gonzales. On July 26, 2004, Baldwin spoke at the 2004 Democratic National Convention in prime time on the issue of health care. "Baldwin was one of 22 members of Congress to vote against a 2006 resolution honoring victims of the September 11 attacks on the fifth anniversary of 9/11. (The resolution passed 395-22.) Baldwin says she voted against the resolution because it used divisive language amounting to an endorsement of the Patriot Act and immigration bills she characterized as overly harsh." "In January 2015, it was reported that the senator had for months failed to act on findings of extremely high numbers of opiate prescriptions

at the Veterans Affairs Medical Center in Tomah, Wisconsin." http://
bit.ly/1RwOckb, http://bit.ly/1RwO7gl

First, I find it interesting that every Senator that is listed as
a Communist is also a Democrat. You will also note that every
Representative that I list is also a Democrat.

Second, each one has been in office for several terms, and not one
of them has been vetted by any opponent running against them, by
the media, or the public at large. None of the articles googled will
say that they are a member of the Communist Party even though the
Communist Party of the United States lists them as party members.
Some articles will say they are liberals or progressives or may even say
socialist, but not one member of the media has bothered to do the real
research when it is in black and white and says they are communists.
Or is it that it does not bother the people of this country any longer?
Does the word "communism" not mean anything to America in this
generation? Is History no longer being taught in schools?

More than one-tenth of our United States Senators are Communists.
That bothers me. Doesn't that bother anyone else in the least? Let's go
through the House of Representatives. There are 435 members of the
House of Representatives. I do not have the name of every Communist
party member, but here are a few.

Luis Gutierrez is a member of the Democratic Party and the
Congressional Progressive Caucus from Illinois. Gutiérrez is also
an outspoken advocate of workers' rights, LGBT rights, gender
equality, and other liberal and progressive causes. He was elected to
the House in 1992.

Marcy Kaptur, a Democrat from Ohio, serving in the House of
Representatives since 1983. Kaptur is a member of the Congressional
Progressive Caucus.

[Congressional Progressive Caucus is a Progressive organization of
which Nancy Pelosi is the leader. http://cpc.grijalva.house.gov/what-is-cpc/

2015 members
Co-Chairs

Keith Ellison co-Chair – An African-American Democrat, servicing
in the House of Representatives for the State of Minnesota since
2007. He is co-chair of the Congressional Progressive Caucus and

Chief Deputy Whip of Congress. He is the first Muslim to be elected to Congress. He was raised Roman Catholic. He garnered national attention with his decision to use an English translation of the Qur'an that once belonged to President Thomas Jefferson for his reenacted swearing-in ceremony.

Raúl Grijalva co-chair - a Democrat serving in the House of Representatives from the State of Arizona. Mr. Grijalva co-chairs the Congressional Progressive Caucus with Keith Ellison. Grijalva has a pro-choice voting record and voted against the Partial-Birth Abortion Ban Act. Grijalva supports increasing restrictions on the purchase and possession of guns and increasing enforcement of existing restrictions on gun purchase and possession. He was one of the 67 co-sponsors of the 2007 Assault Weapons Ban, HR 1022. Grijalva has an F rating from the NRA.

First Vice Chair

Mark Pocan, a Democrat serving in the House of Representatives from the State of Wisconsin. He won the election in 2012, replacing Tammy Baldwin. Pocan is openly gay and was married to partner Philip Frank in Canada.

Vice Chairs

Matt Cartwright, a Democrat serving in the House of Representatives from the State of Pennsylvania.

Judy Chu, a Democrat, serving in the House of Representatives from the State of California since 2009 and is an advocate for abortion rights.

David Cicilline, a Democrat serving in the House of Representative from the State of Rhode Island. Upon being sworn in, Cicilline became the fourth openly gay member of Congress.

Ruben Gallego, a Democrat serving in the House of Representative from the State of Arizona. His birth name was Ruben Marinelarena, but he was raised by a single mother, so he changed his name to Gallego to honor his mother.

Michael Honda, a Democrat serving in the House of Representatives from the State of California. He is third-generation Japanese-American. When he was one-year-old, he and his family were sent to

Camp Amache, a Japanese American internment camp in southeastern Colorado. In 1953, his family returned to California, where they became strawberry sharecroppers in Blossom Valley in San Jose. Honda has been a defender of the civil rights of American Muslims. Soon after the September 11 attacks in 2001, Honda spoke at a convention of the American Muslim Alliance (AMA) on October 2001. He told those in attendance not to change their identity or name. "My last name is Honda. You cannot be more Japanese than that."

Sheila Jackson Lee, a Democrat from Texas, serving in the House of Representatives since 1995. *The Washingtonian* Magazine and *Huffington Post* list her as the meanest member of the House of Representatives and the worst boss. She said that repealing Obamacare would be in violation of the Constitution. *Front Page Magazine* had this to say: "When Enron wanted someone to use as a puppet, they picked Sheila Jackson-Lee. They wanted a woman who didn't have a mind of her own. Enron executives described her as "agreeable", which was a polite way of saying, "dumber than a bunch of rocks caught in the hubcaps of a slow bus going the wrong way on a one-way street in the middle of a flood." http://bit.ly/1nQRzls

Janice Schakowsky, a Democrat in the House of Representatives from the State of Illinois. Her parents were Jewish immigrants, her father from Lithuania and her mother from Russia. She is considered the most progressive member of the current US Congress. She is a member of the Congressional Progressive Caucus. She frequently gains ratings of between 90 and 100 from liberal and progressive interest groups and lower ratings from conservative groups. She is co-chair of the Congressional Caucus for Women's Issues.

Mark Takano, a Democrat in the House of Representative from the State of California. He is the first openly gay non-white person in Congress. His family was relocated and interned from California to a "War Relocation Camp" during World War II. He is Sansei, that is, the grandson of people born in Japan who immigrated to the United States.

Whip

Barbara Lee, a Democrat in the House of Representatives from the State of California. Lee was the Chair of the Congressional Black

Caucus and was the Co-Chair of the Congressional Progressive Caucus. While a student at Mills College, she was a volunteer at the Oakland chapter of the Black Panther Party's Community Learning Center and worked on Panther co-founder Bobby Seale's 1973 Oakland mayoral campaign. Lee endorsed Senator Barack Obama for president in the 2008 primary.

Senate Member

Bernie Sanders, Democrat Junior Senator from the State of Vermont. Sanders is the longest-serving independent in U.S. congressional history. A self-described democratic socialist. He is presently a candidate for the Democratic nomination for the 2016 Presidential nomination. His supporters include the Citizens Party, Progressive Coalition, and the Vermont Progressive Party.

House Members

Alma Adams, a Democrat in the House of Representatives from the State of North Carolina. Her claim to fame: She owns 900 hats.

Karen Bass, a Democrat in the House of Representatives from the State of California.

Xavier Becerra, a Democrat in the House of Representatives from the State of California. Becerra is pro-choice and supports the right of access to abortion.

Don Beyer, a Democrat in the House of Representatives from the State of Virginia. During 2007–08, he endorsed and campaigned extensively for presidential candidate Barack Obama. He served as chairman of the Mid-Atlantic Finance Council of Obama for America campaign and served on the campaign's National Finance Council. Following the 2008 election, President-elect Obama asked Beyer to head up the transition team at the Commerce Department. Obama nominated Beyer for the post of United States Ambassador to Switzerland and Liechtenstein on June 12, 2009. In December 2010, Beyer attracted public attention when it was reported that he had warned the Swiss government against offering asylum to WikiLeaks publisher Julian Assange.

Suzanne Bonamici, a Democrat in the House of Representatives from the State of Oregon. She is married to a Jewish Federal Judge.

Corrine Brown, a Democrat in the House of Representatives from the State of Florida. In terms of interest group ratings, Brown holds high percentages in pro-choice groups such as the Florida Alliance of Planned Parenthood Affiliates - Positions on Reproductive Rights (for which she has a 100% rating), NARAL Pro-Choice America – Positions (100%), National Family Planning & Reproductive Health Association - House of Representatives Score (100%). On June 9, 1998, the Congressional Accountability Project voted to conduct a formal inquiry regarding Brown. The Project called for the U.S. House Committee on Standards of Official Conduct to determine if Brown had violated House Rule 10. One of the complaints was that Brown's adult daughter, Shantrel Brown, had received a luxury automobile as a gift from an agent of a Gambian millionaire named Foutanga Sissoko. Sissoko, a friend of Congresswoman Brown, had been imprisoned in Miami after pleading guilty to charges of bribing a customs officer. Brown had worked to secure his release, pressuring U.S. Attorney General Janet Reno to deport Sissoko back to his homeland as an alternative to continued incarceration. The Project held this violated the House gift rule, but Brown denied she had acted improperly. The congressional subcommittee investigating Brown found insufficient evidence to issue a Statement of Alleged Violation but said she had acted with poor judgment in connection with Sissoko. In June 2007, Citizens for Responsibility and Ethics in Washington released a report listing Brown's daughter Shantrel Brown-Fields as a congressional lobbyist; the organization maintains that Congressional relatives working as lobbyists for special interests are a conflict of interest for lawmakers. Brown-Fields is employed by Alcalde & Fayte, with clients including ITERA, Miami-Dade County Commission, and Edward Waters College. In 2006, Brown's campaign committee paid her daughter's husband, Tyree Fields, $5,500 for political consulting work. Rep. Brown has earmarked millions of dollars in federal funding for her daughter's client Edward Waters College. In 2010, she again received criticism for requesting earmarks for an organization her daughter lobbies for.

Michael Capuano, a Democrat serving in the House of Representatives from the State of Massachusetts. Capuano is pro-choice and supports open access to abortions.

Andre Carson, a Democrat serving in the House of Representatives from the State of Indiana. He is the second Muslim to be elected to Congress behind Keith Ellison. Carson is a member of the Congressional Progressive Caucus, New Democrat Coalition and the youngest member of the Congressional Black Caucus. Among others, he is also a member of the Congressional Automotive Caucus, Cancer Action Caucus, Children's Caucus, Climate Change Caucus, Human Rights Caucus, International Conservation Caucus, Labor and Working Families Caucus, Study Group on Public Health, Democratic Budget Group, LGBT Equality Caucus, Military Family Caucus and Renewable/Efficient Energy Caucus. He also serves as the Congressional Black Caucus liaison to the Sustainable Energy and Environment Coalition (CBC Liaison). In the 2008 Presidential Election, Carson endorsed Senator Barack Obama in April 2008, and later won Obama's endorsement for his own May 2008 Democratic primary battle. Carson was the first member of Indiana's Congressional Delegation to announce his support for then-candidate Obama.

Donna Christensen, a non-voting Delegate member of the House of Representatives from the United States Virgin Islands. Christian-Christensen has supported Obama's Patient Protection and Affordable Care Act. Shortly before the Supreme Court affirmed the legislation, she said, "For 99 years, presidents have been trying to do this. Finally, our president has made it possible for each and every American." Donna Christian-Christensen is a member of the Congressional Black Caucus and the Congressional Progressive Caucus. She was featured on The Colbert Report's Better Know a Protectorate segment. She is also the first female physician to win a congressional election.

Yvette Clarke, a Democratic member of the US House of Representatives from New York. She is ranking member of the Homeland Security Subcommittee on Emerging Threats. Clarke is pro-choice and has consistently voted against legislation that would place restrictions on abortion rights. She is a member of Congressional Black Caucus (Secretary) and the Progressive Democratic Caucus.

Steve Cohen, a Democrat member of the House of Representatives from Tennessee. He is the grandson of Jewish immigrants from Lithuania and Poland. Cohen supports a ban on the gun show loophole and on 'fire sales' of firearms. However, he does support citizen's rights to bear concealed firearms. He supports educating children on gun safety through a school program. Cohen was also one of eighty House members to sign a letter written to President Obama urging him to ban the importation of military-style semiautomatic firearms. He supports legal abortion. He is a member of Congressional Caucus on Turkey and Turkish Americans, Congressional Progressive Caucus, International Conservation Caucus, and Congressional Arts Caucus.

Bonnie Watson Coleman, a Democrat serving in the House of Representatives from the State of New Jersey. She participated with fellow Democrats in the boycott of the speech delivered by Israeli Prime Minister Benjamin Netanyahu to Congress.

John Conyers, a Detroit, Michigan Democrat has been in the House of Representatives since 1965. Conyers is one of the 13 founding members of the Congressional Black Caucus. "Conyers has proposed House Resolution 288, which condemns "religious intolerance" but emphasizes Islam as needing special protection from acts of violence and intolerance. It states that "it should never be official policy of the United States Government to disparage the Quran, Islam, or any religion in any way, shape, or form," and "calls upon local, State, and Federal authorities to work to prevent bias-motivated crimes and acts against all individuals, including those of the Islamic faith." The bill was referred to the House Subcommittee on the Constitution in June 2005." "In letters sent separately to the House Ethics Committee, the FBI, and the US Attorney's office, two former aides of Conyers alleged that Conyers used his staff to work on several local and state campaigns, and forced them to baby-sit and chauffeur his children." "In late July 2009, Conyers, commenting on the healthcare debate in the House, stated: "I love these members, they get up and say, 'Read the bill'... What good is reading the bill if it's a thousand pages and you don't have two days and two lawyers to find out what it means after you read the bill?" "On June 16, 2009, the United States Attorney's Office said that two Synagro Technologies representatives had named Monica Conyers as the recipient of bribes from the company totaling more than $6,000, paid to influence passage of a contract with the City of Detroit. The information was gathered during an FBI investigation into political corruption in the city. She was given a pre-indictment letter and offered a plea bargain deal in the case. On June 26, 2009, she was charged with conspiring to commit bribery. She pleaded guilty. On March 10, 2010, she was sentenced to 37 months in prison, and also received two years of supervised probation. She ended up serving just over 27 months at the Alderson Federal Prison Camp and was released from federal custody officially on May 16, 2013." http://en.wikipedia.org/wiki/John_Conyers

Elijah Eugene Cummings, a Democrat serving in the House of Representatives from the State of Maryland.

Danny Davis, a Democrat serving in the House of Representatives from the State of Illinois. Davis ran on the progressive Democratic platform popular in the district. He was pro-choice and supported gay rights, the ERA, single-payer health care, and some federal support for child nutrition and care. Davis expressed interest in being President Barack Obama's replacement in the U.S. Senate, and Illinois Governor in late 2008 before Blagojevich's major scandal erupted. In a December 31, 2008, article published on the website of The New York Times, Davis said that he turned down an offer from representatives of Blagojevich to appoint him to the Senate. Instead, Blagojevich appointed Roland W. Burris.

Nancy Pelosi, Democrat from California, the Minority Leader of the United States House of Representatives and served as the 60th Speaker of the United States House of Representatives from 2007 to 2011. When the Democrats wanted to impeach Bush in 2007 because weapons of mass destruction were not found in Iraq, Pelosi held firmly against it. "In November 2011, 60 Minutes alleged that Pelosi and several other member of Congress had used information they gleaned from closed sessions to make money on the stock market. The program cited Pelosi's purchases of Visa stock while a bill that would limit credit card fees was in the House. Pelosi denied the allegations and called the report "a right-wing smear." Pelosi was a founding member of the Congressional Progressive Caucus. Pelosi stands in favor of increased background checks for potential gun owners, as well as the controversial banning of assault weapons. In February 2013, she called for the "Boldest possible move" on gun control, similar to a stance made just weeks earlier by former Representative, mass shooting victim, and fellow gun control advocate. http://en.wikipedia.org/wiki/Nancy_Pelosi

Peter DeFazio, an Oregon Democrat serving in the House of Representatives since 1987. "DeFazio has a progressive voting record. He voted against the Telecommunications Act of 1996—one of only 16 congressmen to do so. DeFazio particularly objected to a provision that deregulated the cable television industry. According to DeFazio, many of his fellow Democrat congressmen later realized "they were idiots" for backing the bill. He was also the only Oregonian, who voted against both NAFTA and GATT. In 1995, he challenged President Bill Clinton's stance on Bosnia, claiming Clinton and his Cabinet did not make a convincing claim for the operation. On the issue of abortion, DeFazio is strongly pro-choice, earning a 100 percent rating from Planned Parenthood in 2010. He is a founding member of the Congressional Progressive Caucus and was its chairman from 2003 to 2005." Although he spent four years in the Air Force, DeFazio has shown a propensity to vote against legislation that would increase the militarism of the United States. In 2000, he voted no on legislation to create a national missile defense network, describing the system as a "comic book fantasy." He has consistently voted against the Patriot Act, including its inception after 9/11 and the recurring reauthorization bills, citing the infringement on the civil rights of Americans. He voted multiple times to set an itinerary for exiting Iraq and to bring the troops home. "Speaking on the House floor, DeFazio said, "Something is happening. Something in this land is happening. I call it the 'American Awakening.'" He added that "I think the young people and the others who are joining them on Wall Street get it. They may not be totally focused, but they know that this is not a country that gives them a fair shot at the American dream anymore — it is a stacked deck." "DeFazio opposed the Lowering Gasoline Prices to Fuel an America That Works Act of 2014 (H.R. 4899; 113th Congress), a bill that would revise existing laws and policies regarding the development of oil and gas resources on the Outer Continental Shelf. The bill is intended to increase domestic energy production and lower gas prices."

Rosa DeLauro, a Democrat serving in the House of Representatives from the State of Connecticut. Her father, and all of her grandparents were Italian immigrants. DeLauro is one of the most liberal members of the House. She is a founding member of the Congressional Progressive

Caucus. DeLauro is pro-choice. She supports the availability of abortions in all cases. Additionally, Representative DeLauro supports the use of federal subsidies for abortion procedures. She has consistently voted in support of stronger regulation of firearms in the United States. In 2006, she voted against the Trigger Lock Amendment that ends the use of funds from the Commerce Department FY2007 Appropriation bill to enforce laws requiring guns to be sold with locks. Additionally, DeLauro voted in 1999 to increase the amount of time given to perform background checks from 24 hours to 72 hours. Earlier, in 1998 she voted to increase the minimum gun crime sentence. On 14 January 2013, she introduced a bill allowing for the voluntary surrender of assault-type weapons with compensation to come in the form of tax credits. DeLauro is one of the fifty richest members of Congress.

Mark DeSaulnier, a Democrat serving in the House of Representatives from the State of California.

Sam Farr, a Democrat serving in the House of Representatives from the State of California. Rep. Farr, like most Progressive Democrats in Congress, opposes the USA PATRIOT Act and is pro-choice. He received a 91% progressive rating by Progressive Punch, ranking him the 42nd most progressive member of Congress.

Chaka Fattah, a Democrat serving in the House of Representatives from the State of Pennsylvania. Chaka was born Arthur Davenport. Fattah has lived all his life in the city, attending Overbrook High School, the Community College of Philadelphia and the University of Pennsylvania's Fels Institute of Government, where he received an MGA in 1986. He is a member of Alpha Phi Alpha fraternity. His adoptive father, David Fattah, and mother, Falaka Fattah (born Frances Brown, also known as Queen Mother Falaka Fattah), are community activists in West Philadelphia, where they are building an "urban Boys' Town" through their organization, the House of Umoja. He has five brothers. Fattah is married to his third wife, Renee Chenault-Fattah, a local Philadelphia television news broadcaster on WCAU-TV (NBC 10). They have one young daughter, Chandler Fattah. He is stepfather to her daughter Cameron Chenault. With other women, he is the father of another daughter, Frances ("Fran"), and one son, Chaka Fattah Jr., known as "Chip" (31 years old in March 2015. In 2002, he was named to the PoliticsPA list of Best Dressed Legislators, noting his "excellence in haberdashery." He has also proclaimed that NASA's voting contest for naming rights for a module on the International Space Station should be honored by naming one "Colbert" in honor of TV personality Stephen Colbert. On July 29, 2015, Fattah and four of his associates were indicted for their alleged roles in a racketeering conspiracy involving several schemes that were intended to further the political and financial interests of the defendants and others by, among other tactics, misappropriating hundreds of thousands of dollars of federal, charitable and campaign funds. The FBI further alleged that Fattah accepted an $18,000 bribe from a man seeking an ambassadorship. https://en.wikipedia.org/wiki/Chaka_Fattah

Lois Frankel, a Democrat serving in the House of Representatives for the State of Florida. Frankel was criticized for acceptance of $20,000.00 from Digital Domain Media Group for her election campaign five months after that company was awarded a downtown project which included incentives from the city of West Palm Beach, and in response vowed to give the contribution to charity.

Marcia Fudge, a Democrat serving in the House of Representatives for the State of Ohio. Fudge is an avid Obama supporter.

Alan Grayson, a Democrat serving in the House of Representatives for the State of Florida. Grayson is ranked the eleventh wealthiest member of Congress.

Luis Gutierrez, a Democrat serving in the House of Representatives for the State of Illinois. Gutiérrez is also an outspoken advocate of workers' rights, LGBT rights, gender equality, and other liberal and progressive causes.

Janice Hahn, a Democrat serving in the House of Representatives for the State of California.

Jared Huffman, a Democrat serving in the House of Representatives for the State of California. He was a member of the Congressional Progressive Caucus, a left-leaning organization that works to advance progressive and liberal issues and positions.

Hakeem Jeffries, a Democrat serving in the House of Representatives for the State of New York.

Eddie Bernice Johnson, a Democrat serving in the House of Representatives for the State of Texas. She is the first registered nurse elected to Congress. She is a member of the Congressional Progressive Caucus, as well as several other caucuses.

Hank Johnson, a Democrat serving in the House of Representatives for the State of Georgia. He is one of only three Buddhists, the others being Hawaii's Mazie Hirono and Colleen Hanabusa, to serve in the United States Congress. In December 2009, Johnson revealed that he had been battling Hepatitis C (HCV) for over a decade, which resulted in slow speech and a tendency to regularly get "lost in thought in the middle of a discussion." This is the Representative that thought the island of Guam would become so overly populated that it would tip over.

Joe Kennedy III, a Democrat serving in the House of Representatives for the State of Massachusetts.

Brenda Lawrence, a Democrat serving in the House of Representatives for the State of Michigan.

John Lewis, a Democrat serving in the House of Representatives for the State of Georgia. He is Senior Chief Deputy Whip, leading an organization of chief deputy whips and serves as the primary assistant to the Democratic Whip. Lewis is a member of the Congressional Progressive Caucus and an Obama supporter.

Ted Lieu, a Democrat serving in the House of Representatives from the State of California. Lieu was born in Taipei, Taiwan. He holds the rank of Lieutenant Colonel in the United States Air Force Reserves.

David Loebsack, a Democrat serving in the House of Representatives from the State of Iowa. He has voted consistently to protect a woman's right to get an abortion.

Alan Lowenthal, a Democrat serving in the House of Representatives for the State of California.

Carolyn Maloney, a Democrat serving in the House of Representatives for the State of New York. A bill, reintroduced in 2014 and 2015, would require gun owners to maintain liability insurance, just as most car owners must do. In 2014, she joined with Senator Ed Markey in sending a letter to President Barack Obama asking him to insert $10 million into the budget for the Center for Disease Control and Prevention to resume research on gun violence and "conduct scientific research on the causes and prevention of gun violence."

NARAL Pro-Choice America gives her a 100. Planned Parenthood gives her a 100.

Jim McDermott, a Democrat from Seattle, Washington, serving in the House of Representatives since 1989 and is a member of the House Progressive Caucus. "On April 28, 2004, Congressman McDermott omitted the phrase "under God" while leading the House in reciting the Pledge of Allegiance. The incident occurred after atheist Michael Newdow lost his court case to have the phrase "under God" dropped from the Pledge, and after McDermott had voted against a congressional resolution that called for overturning a court ruling that declared the phrase unconstitutional. In 1954, during the McCarthy era and communism scare, Congress had passed a bill, which was signed into law, to add the words "under God."

James McGovern, a Democrat serving in the House of Representatives for the State of Massachusetts. He is a member of the Congressional Progressive Caucus and has been ranked as one of the most liberal members of Congress. He supports pro-choice, and he supports stem cell research. McGovern has aligned himself with liberal and progressive causes. "It's no secret that I'm a liberal," he said in 2010.

Gwen Moore, a Democrat serving in the House of Representatives for the State or Wisconsin. She is also the second woman after Tammy Baldwin and the first African-American elected to Congress from Wisconsin. Moore supports same-sex marriage in the United States.

Jerrold Nadler, a Democrat serving in the House of Representatives for the State of New York. Nadler is a member of the Congressional Progressive Caucus and has a liberal voting record.

Grace Napolitano, a Democrat serving in the House of Representatives for the State of California.

Rick Nolan, a Democrat serving in the House of Representatives for the State of Minnesota. Nolan supports the Affordable Care Act and said he would not vote to repeal it

Eleanor Holmes Norton, a Democrat Delegate serving in the House of Representative for the District of Columbia. She may serve on committees or speak on the floor, but she is not permitted to vote on the final passage of any legislation. Though she often refers to herself as "Congresswoman," Norton was elected in 1990 as a Democratic delegate to the House of Representatives.

Frank Pallone, a Democrat serving in the House of Representatives for the State of New Jersey. He is a Progressive Caucus member. He also serves as a co-chairman of the Congressional Caucus on Armenian Issues. He was one of the 31 who voted in the House to not count the electoral votes from Ohio in the 2004 United States presidential election.

Chellie Pingree, a Democrat serving in the House of Representatives for the State of Maine. She receives high marks from unions and pro-choice.

Jared Polis, a Democrat serving in the House of Representatives for the State of Colorado. Polis is the first openly gay parent in Congress. He is the owner of Bluemountain.com a free greeting card website Excite@Home in 1999 for $430 million in stock and $350 million in cash. Polis had founded a number of companies and is one of the ten richest members of the United States Congress, estimated to be worth at least $65.91 million. He is a member of Congressional Progressive Caucus, LGBT Equality Caucus, Mexico Caucus (Co-chair), and Nepal Caucus (Co-chair). Polis is currently one of seven openly gay members of the 113th Congress and caucuses in the LGBT Equality Caucus. Polis and his partner, Marlon Reis, have two children: son Caspian Julius, born on September 30, 2011, and daughter Cora Barucha, born July 4, 2014.

Charles Rangel, a Democrat in the House of Representatives, serving since 1971 from the States of New York. He is also a founding member of the Congressional Black Caucus. He earned a Purple Heart and a Bronze Star for his service in the U.S. Army during the Korean War, where he led a group of soldiers out of a deadly Chinese army encirclement during the Battle of Kunu-ri in 1950.

Lucille Roybal-Allard, a Democrat in the House of Representatives for the State of California. Her husband is a Marine Corps Captain.

Jose Serrano, a Democrat serving in the House of Representatives for the State of New York. He is widely regarded as one of the most progressive members of Congress. He has been questioned about his pork barrel spending by some fiscal conservative members of Congress. In the aftermath of the death of Hugo Chávez, Congressman Serrano wrote condolences to Chavez via Twitter describing him as a leader who "understood the needs of the poor. He was committed to empowering the powerless. R.I.P. Mr. President." However, the comments proved controversial with some twitterers and political commentators and prompted a response from the Republican National Committee that described Serrano's tweet as "simply insulting that a Democrat Congressman would praise the authoritarian ruler Hugo Chávez.

Louise Slaughter, a Democrat serving in the House of Representatives for the State of New York.

Mark Takai, a Democrat serving in the House of Representatives for the State of Hawaii. He is a Lt. Col. In the Army National Guard. He took part in Operation Iraqi Freedom in 2009. Takai received the Meritorious Service Medal from the United States Army in 2009, the Distinguished Service Medal from the National Guard Association of the United States in 2011, and the Hawaii Distinguished Service Order in 2012.

Bennie Thompson, a Democrat serving in the House of Representatives for the State of Mississippi. He was one of the 31 who voted in the House to refuse to count the electoral votes from Ohio in the 2004 presidential election.

Nydia Velazquez, a Democrat serving in the House of Representatives for the State of New York. Velazquez is a progressive fighting for Latino rights.

Maxine Waters, a Democrat serving in the House of Representatives for the State of California. Waters was charged, and exonerated, by the House's subcommittee on ethics with violations of the House's ethics rules in 2010. Waters had a confrontation over an earmark in the United States House Committee on Appropriations with fellow Democratic Congressman Dave Obey in 2009. The funding request was for a public school employment training center in Los Angeles that was named after her. Waters has visited Cuba a number of times, praised Fidel Castro, and demanded an end to the U.S. trade embargo. In 1998 Waters wrote a letter to Castro citing the 1960s and 1970s as "a sad and shameful chapter of our history," and thanked Castro for providing help to those who needed to "flee political persecution." According to Chuck Neubauer and Ted Rohrlich writing in the LA Times in 2004, Maxine Waters' relatives had made more than $1 million during the preceding eight years by doing business with companies, candidates and causes that Waters had helped. They claimed she and her husband helped a company get government bond business, and her daughter Karen Waters and son Edward Waters have profited from her connections. Waters replied that "They do their business, and I do mine." http://bit.ly/1IMITpB

Peter Welch, a Democrat serving in the House of Representatives from the State of Vermont. One area where Welch has been at odds with vocal constituents is the matter of impeachment of President Bush and Vice President Cheney. Welch supports a Progressive Democratic position on most issues. On the issue of abortion, Welch was given a 100% rating from Planned Parenthood and NARAL Pro-Choice America.

Frederica Wilson, a Democrat serving in the House of Representatives from the State of Florida. She has a large collection that includes hundreds of hats of all different varieties. She wears one every day to honor her late grandmother. She has asked House Speaker John Boehner to waive the rule prohibiting the wearing of hats on the floor of the House of Representatives, a rule in place since 1837. Frederica Wilson has taken a vocal opposition to the Tea Party. At a Miami town hall meeting, she told citizens to remember that the Tea Party is the real enemy and that they hold Congress hostage. She expressed her belief that they have one goal in mind: "to make President Obama a one-term president." http://bit.ly/1PKxj64

It appears to me that if you did or did not want something to pass all you had to do was get all of the Communists together and vote yes or no.

Obama wants to not only complete his mission to bring America down to her knees and humiliate the United States in the eyes of the world, but to prove to the Democrat party real socialism cannot be stopped.

It was the Democrats that booed God on National Television during the Democratic National Convention in 2012 when a large group shouted "no" when a vote was called three times to restore to the platform a reference to God and recognition of Jerusalem as Israel's capital before Los Angeles Mayor Antonio Villaigosa announced the ayes have it. Many in the crowd booed after he determined the language would be restored. A Senior Official said that President Obama personally intervened to change the language on the God reference.

Has this country come so far that when someone runs for office now, and particularly for one of the highest offices in the United States of America, that it is no longer important and no one questions whether that candidate is a socialist/progressive/Marxist/communist? Are we so naïve that we do not believe that their being a socialist/progressive/Marxist or communist will not make a difference to our lives in the future?

Look at where our country is today – right now. Everyone listed above that was elected to the United States Senate and the United States House of Representatives are elected officials, and they all are socialists/progressives/Marxists/communists employed in our United States Government. They were elected because we, the people, and the Media, did not do our job and vet the candidates. We either did not vet the candidates, or we did not care that they were communists. Which was it? Is it okay with you that the United States has becoming a communist country? We already are a socialist country. I have proven that to you in *The Lyin Kings*. It will continue if you elect another Democrat.

How did it all begin? Well, I once received an Anthropological Theory that you may find amusing – or not. It has a lot of truth in it.

"Humans originally existed as members of small bands of nomadic hunter/gatherers. They lived on deer in the mountains during the summer and would go to the coast and live on fish and lobster in the winter.

The two most important events in all of history were the invention of beer and the invention of the wheel.

Beer required grain and that was the beginning of agriculture.

Neither the glass bottle nor aluminum can was invented yet, so while our early humans were sitting around waiting for them to be invented, they just stayed close to the brewery. That's how villages were formed.

The wheel was invented to get man to the beer.

These two were the foundation of modern civilization and together were the catalyst for the splitting of humanity into two distinct subgroups:

1. Liberals.
2. Conservatives.

Some men spent their days tracking and killing animals to BBQ at night while they were drinking beer. This was the beginning of what is known as the Conservative movement.

Other men who were less skilled at hunting learned to live off the conservatives by showing up for the nightly BBQ's and doing the sewing, fetching, and hair dressing. This was the beginning of the Liberal movement.

Some of these liberal men evolved into women (i.e., some say like Bruce Jenner). Others became known as girlie-men. Some noteworthy Liberal achievements include the domestication of cats, the invention of group therapy, group hugs, and the concept of democratic voting to decide how to divide the meat and beer that Conservatives provided.

Over the years, Conservatives came to be symbolized by the largest, most powerful land animal on earth, the elephant. Liberals are symbolized by the jackass for obvious reasons.

Modern Liberals like lite beer (with lime added), but most prefer white wine or imported bottled water. They eat raw fish but like their beef well done. Sushi, tofu, and French food are standard Liberal fare.

Another interesting evolutionary side note: many Liberal women have higher testosterone levels than their men.

Most college professors, social workers, personal injury attorneys, journalists, film makers in Hollywood, group therapists, and community organizers are Liberals. Liberals meddled in our national pastime and invented the designated hitter rule because it wasn't fair to make the pitcher also bat.

Conservatives drink real beer. They eat red meat and still provide for their women. Conservatives are big game hunters, rodeo cowboys, lumberjacks, construction workers, firemen, medical doctors, police officers, dentists, engineers, corporate executives, athletes, members of the military, airline pilots, and generally anyone who works productively.

Conservatives who own companies hire other conservatives who want to work for a living.

Liberals produce little or nothing. They like to govern the producers and decide what to do with the production. Liberals believe Europeans are more enlightened than Americans. That is why most of the Liberals remained in Europe when Conservatives were coming to America.

They crept in after the Wild West was tamed and created a business of trying to get more for nothing.

Here ends today's lesson in world history. It should be noted that a Liberal may have a momentary urge to angrily respond. A Conservative will simply laugh and be so convinced of the absolute truth of this history that they will tell other true believers just to tick off more Liberals."

Let your next action reveal your true self. I'm going to have another Bud.

XXI

VETERANS

Who has given more for this Country, who has sacrificed more personally, who has given you more freedom than our Veterans? I salute and thank every one of you for your service and my freedom.

Now it is time that Big Government give back to our Veterans instead of continuing to take away from them in the form of medical services and pension funds and disability funds while giving free services to illegal aliens and drug abusers.

No President has ever treated our military as bad as this administration. This is the most corrupt administration I have ever witnessed in all my seventy-four years of living.

This is the most corrupt media I have ever witnessed. Most do not even bother to get up from their desks to investigate and cover stories and scandals anymore. Very few of them investigate a story their self but have a staff that does the leg work or computer research for them.

Our Congress is very quick to spend money, and when it comes time to find where to get the money they want to spend, they look for cuts from the retired military and cuts from programs from the elderly. The problem is these are the ones least able to afford such cuts and Congress, and foreign countries are the most able to afford such a cut.

At the beginning of each session of Congress, the first order of business is to give members of Congress a raise. However, Congress never adds hours to their employment schedule. They work approximately two weeks per month and less some months. All that for a six-figure salary and a lot of arrogance, because they do not listen to the people that vote them into office.

Veterans Administrations' errors and bureaucracy have killed over 500 veterans. Independent legal analysts say the nearly 1,000 wrongful death payments in the decade after 9/11 represent a small percentage of the veterans who have died because of malpractice by the Department of Veterans Affairs.

Sarah Palin got it right when she said, "The reason you don't hear about them is because our vets don't whine," she said. "They're not wired to complain. That's why this ran under the radar for so long."

As of April 2015, 847,882 veterans were awaiting health care and 238,657 of them were already dead, but still in the system. That is 28% of the list! These numbers came out of the VA's Health Eligibility Center in Atlanta, GA. Every year thousands of Veterans lose their eligibility for VA health care due to the agency's inaction. People who are sick and need treatment are forced to wait for the cases of the deceased veterans to be resolved before their number is called. 10.6% of the people on this list who are deceased are still active within the VA's system. Some people go on to fill prescriptions and make appointments from the grave! The VA's inaction is only making the waiting list grow longer. http://bit.ly/17CjnqK

Most of our veterans wait unending months for the Department of Veterans Affairs to process their disability claims. The excuse is a backlog of claims. However, no effort is made to fix the problem. Representative Jeff Miller said, "It's time to end that culture of complacency that has developed among some VA employees and replace it with a culture of accountability." I agree with him when he said it is time that instead of moving a bad employee to another VA office that you remove them from the VA altogether. Our veterans are being short changed and not getting the service they have been promised. I think it is time to remove them from working for any government office.

If you decide to write to your Senator to get help with a VA claim that you have, this is not going to speed up your claim. This is what is really going to happen.

You call your US Senator & speak to an aid.

The aid asks you to fill out a release of information.

The aid sends your release of information and a canned letter to the VA RO your claim is in.

The VA has a paid person called a Congressional Liaison. Their job is to answer letters from US Senators. When your request reaches their desk two things that I know of happen. They (1) pull your file to document where your claim is in the process, and (2) open a "claim" on benefits as a "special inquiry".

After they review your claim they write a claim specific letter back to the senator telling you your claim has to wait in line, it's in XYZ phase, and you can increase your time by submitting hardship. They thank the senator for his understanding and rubber stamp it.

Your claim is then put back in its file cabinet and continues on its merry way. The only problem with this is in the rare chance that your claim comes up for review, and the congressional liaison has it out there could be a conflict that causes a delay in your rating.

So...... long and short is your claim will not really get any help by filing, however the U.S' Senators do track these numbers and the more veterans that bitch about slow times will likely cause a bill in the future to be passed helping out current/future veterans going through this hell. It's completely up to you if you want to request help, but in all reality it's not going to speed up your claim. http://bit.ly/1XRST7Z

The above website did say that it depended on how diligent your Senator was. Some Senators have higher aspirations and might contact the VA and pursue the matter further on behalf of the veteran. If that is done, the VA will move on behalf of the veteran because for all the VA knows, that Senator might become the next President.

On the last day of the fiscal year of 2013, the VA in Augusta, Georgia spent more than $3.5 Million and the VA also awarded a five-figure bonus to the executive who oversaw the Memphis facility, yet appointments were delayed to veterans for cancer screenings in South Carolina causing six veteran deaths.

In a report submitted to Congress, it was said that a review was made where 250 million cases were reviewed dating back to 1999 and that only 23 veterans had died from gastrointestinal cancers under questionable circumstances. Later the department said they actually had reviewed only 11,000 cases over a two-year period from 2009 through 2011 and found that 24 veterans had died.

The VA Hospital in Phoenix, Arizona was investigated and found wanting. Several hospital whistleblowers came forward claiming the administrators ordered thousands of appointment requests be diverted to a secret unofficial list not to be reported. If the patients died, their names would disappear. Dr. Samuel Foote, who spent decades working for the VA, was the first to allege that in an effort to improve their record, hospital officials kept a secret unofficial list of veterans who sought medical care. "This was basically an elaborate scheme to cover up patient wait times," Foote told NBC News. "The main problem was we had a huge demand, and we had a relatively limited supply of service." Foote added, "Rather than dealing with the problem, they were just covering it up." http://nbcnews.to/1iwosTK

In January 2013, CBS News reported that a Veterans Affairs hospital in Pittsburgh knew for more than a year it had an outbreak of Legionnaires' disease but failed to warn patients. VA officials testified before Congress on February 5, 2013, blaming the facilities' old water system for the outbreak.

Hospital staff had received lab tests indicating that the hospital's water system had tested positive for the lethal bacteria that causes Legionnaires' disease. The hospital never acknowledged it had an outbreak until an 87-year-old patient named William Nicklas died after testing positive for Legionnaires' disease in November of 2012 – even though a memo shows that just four months before he fell ill, the Pittsburgh VA's director Terry Gerigk Wolf was aware that sites in the hospital were still testing positive for Legionella bacteria. CBS News reported in January 2013 that there were at least four infections before Nicklas died, and the bacteria had been reported in the hospital's water nearly a year before his death.

Ultimately, at least six patients died and 22 were sickened by the outbreak. http://cbsn.ws/1gvdnx8

Our veterans are a precious commodity of this country. They gave their all. They deserve much better than what this administration and Congress is giving them in their retirement.

An investigation into the Obama Administration's Order that Veterans deemed "incompetent" must give up their weapons is worse than expected. People who live with the veterans are being ordered not to possess a gun.

Some Veterans are being told they can buy back their Second Amendment rights by giving up their Veteran's benefits. Sounds like extortion and tyranny to me.

Veterans are being sent letters telling them they are being classified as incompetent, and the government is assigning someone to help them handle their benefits and payments. Consequently, they were told, they could no longer own weapons, under penalty of fines and jail time. The problem with this is that the veterans are being determined guilty without a hearing regarding the potential loss of their constitutional rights.

WND broke the story that the Obama administration insisted it was routine for officials to send out letters informing veterans that an unidentified "report" indicated they may be declared incompetent and consequently stripped of their Second Amendment rights. http://bit.ly/1QAA0Tg

Why are we cutting benefits for our veterans, no pay raises for our military and cutting our army to a level lower than before WWII, but we are not stopping payments to illegal aliens such as monthly payments for each child, money for housing, food stamps, free education including college and also the right to vote?

Barack Obama's non-allegiance to our Military began on the evening of his first inauguration in 2009 when he attended every Ball, except the Military Ball. He has disrespected the military in innumerable ways since his election, but rarely has he shown such disdain and held them in such contempt, and has America felt equal contempt for this President, as when Obama showed a lack of response to our five servicemen that were attacked in Chattanooga.

The matter was worse when it became known that Lt. Cmdr. Timothy White, a Navy officer and Marine, reportedly returned fire at the shooter, even though current policy does not permit military members to carry firearms on facilities such as those where the attack occurred. America, of course praised Lt. Cmdr. White for saving many other lives and considered him a hero. But not this Administration. The United States Navy decided to bring charges against Lt. Cmdr Timothy White for illegally discharging a firearm on federal property.

What has become of our old military? If our soldiers were armed there would not be shootings and Muslims madmen on our bases. Lt. Cmdr. White deserves a medal for saving many lives.

Let's take the guns away from the Secret Servicemen that guard the President like we take away the guns of our servicemen. Will Obama then see the need for security?

The Obama Administration did nothing except issue an order that military recruiters refrain from dressing in uniform. But in Maricopa County, Arizona, The Army Reserve Center was safe. Sheriff Joe Arpaio came to the rescue and sent his all volunteer posse to stand guard outside the recruitment center. Furthermore, Arpaio planned to do this again for the second week in a row, despite objections from the Obama administration, which apparently preferred that our recruiters remain defenseless. http://bit.ly/1NARPPV

According to Breitbart, the sheriff did the same for black churches in Maricopa County after the mass murder in Charleston, S.C., by alleged shooter Dylann Roof.

To have this President defend black criminals such as Trayvon Martin, or fly our nation's flag at half-mast for someone that died of a drug overdose, or light up the White House in rainbow colors, and then run out on our nation's heroes is a cowardly and despicable act of the worst kind. If we try to erase these truths, we are destined to repeat them.

"Would you encourage your son or daughter to enlist in the military with Obama as commander-in-chief?" Even the best domestic programs and the friendliest foreign relations cannot make up for failing to keep the American people safe. Barack Obama is a failure as America's commander-in-chief. He appears to hate the military. Since taking office in his first term, President Obama has shown nothing but disdain for the military, veterans, and their families. Under Obama veteran's care has been atrocious, the military's budget has been pole axed, and the morale of active duty personnel has dropped through the floor. Barack Obama's only use for the military seems to be as a laboratory for social experiments focused on advancing the agendas of the homosexual and transgender movements.

'His attitude is lackadaisical at best when talking about military matters, but when talking about entitlement programs, reforming healthcare, government bailouts, new federal regulations, the redistribution of wealth, how Islam is a peace-loving religion, the supposed failings of George W. Bush, heartless Republicans, gun control, or the socialization of America's economy Barack Obama can be animated to the point of exuberance. The president calls to mind a football coach who is so focused on one aspect of the game that he ignores all of the others. Teams with this type of coach lose, and that is what's happening to America on the global stage: we are losing. Frankly, if Barack Obama were a football coach he would have been fired by now." http://bit.ly/1TsZKU5

XXII

THE PATRIOT ACT
THE USA FREEDOM ACT

The USA Patriot Act is an Act of Congress that was signed into law by President George W. Bush on October 26, 2001. Its title is a ten-letter backronym (USA PATRIOT) that stands for "Uniting and Strengthening America by Providing Appropriate Tools Required to Intercept and Obstruct Terrorism Act of 2001".

On May 26, 2011, President Barack Obama signed the PATRIOT Sunsets Extension Act of 2011, a four-year extension of three key provisions in the USA PATRIOT Act: roving wiretaps, searches of business records (the "library records provision"), and conducting surveillance of "lone wolves"—individuals suspected of terrorist-related activities not linked to terrorist groups. http://en.wikipedia.org/wiki/Patriot_Act

Overview of the Patriot Act

History, Information

The Patriot Act allowed law enforcement sweeping authority to monitor electronic communications with little oversight. It also allows law enforcement to engage in the use of roving wiretaps, sneak and peek warrants and other provisions. Essentially, what worries civil liberties advocates at all points along the political spectrum is that the government could be spying on any U.S. citizen without that citizen even knowing, if the government decides that the citizen is a "suspected terrorist".

Electronic Consequences

The government has already been caught gathering information on Internet traffic on a wide-net basis, most famously in San Francisco when a telecom employee blew the whistle on a clandestine monitoring operation by the NSA. This has led many people who have valid concerns about how much privacy they really have online. Would texting something with the words "Al Qaeda" in it result in you being monitored? Does a peaceful political organization that you belong to fit the definition of a "terrorist organization" by government standards? Would you even know if you were being spied on? Probably not.

Privacy

In reaction to the Patriot Act—and other acts, including SOPA and PIPA—many US citizens have taken measures to protect their privacy. These include using VPN connections, which encrypt all communication so that it cannot be read and so that it does not trigger filters that sort through data looking for specific keywords of other information. Proxy servers are also used to protect communication by concealing the IP address of origin, though they do nothing actually to encrypt information, in most cases.

The Patriot Act remains controversial today. Some sources say that it stopped as many as ten terrorist plots. Others say that law enforcement already had the tools that they needed and merely used the Patriot Act as a way to get even more sweeping powers that they simply wanted, but that only constitute invasions of citizen privacy. http://bit.ly/1PEaMDf/

Main Provisions of the Patriot Act

The Patriot Act's full title is Uniting and Strengthening America
by Providing Appropriate Tools Required to Intercept and Obstruct
Terrorism Act of 2001. It's split into ten parts, and it covers a lot of
ground. Here is a summary.

Title I - This section pertains to the protection of civil liberties. It
authorizes Federal money to accomplish much of the act's provisions
and authorizes the Secret Service to create a nationwide electronic
crime task force. This section also gives the president the authority to
confiscate the property of any foreign person who is believed to have
aided in a war or attack on the United States. Such seizures can be
submitted secretly to courts as evidence.

Title II - This section broadens the ability of law-enforcement
agencies to conduct surveillance on "agents of foreign powers." It
allows the interception of communications if they're related to terrorist
activities and allows law-enforcement agencies to share information
related to terrorist activities with federal authorities. In addition,
Title II authorizes roving surveillance – that is, a court order allowing
surveillance on a particular person allows officers to use any means
available to intercept that person's communications, regardless of where
the person goes. Previously, a court order would only allow a wiretap
on a specific line in one location. Further, it allows the government
to order files from the providers of communications services with
details about specific customers' use of the service. For example, an
Internet service provider can be ordered to provide information on
IP addresses, login times and sites visited. Title II also allows delayed
notification of search warrants, meaning a suspect's house could be
searched while the suspect isn't present, and the suspect would not be
notified of the search until after it was carried out. The wide-ranging
Title II included many other relatively minor clauses. Title II also
contained the sunset clause that would have caused many of the act's
provisions to expire in 2005 had they not been renewed. We'll discuss
more on the sunset clause later.

Titles III-X of the Patriot Act

Title III - This section of the Patriot Act is aimed at cutting off the
financial support of terrorist groups. It has provisions requiring banks
to take steps to prevent money laundering, allows law-enforcement

agencies to gather information from banks and creates longer prison terms for money laundering and smuggling.

Title IV - This section has provisions intended to strengthen border security. It authorizes increased funding for border patrols, customs officials, and immigration officials. Foreigners with ties to terrorist organizations are banned from entering the United States, and Title IV expands the monitoring of foreign students.

Title V - The most important part of Title V is the use of National Security Letters (NSL). An NSL is a demand for the release of information and paperwork related to a person under investigation. The Patriot Act makes NSLs much stronger, allows them to be used against U.S. citizens and contains a gag order preventing the target of the NSL from ever knowing about it or telling anyone else about it. There is no judicial review or need for probable cause when an NSL is requested and issued.

Title VI - This section contains provisions for providing financial compensation to victims of terrorism and their families.

Title VII - Authorization and budgeting for increased sharing of information between law-enforcement agencies and jurisdictions are contained in this section.

Title VIII - This portion of the Patriot Act adds several crimes to the list of things considered acts of terrorism, including attacking a mass transit system, using a biological weapon, supporting terrorism and computer hacking. The penalties for terrorist crimes are also increased.

Title IX - This section creates a method for the sharing of national intelligence information among government agencies.

Title X - The final section of the Patriot Act contains a number of relatively minor, miscellaneous provisions.

Note: Anyone think the government does not know everything they are doing every minute of the day anyway?

The USA Freedom Act

The USA Freedom Act is a law that was originally introduced in both houses of the U.S. Congress on October 29, 2013. Following the expiration of several provisions of the Patriot Act, the Act was passed on June 2, 2015. The title of the act is a ten-letter backronym (USA FREEDOM) that stands for "Uniting and Strengthening America by

Fulfilling Rights and Ending Eavesdropping, Dragnet-collection and Online Monitoring Act."

When the bill was re-introduced in the 114th Congress (2015-2016), it was described by the bill sponsors as "a balanced approach" while being questioned for extending the Patriot Act through the end of 2019. Supporters of the bill said that the House Intelligence Committee and House leadership would insist on reauthorizing all Patriot Act powers except bulk collection under Section 215 of the Patriot Act. Critics assert that mass surveillance of the content of Americans' communication will continue under Section 702 of FISA which does not expire until 2017 and Executive Order 12333 due to the "unstoppable surveillance-industrial complex" despite the fact that a bipartisan majority of the House had previously voted to close backdoor mass surveillance.

Section 215 bulk collection authority expired June 1, 2015, but in the event that the Obama administration is successful in restarting it, USA Freedom enacts a ban on such collection activities which "shall take effect on the date that is 180 days after the date of the enactment of this Act".

According to supporters of the USA Freedom Act, the USA Freedom Act was meant to end the bulk collection of Americans' metadata by the NSA, end the secret laws created by the FISA court, and introduce a "Special Advocate" to represent public and privacy matters. However, opponents of the bill cite that the USA Freedom Act does allow the bulk collection of Americans' metadata by phone companies, which is then accessible by the NSA; it also does not address other laws that have purportedly challenged Americans' Fourth Amendment rights. Other proposed changes included limits to programs like PRISM, which retains Americans' Internet data, and greater transparency by allowing companies such as Google and Facebook to disclose information about government requests for information. http://bit.ly/1N43rxT

To quote Judge Napolitano on the Freedom Act - Judge Napolitano has much to say about the so-called FREEDOM Act. Let's listen to the good Judge and lover of Liberty now …

"In their continuous efforts to create the impression that the government is doing something to keep Americans safe, politicians in Washington have misled and lied to the public. They have violated their oaths to uphold the Constitution. They have created a false sense of security. And they have dispatched and re-dispatched 60,000 Federal agents to intercept the telephone calls, text messages and emails of all Americans all the time.

'In the process, while publicly claiming they only acquire identifying metadata — the time, date, location, duration, telephone numbers and email addresses of communications — they have, in fact, surreptitiously gained access to the content of these communications."

The Patriot Act has failed to protect our freedom. The Boston Marathon Bombing and the Fort Hood Massacre are good examples of that. The data collection process by the government is too massive that the government cannot sift through it quickly or effectively enough to gain intel to stop such events from happening. This just gives Americans a false sense of security.

So why do it? (1) The Feds want to give the Americans the idea they are doing something even though their spying has failed to increase our safety; and (2) "It also has failed to protect our freedoms. The Constitution requires probable cause as a precondition for all search warrants. That is a level of evidence about the place to be searched or the person or thing to be seized sufficient to induce a judge to conclude that a crime probably has been committed. Without this probable cause requirement, nothing would stop the government from searching and seizing whatever it wants. Yet that is where we are today. The NSA's unconstitutional standard of "government need" reinstitutes the general warrants — search where you wish and seize what you find — which the Fourth Amendment was written to prohibit." http://bit.ly/1ljDHok

Both the Patriot Act and the Freedom Act, the substitute law enacted by Congress, do away with the probable cause requirement. Both of those laws permit the Foreign Intelligence Surveillance Act (FISA) court to issue general warrants based on the government's needs, rather than probable cause. It is the government-need standard, which is no standard at all that has resulted in spying on all persons all the time.

XXIII

RELIGION IN AMERICA

We Recognize No Sovereign but God, and no King
but Jesus! [April 18, 1775]" –John Hancock.

On the one hand, Obama claims to be a Christian, but all of
his actions say that he is a Muslim. And he speaks against
the Christians and for the Muslims. What has happened since this
Administration has been in office?

In *United States v. MacIntosh* (1931) The Supreme Court declared,
"We are a Christian people…according to one another the equal right
of religious freedom, and acknowledging with the reverence the duty
of obedience to God."

"The black robed tyrants are like a bunch of pigeons picking at peas.
They pick the cases they do not want to hear and choose the ones they
do. It is their duty and obligation to interpret law against crime, not
promote crime (1 Peter 2:14)."

The members of our military are called on to resign and sometimes
fired for using the name of God in a speech. Often one has gone so
far as to sought to be "aggressively and very visibly brought to justice
for his unforgivable crimes and transgressions" by a court-martial,
adding that any other service members who helped him should be

investigated and punished "to the full extent of military law." http://
www.teaparty.org/push-court-martial-general-mentioning-god-
99353/#sthash.hu7FDINt.dpuf

Not only does this Administration want America to change their
religious views towards gay rights, but gender identity is now to be
taught in schools. Your children are going to be taught that there is no
such thing as a 100% girl or 100% boy.

Long-time conservative activist, nationally syndicated columnist,
and best-selling author Phyllis Schlafly said that gay marriage advocates
are targeting Christian businesses, such as bakeries and wedding
planners, and not targeting similar Muslim businesses because the
ultimate goal of homosexual marriage is to "wipe out the Christian
religion." http://bit.ly/1NOF2zQ

"Human beings are created male and female. But the current
transgender ideology goes way beyond that. They're telling us you can
be both genders, you can be no gender, you can be a gender that you
make up for yourself. And we're supposed to affirm all of it."

"Students will be provided definitions for sexual orientation terms
heterosexuality, homosexuality and bisexuality; and the gender identity
term transgender," the district's recommendations state. "Emphasis will
be placed on recognizing that everyone is experiencing changes and
the role of respectful, inclusive language in promoting an environment
free of bias and discrimination."

Eighth graders will be taught that individual identity "occurs over
a lifetime and includes the component of sexual orientation and
gender identity."

"Individual identity will also be described as having four parts –
biological gender, gender identity (includes transgender), gender
role, and sexual orientation (includes heterosexual, bisexual,
and homosexual)."

The district will also introduce young teenagers to the "concept that
sexuality is a broader spectrum." By tenth grade, they will be taught
that one's sexuality "develops throughout a lifetime."

"Emphasis will be placed on an understanding that there is a
broader, boundless, and fluid spectrum of sexuality that is developed
throughout a lifetime," the document states. "Sexual orientation and

gender identity terms will be discussed with focus on appreciation for individual differences."

'To make matters worse, Lafferty contends parents will not be able to opt their children out of the classes because the lessons will be a part of the mandatory health curriculum." http://fxn.ws/1KcETTN

I rarely quote an entire article, but this one bears repeating, and you will probably find it quite interesting:

"Author and activist Ryan Sorba recently released an undercover video showing "gays" freely contradicting prevailing dogma on the subject of homosexuality. Shot at various "gay" bars in the very LGBT-friendly desert oasis of Palm Springs, California, Sorba posed as a homosexual in order to elicit honest answers to a very important question. The question was neither difficult nor misleading, and it wasn't a "gotcha" question as some have suggested, but it was a question that few homosexuals would answer truthfully unless they believed they were speaking off the record.

"Do you believe being gay is strictly genetic?" Sorba asked. The responses he received certainly didn't carry the Dan Savage seal of approval.

'Three male homosexuals connected the genesis of their sexuality to childhood sexual abuse. All of the men volunteered this information without any prompting from Sorba. Another man admitted that he turned to homosexuality because he was "depressed [and] stressed." After a bad breakup with a girlfriend he loved, he found little satisfaction in relationships with women, but then men propositioned him, and he began to experiment. When asked if "being gay" was strictly genetic, he said it was not. "The thing is I was never gay. Now I am, and I'm proud. I am who I am now." When Sorba asked another man, "So you believe you became gay from the culture?" he responded, "Yeah, but I'm proud of it." An older man declared categorically that "None of us was born gay." One woman claims that she had a girlfriend who became a lesbian only after she was raped at gunpoint by her boyfriend. When Sorba said that his sister went the other way—from lesbian to heterosexual—the woman didn't doubt that such a thing was possible. "That's her choice," she replied.

'Her "choice." That's really quite queer, I mean strange, because the overwhelming media message today is that sexuality is genetically determined and, therefore no more of a choice than eye color or height. Furthermore, it can't be changed no matter how much one tries. The burden of proof never rests on the proponents of these dubious assertions, but on the rest of us to prove that they aren't true.

'The idea that people choose homosexuality, or that it might be the result of negative environmental factors such as sexual trauma, is often portrayed as the ramblings of clueless straight people who are almost uniformly religious and uncomfortable with modern science; people like Michele Bachman and Ben Carson, for example. How odd it is then to hear homosexuals talking very much like Ben Carson, or at least admitting that he's right.

'This just in: Sex is a volitional behavior. How anyone can be shocked this revelation is beyond me.

'I first became aware of Ryan Sorba and his work in 2008 when he lectured on "the Born Gay Hoax" at Smith College in Northampton, Massachusetts. Smith is known as a citadel of lesbianism, so I knew Mr. Sorba would receive a chilly welcome, yet even I was shocked to see how he was treated. At the time, I was naïve to the homosexual movement's fascistic tendencies. No longer.

'The grotesque horde of shrieking lesbians closely resembled a lynch mob. They crawled in through the windows, stormed the podium and shouted Sorba down. The police stood idly by, refusing to arrest anyone for disorderly conduct. Ironically, one halfwit student in the crowd carried a sign that read: "Lesbian Cuz I Wanna. Oh What Now?" Apparently she didn't understand that she was actually reinforcing Sorba's point. And to think that in the old days you had to be smart to go to Smith.

'The Gaystapo thinks they won that battle because they forced the "bigot" to shut up and go home. That's always a win in their book. Yet I believe Sorba emerged victorious because he exposed the homofascist horde as weak and insecure. Their panicky response made it clear that the central idea of their movement—that they're "born that way"—is built on a precariously shaky foundation. They were terrified that, given the chance, Sorba would demolish their argument.

'Why is the genetic basis of homosexuality so important? Plenty of homosexuals will admit that the "born that way" message carries certain political benefits that are just too important to forgo. Dr. Lillian

Faderman, a professor of lesbian literature, let slip an inconvenient truth in the pages of *The Advocate*, a homosexual newspaper. "The concept of gay and lesbian identity may be nothing but a social construct," she wrote, "but it has been crucial, enabling us to become a political movement and demand the rights that are due to us as a minority. What becomes of our political movement if we openly acknowledge that sexuality is flexible and fluid, that gay and lesbian does not signify 'a people' but rather a 'sometime behavior'?"

'What Lillian Faderman was expressing in the above passage is her cognitive dissonance. She understands that two types of behavior do not create two classes of people. Deep down inside she knows that the "bigots" are right, that her sexual conduct is just that—conduct, not identity. But she also wants society to heed the demands of a well-organized and well-funded political movement, which requires her to publicly advocate an idea she knows to be a lie.

'If you listen to what homosexuals say when they think they're speaking to a friendly audience, you'll find that they fret a lot about what should be said in public and what is better kept entre nous. Certain lies must be preserved because they have the power to liberate. While most people have probably heard that "The truth shall set you free," homosexuals take exactly the opposite position. They believe that falsehoods will set them free, which explains why they despise truth-tellers more than the plague.

'Benoit Denizet-Lewis is another homosexual journalist/activist (what's the difference these days?) who understands the importance of staying on script. In an article about bisexuality, the "gay"-identified reporter admitted that he feels uncomfortable with ambiguity in sexual labels. "That kind of publicly shared uncertainty is catnip to the Christian Right…As out gay men and lesbians, after all, we're supposed to be sure — we're supposed to be 'born this way.' It's a politically important position (one that's helping us achieve marriage equality and other rights), but it leaves little space for out gay men to muddy the waters…"

'Does Denizet-Lewis ever lose any sleep on account of his hypocrisy? I doubt it. He's essentially admitting that the Ryan Sorbas of this world are onto something, but because they're evil bigots, he is duty-bound to perpetuate the "born gay" charade.

'What Denizet-Lewis has in common with Dr. Faderman, and what they both have in common with prominent homosexual opinion leaders, is that they all believe in the power of the Liberating Lie. Such is the thinking of the reprobate mind. Their lies are politically calculated and it appears they've calculated well because their shameless fibbing is winning the culture wars." http://bit.ly/1OaKxTN

Obama must constantly stir up Americans. When the Pope decided to visit Cuba and the United States, Obama invited him to the White House and promptly extended invitations to a transgender activists, a gay Episcopal Bishop, and the leader of a group of nuns that want changes to Catholic teachings on abortion and euthanasia. Of course the Vatican is not happy with America's attempt to lecture the Pope about catechesism and Catholics and the rest of America is not happy with the lack of class and dignity and outright abomination displayed by the leader of this country towards a holy man.

Pope Francis has said that he doesn't believe in judging persons and is ready to welcome anyone in Christ's name, he has also said that Catholics do not accept the modern mentality of transgenderism and once said that gay marriage is the devil's "attempt to destroy God's plan."

This year the Vatican officially prohibited transgender persons from being baptismal godparents posing as the opposite sex from which they were born. The Vatican Doctrinal Congregation said that "transsexual behavior publicly reveals an attitude contrary to the moral imperative of resolving the problem of one's sexual identity according to the truth of one's sexuality."

"An intermediary for several of the invitations to greet the Pope was Vivian Taylor, a 30-year-old male transvestite who acted as Executive Director of Integrity USA, a homosexual and transgender activist wing of the Episcopal Church, until last March.

"A few months ago I received an invitation from the White House to attend the reception for Pope Francis," Taylor told CNS News. "I was told I could bring several friends with me," adding that he is "glad we can bring some LGBT representation to the event." http://bit.ly/1LyIxTZ

Then there is the matter of religion in schools. A little fifth grader in Florida received a Bible as a Christmas gift. He took it to school with him. His teacher told him that Bibles were not allowed in her classroom and instructed him not to bring it back to school in the future. The boy asked her to contact his father. The father was unable to get the ruling overturned. He went to the Liberty Institute.

This is strictly about a little boy being able to read a religious book during his free time at school. The case has not yet been settled. : http://bit.ly/1XKRTYu.

Retired US Marine Jordan Matson joined the YPG Kurdish fighters to fight ISIS in September 2014. Jordan said that there are 40-50 Americans fighting with Kurdish forces against ISIS.

He also said the Kurds are very hospitable to Christians. British ex-soldiers are also fighting with Kurdish forces against the Islamic State.

James Hughes, 26, and Jamie Read, 24, are fighting alongside other foreign volunteers with the Kurdish People's Protection Units.

This week Obama gave a green light to Turkey to bomb the Kurds. Turkish jets struck camps belonging to Kurdish militants in northern Iraq this weekend. This was Turkey's first strike on the Kurds since a 2013 peace deal. Americans and British soldiers are fighting with Kurds against ISIS.

Which side is Obama on? http://bit.ly/1XKRKV4

The Reverend Franklin Graham was speaking at the First Baptist Church in Jacksonville, Florida when he said America will not come back.

He said:

The American Dream ended (on November 6th, 2012) in Ohio. The second term of Barack Obama will be the final nail in the coffin for the legacy of the white Christian males who discovered, explored, pioneered, settled and developed the greatest Republic in the history of mankind.

A coalition of Blacks, Latinos, Feminists, Government Workers, Union Members, Environmental Extremists, The Media, Hollywood, uninformed young people, the "forever needy," the chronically unemployed, illegal aliens and other "fellow travelers" have ended Norman Rockwell's America.

The Cocker Spaniel is off the front porch... The Pit Bull is in the back yard. The American Constitution has been replaced with Saul Alinsky's "Rules for Radicals" and Chicago shyster, David Axelrod, along with international Socialist George Soros will be pulling the strings on their beige puppet to bring us Act 2 of the New World Order.

Our side ran two candidates who couldn't even win their own home states, and Chris Christie helped Obama over the top with a glowing "post Sandy" tribute that elevated the "Commander-in-Chief" to Mother Teresa status. (Aside: with the way the polls were run, he didn't need any help!)

People like me are completely politically irrelevant and I will never again comment on or concern myself with the aforementioned coalition which has surrendered our culture, our heritage and our traditions without a shot being fired.

You will never again out-vote these people. It will take individual acts of defiance and massive displays of civil disobedience to get back the rights we have allowed them to take away. It will take Zealots, not moderates and shy, not reach-across-the-aisle RINOs, to right this ship and restore our beloved country to its former status.

Those who come after us will have to risk their lives, their fortunes and their sacred honor to bring back the Republic that this generation has timidly frittered away due to "white guilt" and political correctness.

An American Veteran......... Semper-Fi

XXIV

JADE-HELM AND CONCENTRATION CAMPS

There are Jade Helm exercises going on in seven Western states. Some are hostile exercises and some permissive.

Coast-to-coast sinister government vehicles park outside of a Wal-Mart store and elsewhere as the government's agenda known as Jade Helm unfolds in America. Military convoys are seen in an endless series of utube videos, the footage of the first video being the courtesy of the Department of Defense, who is now pushing on the public their martial law plans right out in the open so that the public will see it and accept what is coming.

"These are the U.S. Marines from 1st Battalion, 5th Marine Regiment, 1st Marine Division practicing "assault support tactics" in Yuma Arizona as part of a 7 week exercise prior to the Jade Helm 15 Exercises. It is "Pretty hard to miss the children behind the same fencing as the mock demonstrators." http://bit.ly/1ljCM7b "Role players chant for food and water during alarming exercise

'(Infowars) – Alarming video footage from a U.S. Marines training drill which took place in Arizona last month shows armed troops chasing down unruly citizens inside a mock internment camp while role players chant for food and water.

'The exercise, which involved U.S. Marines from 1st Battalion, 5th Marine Regiment, 1st Marine Division, took place on April 18 in Yuma, Arizona and revolved around "assault support tactics" training.

'The drill was part of, "standardized tactical training and certification of unit instructor qualifications to support Marine Aviation Training and Readiness," according to the description accompanying the video.

'In plain English, the exercise was about subduing, arresting and incarcerating irate citizens during a martial law-style scenario.

'The video shows Marines landing in helicopters on a field next to a busy highway. Locals watch the exercise behind a perimeter fence while role players prepare to take part in the drill.

'The Marines then practice apprehending unruly citizens, one of whom is carried away on a stretcher.

'One of the role players simulates attempting to escape the enclosure before he is chased down and handcuffed by an armed Marine.

'Other role players are then heard chanting "food and water" while rattling the perimeter fence as Marines look on. The video then shows more role players being chased and hauled away. One of the role players is subsequently heard to shout, "let me out!"

'More physical struggles and chases ensue between role players and Marines before some of the citizens receive mock medical treatment, with one Marine heard describing one of the injuries as "gunshot wounds to the chest."

'Some of the victims are then loaded onto the chopper before the video clip ends.

'The Marines will undoubtedly claim that these exercises are to prepare for overseas combat and occupation missions, but U.S. Army manuals have made it clear that such operations also apply to the Continental United States (CONUS), and will be used against American citizens during a national emergency.

'Concerns over such exercises have been raised after the announcement of Jade Helm, a nationwide military exercise set to begin in July during which troops will operate undercover amongst local populations.

'Innumerable videos showing similar drills taking place across the United States have emerged in recent months, although this footage is easily the most alarming.

'Another video out of Fort Lauderdale, Florida which emerged in March, also showed military and law enforcement practicing the internment of citizens during martial-law style training." http://bit.ly/1QnBqDJ

In my book *The Lyin Kings*, I told you about the 800 FEMA Concentration Camps throughout the United States and told you where each one was located and what each camp contained. Each camp is presently manned and ready to receive occupants and now the government, which has purchased millions of rounds of ammunition is practicing for when the administration will call Martial Law and begin rounding up citizens for the camps. Any citizen declared a terrorist can now be beheaded as the government has just purchased 30,000 guillotines.

The FEMA camps have railroad facilities, as well as roads running to and from the detention camps. Many of them also have an airport nearby. The majority of the camps can house upwards of 20,000 prisoners. The largest one is just outside of Fairbanks, Alaska. It is a mental health facility and can hold two million occupants.

With the stroke of the President's pen, the following orders can be enacted at once.

EXECUTIVE ORDER 10990 allows the government to take over all modes of transportation and control of highways and seaports.

EXECUTIVE ORDER 10995 allows the government to seize and control the communication media.

EXECUTIVE ORDER 10997 allows the government to take over all electrical power, gas, petroleum, fuels and minerals.

EXECUTIVE ORDER 10998 allows the government to seize all means of transportation, including personal cars, trucks or vehicles of any kind and total control over all highways, seaports, and waterways.

EXECUTIVE ORDER 10999 allows the government to take over all food resources and farms.

EXECUTIVE ORDER 11000 allows the government to mobilize civilians into work brigades under government supervision.

EXECUTIVE ORDER 11001 allows the government to take over all health, education and welfare functions.

EXECUTIVE ORDER 11002 designates the Postmaster General to operate a national registration of all persons.

EXECUTIVE ORDER 11003 allows the government to take over all airports and aircraft, including commercial aircraft.

EXECUTIVE ORDER 11004 allows the Housing and Finance Authority to relocate communities, build new housing with public funds, designate areas to be abandoned, and establish new locations for populations.

EXECUTIVE ORDER 11005 allows the government to take over railroads, inland waterways and public storage facilities.

EXECUTIVE ORDER 11051 specifies the responsibility of the Office of Emergency Planning and gives authorization to put all Executive Orders into effect in times of increased international tensions and economic or financial crisis.

EXECUTIVE ORDER 11310 grants authority to the Department of Justice to enforce the plans set out in Executive Orders, to institute industrial support, to establish judicial and legislative liaison, to control all aliens, to operate penal and correctional institutions, and to advise and assist the President.

EXECUTIVE ORDER 11049 assigns emergency preparedness function to federal departments and agencies, consolidating 21 operative Executive Orders issued over a fifteen-year period.

EXECUTIVE ORDER 11921 allows the Federal Emergency Preparedness Agency to develop plans to establish control over the mechanisms of production and distribution, of energy sources, wages, salaries, credit and the flow of money in U.S. financial institution in any undefined national emergency. It also provides that when a state of emergency is declared by the President, Congress cannot review the action for six months. The Federal Emergency Management Agency has broad powers in every aspect of the nation. General Frank Salzedo, chief of FEMA's Civil Security Division stated in a 1983 conference that he saw FEMA's role as a "new frontier in the protection of individual and governmental leaders from assassination, and of civil and military installations from sabotage and/or attack, as well as prevention of dissident groups from gaining access to U.S. opinion, or a global audience in times of crisis." FEMA's powers were consolidated by President Carter to incorporate the National Security Act of 1947 allows for the strategic relocation of industries, services, government and other essential economic activities, and to rationalize the requirements for manpower, resources, and production facilities. 1950 Defense Production Act gives the President sweeping powers over all aspects of the economy. Act of August 29, 1916, authorizes the Secretary of the Army, in time of war, to take possession of any transportation system for transporting troops, material, or any other purpose related to the emergency. International Emergency Economic Powers Act enables the President to seize the property of a foreign country or national. These powers were transferred to FEMA in a sweeping consolidation in 1979.

Note: Special Agent Ted Gunderson wrote the original of this article prior to his death in 2011. http://bit.ly/1OGHNlE, http://bit.ly/1m4xA7k, and http://bit.ly/1NAQB7w

XXV

GUNS AND THE SECOND AMENDMENT – AGAIN

(A tribute to two CIA Officers)

Obama does not intend to give up on taking away your guns or at least making it as difficult as possible for you to own one. The Justice Department is working on more than a dozen new gun control regulations it plans on implementing apart from Congress. Some will be put in place by November of 2015 and others by the end of the Obama Administration term.

The regulations range from restrictions on high-powered pistols to gun storage requirements and new criteria for people who do not qualify for gun ownership. For instance, anyone convicted of domestic violence – could be someone who spanked his kid, yelled at his wife, or a wife who slapped her husband.

The new regulation also includes mental health criteria such as someone who has seen a psychologist because most mentally ill people pose no threat to society, the new regulation will actually become a snare for masses of mostly harmless individuals.

It would appear one of the U.S. Benghazi secrets was that the U.S. was running guns between Benghazi to Syria before the attack on the U.S. Consulate on September 11, 2012. As you will recall, Ambassador Stevens and three others were killed during that terrorist attack.

The following story was given by a cousin of Ambassador Stevens, Dr. Charles R. Roots, Senior Pastor, Former Staff Sergeant, USMC Captain, U. S. Navy Chaplain Corps (Ret.).

"A week out the Embassy in Tripoli began receiving multiple tips about an Al Qaeda cell in the area planning an attack on 9/11 in response to the killing of Bin Laden. For the next several days, the State Dept. and WH were asked for a security force and were denied at least six times. Ambassador Stevens and his team were given the all clear that the Consulate in Benghazi was safe and there was no need for a security force other than his 3 personal guards (One being my cousin) and a few Libyans who were not armed. Then the attack and murders occurred.

Immediately the White House claimed it was a protest gone bad over a you tube video. Obama made a quick speech in the Rose Garden on Sept.12 before catching a plane to Vegas to campaign. He made a generic statement at the end of his speech after placing the blame on an overheated protest over the video. He said: "No act of terror will shake the resolve of America."

"Later that day and over the next 2 days, the liberal media began saying Ambassador Stevens and the other 3 men died of smoke inhalation.

'This was not the case.

'Out of respect for my cousin, I'm not going to be specific about his murder. However, Ambassador Stevens was brutally murdered. His genitals were cut off, he was sodomized and beaten and cut and stabbed and burned. He was drug thru the streets and left for dead.

'This is eyewitness testimony of a local Dr. who found the Ambassador in a ditch and tried to save his life. He had no idea who he was.

'The other 3 men, including my cousin, met similar fates. And deaths due to smoke inhalation is a 100% fabricated LIE.

'The next week I drove my aunt and Uncle and 2 others to DC to receive his body. We met with Hillary, Panetta, and Susan Rice. ALL of whom apologized and said it was a protest gone bad over a video and exited the area.

'Next, Obama entered with the same story and didn't apologize and wasn't sympathetic. My aunt cried to this man and all he did was hand her flowers and walk away.

'I tried to get his attention, but didn't. I got upset and yelled liar to him, he kept walking.

'Then a secret service agent grabbed my arm and led me to a room where I was held till the proceedings were over.

'America, I saw firsthand how cold this man is. What kind of liar he is. Most of you haven't a clue about this tyrant and yet you support him. And act like every word he says is Gospel.

'These murders and the fast and furious cover-ups make Watergate look like a kid who told his BFF's secret to the class.

'THIS PART YOU DON'T KNOW, BUT SHOULD. AMERICAN VALOR, BENGHAZI , LIBYA:

'The stunning part of this story is that Tyrone Woods and Glen Doherty killed 60 of the attacking force.

'Once the compound was overrun, the attackers were incensed to discover that just two men had inflicted so much death and destruction.

'The news has been full of the attacks on our embassies throughout the Muslim world, and in particular, the deaths of Ambassador Chris Stevens; Officer Sean Smith; CIA Contractor, Tyrone S. Woods; and CIA Contractor Glen Doherty in Benghazi, Libya.

'However, there's a little known story of incredible bravery, heroics, and courage that should be the top story.

'So what actually happened at the U.S. Embassy in Libya?

'We are learning more about this every day. Ambassador Stevens and Foreign Service officer Sean Smith, along with administrative staff, were working out of temporary quarters due to the fact that in the spring of 2011 during the so-called Arab Spring, the United States cut ties with then president Moammar Gadhafi.

'Our embassy was looted and ransacked, causing it to be unusable. It is still in a state of disrepair.

'Security for embassies and their personnel is to be provided by the host nation.

'Since Libya has gone through a civil war of sorts in the past 18 months, the current government is very unstable, and therefore, unreliable.

'A well-organized attack by radical Muslims was planned specifically targeting the temporary U.S. Embassy building. The Libyan security force that was in place to protect our people deserted their post, or joined the attacking force. Either way, our people were in a real fix.

'And it should be noted that Ambassador Stevens had mentioned on more than one occasion to Secretary of State Hillary Clinton, that he was quite concerned for his personal safety and the welfare of his people.

'It is thought that Ambassador Stevens was on a hit list. A short distance from the American compound, two Americans were sleeping. They were in Libya as independent contractors working an assignment totally unrelated to our embassy. They also happened to be former Navy Seals.

'When they heard the noise coming from the attack on our embassy, as you would expect from highly trained warriors, they ran to the fight. Apparently, they had no weapons, but seeing the Libyan guards dropping their guns in their haste in fleeing the scene, Tyrone Woods and Glen Doherty snatched up several of these discarded weapons and prepared to defend the American compound.

'Not knowing exactly what was taking place, the two Seals set up a defensive perimeter. Unfortunately, Ambassador Stevens was already gravely injured, and Foreign Service officer, Sean Smith, was dead.

'However, due to their quick action and suppressive fire, twenty administrative personnel in the embassy were able to escape to safety. (But all have been silenced and kept away from congress and all investigations on Benghazi!)

'Eventually, these two courageous men were overwhelmed by the sheer numbers brought against them, an enemy force numbering between 100 to 200 attackers which came in two waves.

'But the stunning part of the story is that Tyrone Woods and Glen Doherty killed 60 of the attacking force. Once the compound was overrun, the attackers were incensed to discover that just two men had inflicted so much death and destruction.

'As it became apparent to these selfless heroes, they were definitely going to lose their lives unless some reinforcements showed up in a hurry. As we know now, that was not to be. I'm fairly certain they knew they were going to die in this gunfight, but not before they took a whole lot of bad guys with them!

'Consider these tenets of the Navy SEAL Code:

1) Loyalty to Country, Team and Teammate,
2) Serve with Honor and Integrity On and Off the Battlefield,
3) Ready to Lead, Ready to Follow, Never Quit,
4) Take responsibility for your actions and the actions of your teammates,
5) Excel as Warriors through Discipline and Innovation,
6) Train for War, Fight to Win, Defeat our Nation's Enemies, and...
7) Earn your Trident every day.

'Thank you, Tyrone and Glen. To the very last breath, you both lived up to the SEAL Code. You served all of us well. You were courageous in the face of certain death. And Tyrone, even though you never got to hold your newborn son, he will grow up knowing the character and quality of his father, a man among men who sacrificed himself defending others.

'Dr. Charles R. Roots Senior Pastor, Former Staff Sergeant, USMC Captain, U. S. Navy Chaplain Corps (Ret.)"

A Defense Intelligence Agency report dated September 12, 2012, details that the attack on the compound had been carefully planned by the BOCAR terrorist group "to kill as many Americans as possible." The document was sent to then-Secretary of State Hillary Clinton, then-Defense Secretary Leon Panetta, the Joint Chiefs of Staff and the Obama White House National Security Council. The heavily redacted Defense Department "information report" says that the attack on the Benghazi facility "was planned and executed by The Brigades of the Captive Omar Abdul Rahman (BCOAR)." The intention was to attack the consulate and to kill as many Americans as possible to seek revenge for U.S. killing of Aboyahiye ((ALALIBY)) in Pakistan and in memorial of the 11 September 2001 attacks on the World Trade Center buildings.

The DOD documents also contain the first official documentation that the Obama administration knew that weapons were being shipped from the Port of Benghazi to rebel troops in Syria. An October 2012 report confirms:

Weapons from the former Libya military stockpiles were shipped from the port of Benghazi, Libya to the Port of Banias and the Port of Borj Islam, Syria. The weapons shipped during late-August 2012 were Sniper rifles, RPG's, and 125 mm and 155mm howitzers missiles.

The DIA document further details:

The weapons shipped from Syria during late-August 2012 were Sniper rifles, RPG's and 125mm and 155mm howitzers missiles. The numbers for each weapon were estimated to be: 500 Sniper rifles, 100 RPG launchers with 300 total rounds, and approximately 400 howitzers missiles [200 ea – 125mm and 200ea – 155 mm.]

Another DIA report, written in August 2012 (the same time period the U.S. was monitoring weapons flows from Libya to Syria), said that the opposition in Syria was driven by al Qaeda and other extremist Muslim groups: "the Salafist, the Muslim Brotherhood, and AQI are the major forces driving the insurgency in Syria." The growing sectarian direction of the war was predicted to have dire consequences for Iraq, which included the "grave danger" of the rise of ISIS: http://bit.ly/1ONiwnV

Fox News reported that the United States was sending guns to Banias and Borj Islam, Syria before the terrorist attack. http://bit.ly/1YRg8Bk

Now we all know that President Obama is a Democrat and his cabinet members are Democrats, and all Democrats will hate these next few lines.

"In 1865, a Democrat shot and killed Abraham Lincoln, President of the United States.

In 1881, a left wing radical Democrat shot James Garfield, President of the United States who later died from the wound.

In 1963, a radical left wing socialist shot and killed John F. Kennedy, President of the United States.

In 1975, a left wing radical Democrat fired shots at Gerald Ford, President of the United States.

In 1983, a registered Democrat shot and wounded Ronald Reagan, President of the United States.

In 1984, James Hubert, a disgruntled Democrat shot and killed twenty-two people in a McDonalds restaurant.

In 1986, Patrick Sherrill, a disgruntled Democrat shot and killed fifteen people in an Oklahoma post office.

In 1990, James Pough, a disgruntled Democrat shot and killed ten people at a GMAC office.

In 1991, George Hennard, a disgruntled Democrat, shot and killed 23 people in a Luby's cafeteria in Killeen, TX.

In 1995, James Daniel Simpson, a disgruntled Democrat, shot and killed five coworkers in a Texas laboratory.

In 1999, Larry Asbrook, a disgruntled Democrat, shot and killed eight people at a church service.

In 2001, a left wing radical Democrat fired shots at the White House in a failed attempt to kill George W. Bush, President of the US.

In 2003, Douglas Williams, a disgruntled Democrat, shot and killed seven people at a Lockheed Martin plant.

In 2007, a registered Democrat named Seung - Hui Cho, shot and killed 32 people at Virginia Tech.

In 2010, a mentally ill registered Democrat named Jared Lee Loughner, shot Rep. Gabrielle Giffords and killed six others.

In 2011 a registered Democrat named James Holmes, went into a movie theater and shot and killed 12 people.

In 2012 Andrew Engeldinger, a disgruntled Democrat shot and killed seven people in Minneapolis.

In 2013, a registered Democrat named Adam Lanza, shot and killed 26 people at a school in Newtown, CT.

As recently as Sept 2013, an angry Democrat shot 12 at a Navy ship yard.

Clearly, there is a problem with Democrats and guns. Not one NRA member, Tea Party member, or Republican conservative was involved in any of these shootings and murders. SOLUTION: Maybe it should be illegal for Democrats and Liberals to own guns." It is Democrats that are attempting to remove all guns from the American people.

Behind this façade of a man of the people is an enemy with a threatening agenda. His platform of hope and change has brought about job loss, explosive health care prices, massive unemployment, the greatest racial divide in America's history and now gun confiscation. Obama's treasonous acts and illegal actions must be stopped by Congress. He has flagrantly abused his power and continuously lied to the people. He has abused our taxpayer dollars by funding terrorists, handing guns to criminals and drug cartels and granting defacto amnesty to illegals.

Obama is already on his march towards Martial Law. Jade-Helm has had their practice sessions. All Fema Concentration Camps are manned and ready for the occupants to arrive.

What still excites me is the Second Amendment. What excites me are all of the hunters in America.

A blogger added up the deer license sales in just a handful of states and arrived at a striking conclusion: There were over 600,000 hunters this past season in the state of Wisconsin. Allow me to restate that number: 600,000! Can you grasp that number? Wisconsin's hunters are the eighth largest army in the world. (That is more men, and women, under arms than in Iran. More than France and Germany combined.) These men, deployed to the woods of a single American state, Wisconsin, to hunt with firearms, and NO ONE WAS KILLED. Obama cannot stand to have that many men and women armed, let alone in a single state.

And I would guess some of them were probably even Democrats. 600,000 men and women in one State of these United States are armed. Now do you understand why Obama is so nervous? He cannot control these men and women.

But that number pales in comparison to the 750,000 who hunted the woods of Pennsylvania, and Michigan's 700,000 hunters, all of whom returned home safely after hunting.

That is over two million hunters in just three states carrying guns, and no one was killed.

Then you can toss in a quarter of a million hunters in West Virginia and it literally establishes the fact that the hunters of those four states alone would comprise the largest army in the world.

And then add in the total number of hunters in the other 46 states. It is millions more.

My point?

America will forever be safe from foreign invasion with that kind of home-grown firepower! Hunting... it is not just a way to fill the freezer. It is a matter of national security.

That's why all enemies, foreign and domestic, want to see us disarmed. Food for thought, when next we consider gun control.

Overall it's true, so if we disregard some assumptions that hunters don't possess the same skills as soldiers, the question would still remain.

What army of 2 million would want to face 30 million, 40 million, or 50 million armed citizens? For the sake of our freedom, don't ever allow gun control or confiscation of guns.

This is exactly why the Japanese did not attack inland during World War II.

I found the following murder statistics quite interesting.

World Murder Statistics - From the World Health Organization

The latest Murder Statistics for the world: Murders per 100,000 citizens per year.

Honduras 91.6
El Salvador 69.2
Cote d'Ivoire 56.9
Jamaica 52.2
Venezuela 45.1
Belize 41.4
US Virgin Islands 39.2
Guatemala 38.5
Saint Kitts and Nevis 38.2

Zambia 38.0
Uganda 36.3
Malawi 36.0
Lesotho 35.2
Trinidad and Tobago 35.2
Colombia 33.4
South Africa 31.8
Congo 30.8
Central African Republic 29.3
Bahamas 27.4
Puerto Rico 26.2
Saint Lucia 25.2
Dominican Republic 25.0
Tanzania 24.5
Sudan 24.2
Saint Vincent and the Grenadines 22.9
Ethiopia 22.5
Guinea 22.5
Dominica 22.1
Burundi 21.7
Democratic Republic of the Congo 21.7
Panama 21.6
Brazil 21.0
Equatorial Guinea 20.7
Guinea-Bissau 20.2
Kenya 20.1
Kyrgyzstan 20.1
Cameroon 19.7
Montserrat 19.7
Greenland 19.2
Angola 19.0
Guyana 18.6
Burkina Faso 18.0
Eritrea 17.8
Namibia 17.2
Rwanda 17.1
Mexico 16.9

Chad 15.8
Ghana 15.7
Ecuador 15.2
North Korea 15.2
Benin 15.1
Sierra Leone 14.9
Mauritania 14.7
Botswana 14.5
Zimbabwe 14.3
Gabon 13.8
Nicaragua 13.6
French Guiana 13.3
Papua New Guinea 13.0
Swaziland 12.9
Bermuda 12.3
Comoros 12.2
Nigeria 12.2
Cape Verde 11.6
Grenada 11.5
Paraguay 11.5
Barbados 11.3
Togo 10.9
Gambia 10.8
Peru 10.8
Myanmar 10.2
Russia 10.2
Liberia 10.1
Costa Rica 10.0
Nauru 9.8
Bolivia 8.9
Mozambique 8.8
Kazakhstan 8.8
Senegal 8.7
Turks and Caicos Islands 8.7
Mongolia 8.7
British Virgin Islands 8.6
Cayman Islands 8.4

Seychelles 8.3
Madagascar 8.1
Indonesia 8.1
Mali 8.0
Pakistan 7.8
Moldova 7.5
Kiribati 7.3
Guadeloupe 7.0
Haiti 6.9
Timor-Leste 6.9
Anguilla 6.8
Antigua and Barbuda 6.8
Lithuania 6.6
Uruguay 5.9
Philippines 5.4
Ukraine 5.2
Estonia 5.2
Cuba 5.0
Belarus 4.9
Thailand 4.8
Suriname 4.6
Laos 4.6
Georgia 4.3
Martinique 4.2
And the United States 4.2

All 109 of the countries above America, have 100% gun bans.

It is interesting to note that Switzerland is not on this list because they have no murder occurrence. It is also interesting to note that in Switzerland everyone owns a gun and maintains marksmanship qualifications regularly.

Obama is now attempting to issue a gag order that would ban Americans from talking about guns; specifically, any sort of "technical data" about a firearm such as "blueprints, drawings, photographs, plans, instructions or documentation." Of course, this is a restraint on our First Amendment rights.

Obama has failed at imposing direct gun control on Americans, so now he is attempting to infringe on our right to talk about guns. As a matter of fact, if his proposal becomes law, then Americans who share "technical data" about a firearm without first obtaining permission from the government would face time in jail for up to 20 years and a fine of $1 million.

We are advised not to judge all Muslims by the actions of a few lunatics, but we are encouraged to judge all gun owners by the actions of a few lunatics.

Nazi Germany's Joseph Goebbels believed that "if a lie could be told often enough, the public could be brought to believe it. In his mind, the bigger and more outrageous the lie the better, because it would be easier to discredit those who would call it out for being untrue."

More and more we are being forced to believe that if we live in gun free zones we will all be safe, so everyone should do the empathetic thing and give up their guns. That way, there would be no more violence.

Well, at least the good guys who are not violent anyway, will remain safe around you, but the gangsta and mobster will not be giving up their guns. Goebbels was a Liberal, and this is all a Liberal view. Liberals always get emotional and blame the gun instead of the person behind the gun. Unfortunately, we have cowardly Republicans that sit back and believe the lies instead of disputing them and fighting back with the truth.

Obama wants your guns, and he does not care how he gets them or who he gets them from, as long as he gets them. He is starting his confiscation plan by going after senior citizens that are on social security. This will affect 4.2 million Americans.

Senior Citizens that are on social security have received questionnaires in the mail. If they did not respond to the questionnaires by filling them out and returning them to the government office, they get a personal phone call and must answer the questions over the telephone. I was one of those that pitched the questionnaire and received a telephone call at 8:30 at night.

The questionnaire consisted of questions carefully designed more towards mental capabilities than physical capabilities. The questions were on the line of are you depressed? When you are physically and mentally – and I would interrupt and say "I am not mentally depressed, or I am not mentally or emotionally whatever the question was. Finally, he got irritated with me and said "I have to read the question." I laughed and told him to go ahead. Most questions concerned whether or not I could take care of myself, whether I could take care of my finances, how often did I forget small things. If you are deemed to be "marked subnormal intelligence, or mental illness, incompetent, condition, or disease," they will come after your weapons. The ban also covers anyone who has their finances handled by other members of their family if they are on Social Security.

Obama has not been able to push through stricter background checks. Now when is the last time you read in the paper of a senior citizen going out on a crime spree? When is the last time you heard of a senior citizen needing money and selling all of his/her guns to felons, drug addicts, or illegal immigrants?

Gun stores are required to run the names of potential buyers through a computerized system before every sale. Obama is going after the largest segment of the population – retiring baby boomers. He's using a tactic that was used by Hitler in Nazi Germany and by communists in the Soviet Union. It's the use of psychiatry as a soft enforcement arm of the federal government. The Nazis began a huge propaganda campaign against mentally and physically disabled Germans. They did not fit into the Nazi stereotype of the pure Aryan; that is physically fit with an obedient mind to serve the Reich. In addition, they were viewed as a burden on society, as they were unable to work and drained resources from the state. http://bit.ly/1SG9n1A

There is a saying about Barack Obama. Always watch what his other hand is doing. Every time Obama is making a big speech about gun confiscation, **it is because a Muslim Terrorist has murdered a bunch of Americans and Obama is attempting to deflect the story to make it a gun issue instead of an Islamist Terrorist issue.** Isn't it interesting that it is always the Democrat Liberals that are the ones that go after your guns?

Millions of Senior Americans are living on fixed incomes which do not keep pace with the increased cost of living. Many seniors are forced to find full or part time jobs, some to keep a roof over their heads, or to meet their medical expenses.

About Fifteen Million Seniors could see their Medicare premiums increase by 52%. "Unless Congress or Health and Human Services Secretary Sylvia Mathews Burwell intervenes, an estimated 15 million seniors, first-time beneficiaries or those currently claiming dual Medicare and Medicaid coverage will see their premiums jump from $104.90 per month to $159.30 for individuals, according to an analysis by the Center for Retirement Research at Boston College. Higher-income couples would pay multiples of that increase." $54.40 a month is probably a financial breaking point for some.

"Obama has been at war with senior citizens ever since taking office. The provisions built into Obamacare have only cost seniors more for less medical coverage. It's as if Obama wants older Americans to die sooner so the government doesn't have to help provide for us. He's in favor of killing off the elderly, the unborn, the sick and the disabled so they aren't a burden on society. Kind of sounds like Adolf Hitler's philosophy doesn't it?" http://bit.ly/1NbbnLB

XXVI

THE TWENTY-SECOND AMENDMENT

I s it possible for President Obama to remain in office after 2016? Would that not be against the 22nd Amendment to the Constitution, right? I wrote about that in *The Lyin Kings*.

"Despite the 22nd Amendment, it is possible for Obama to stay in office. Obama has signed more executive orders than any other American president in history. One of those is Executive Order 13603, which he signed on March 16, 2012. EO 13603 also goes by the National Defense Resources Preparedness Order. It gives the President power over many things in case of an emergency. For example, if there is an earthquake, the president would have the power to decide how much food people could buy and be given power over civil transport and the military.

'Under Executive Order 13603, Barack Obama can also stay in office as President of the United States if an emergency occurs. If Obama declares martial law in the event of an emergency, then he can stay in office as long as he wishes.

'Under martial law no election is needed, and political power is handed over to the executive branch and the military, rather than being shared among a balance of the legislative, executive, and judicial branches as laid out in the Constitution.

'Obama is on a slippery slope and seems to be going downhill pretty fast. He has made some pretty serious mistakes and has not been able to hide them. Here are a few:

'Benghazi - To be honest, there so many different versions of this one, it's hard to tell which ones are true. Still, a few things are clear. The United States' Ambassador to the United Nations has stated that the attack was part of a street protest, not a terrorist attack. That is not true. It was a terrorist attack. The truth was not told to the citizens of the United States until it was exposed through an investigation led by Republican members of Congress.

'The IRS - The Internal Revenue Service has been targeting conservative political groups. The IRS stated that the high-level officials knew nothing about it and blamed it on low-level employees who oversee the taxes of most Americans. It was only after being investigated that a high-level IRS official apologized for it.

'Phone Tapping - The Associated Press had their phone records taken by the US Department of Justice. That is interesting: Why would the Department of Justice want their phone records? It seems unlikely that the AP is trying to hide the identity of terrorists. So, why is the Department of Justice targeting them?

'To Sum It All Up...

'Based on these egregious actions by the executive branch under the Obama Administration, many people feel that Obama is going to declare martial law in order to stay in power for as long as possible, beginning in 2016." http://micheletravis.hubpages.com/hub/Can-Obama-Still-Be-The-President-In-2016

As for President Obama, during his July 2015 African trip, he said, "I actually think I'm a pretty good president," Obama said. "I think if I ran, I would win. But I can't."

"I'm still a pretty young man, but I know that someone with new insights and new energy will be good for my country," he said.

XXVII

THE OBAMA LIBRARY

There was a dinner in the private upstairs dining room of the White House. Among the guests were novelist Toni Morrison and Malcolm Gladwell; hedge fund manager, Marc Lasry; Silicon valley venture capitalist John Doerr; Hollywood actress Eva Longoria and Vinod Khosla, a founder of Sun Microsystems; and Reid Hoffman, LinkedIn billionnaire. Altogether, with Obama and Michelle, there were 13 guests.

They discussed proposed locations for the presidential library as well as fund raising.

The president, first lady and a cadre of top aides map out a post-presidential infrastructure and endowment they estimate could cost as much as $1 billion. The president's aides did not ask any of the guests for library contributions after the dinner, but a number of those at the table could be donors in the future.

The $1 billion — double what George W. Bush raised for his library and its various programs — would be used for what one adviser called a "digital-first" presidential library loaded with modern technologies, and to establish a foundation with a worldwide reach.

So far, Mr. Obama has raised just over $5.4 million from 12 donors, with gifts ranging from $100,000 to $1 million. Michael J. Sacks, a

Chicago businessman, gave $666,666. Fred Eychaner, the founder of Chicago-based Newsweb Corp., which owns community newspapers and radio stations, donated $1 million. Mark T. Gallogly, a private equity executive, and James H. Simons, a technology entrepreneur, each contributed $340,000 to a foundation set up to oversee development of the library.

The real push for donations, foundation officials said, will come after Mr. Obama leaves the White House.

Shailagh Murray, a senior adviser, oversees an effort inside the White House to keep attention on Mr. Obama's future and to ensure that his final 17 months in office, barring crises, serve as a glide path to his life as an ex-president. Mr. Obama's recent visit to a federal prison indicates, advisers say, a likely emphasis on criminal justice reform after he leaves office. His eulogy for one of nine African-Americans killed at a church in Charleston, S.C., is a forerunner, they say, of a focus on race relations. Diplomacy with Iran and Cuba could serve as the foundation for foreign policy work.

"His focus is on finishing this job completely, thoroughly," said Valerie Jarrett, one of Mr. Obama's closest confidantes inside the White House. But officials in the West Wing said the president's thinking about some of his signature issues — including health care, economic inequality and fighting climate change — also involves considering their incorporation into his life after January 2017.

The heart of the post-presidential planning is Mr. Obama's own outreach to eclectic, often extraordinarily rich groups of people. Several aides close to Mr. Obama said his extended conversations over the lengthy dinners — guests say his drink of choice at the gatherings is an extra-dry Grey Goose martini — reminded them of the private consultations Mr. Obama had with donors and business leaders as he sought to build a winning campaign.

The process started as early as the week after Mr. Obama's re-election in 2012, when the director Steven Spielberg and the actor Daniel Day-Lewis went to a White House screening of the movie *Lincoln*." Mr. Spielberg held the president spellbound, guests said, when he spoke about the use of technology to tell stories. Mr. Obama has continued those conversations, most recently with Mr. Spielberg and the studio executive Jeffrey Katzenberg over dinner at a Beverly Hills hotel in California in June, according to some of Mr. Obama's close advisers.

The advisers said Mr. Spielberg was focused on helping to develop a "narrative" for Mr. Obama in the years after he leaves office.

Mr. Obama has sought input from an eclectic group including, clockwise from top left, Malcolm Gladwell, Toni Morrison, John Doerr and Eva Longoria. Credit Clockwise from top left: Amy Sussman/ Getty Images; Damon Winter/*The New York Times;* Matt Rourke/ Associated Press; Valery Hace/Agence France-Presse — Getty Images

At a dinner this year at Spruce, a restaurant in the Presidio Heights neighborhood of San Francisco, Mr. Obama urged technology executives to focus their philanthropic efforts on helping government become more efficient, giving some the impression that the topic would most likely be a theme of his agenda after leaving office.

Dinner guests say that post-presidency planning is a big topic of conversation but not the only one. "He loves those sessions," a top adviser said. "They're very nourishing to him."

The next milestone in the library planning will come this month when foundation officials kick off a global search for an architect by releasing a request for proposals to major firms.

The planning for the library is being managed largely out of Chicago, where it will be built. The board for the library foundation includes Mr. Doerr and Julianna Smoot, Mr. Obama's chief campaign fund-raiser in 2008 and 2012. The Chicago library will include an office for the president, but aides said the Obamas could live in Washington while Sasha, 14, their younger daughter, finished high school here. Several said Mr. Obama, who graduated from Columbia University in 1983, may also have a New York office on Columbia's campus.

In Chicago, Mr. Nesbitt, the leader of the planning effort, also runs committees overseeing the future library's architecture, fund-raising and what the organizers call "vision." The vision committee, which solicits ideas from supporters around the country about how Mr. Obama should approach his post-presidency, is run by Lynn Taliento, a McKinsey & Company consultant in Washington who met with Mr. Obama in the Oval Office in February 2014, according to White House visitor logs. The planning is coordinated with the White House by Mr. Obama's deputy chief of staff, Anita Decker Breckenridge.

Among the debates at some of Mr. Obama's dinners: How could technology be used to provide global access to his presidential library? How prominent should Mr. Obama seek to be, especially in the first few years?

One top aide said Mr. Obama respected Mr. Bush's decision to limit his time in public after leaving office, but also admired Mr. Clinton's aggressive use of the spotlight to press his agenda.

"My sense is that he's probably a blend of the two,'" said David Plouffe, one of Mr. Obama's closest former aides and a member of the library foundation board.

In response to a question from Mr. Doerr at the February White House dinner, the president told the group that he wanted to focus on civic engagement and opportunities for youths, pushing guests for ideas about how to make government work better, Mr. Hoffman recalled in an interview. The president asked if social networks could improve the way society confronted problems.

In their conversations with Mr. Obama and his advisers, people from Silicon Valley and Hollywood are pressing for a heavy reliance on cutting-edge technology in the library that would help spread the story of Mr. Obama's presidency across the globe. Ideally, one adviser said, a person in Kenya could put on a pair of virtual reality goggles and be transported to Mr. Obama's 2008 speech on race in Philadelphia.

Some discussions at the dinners have focused on the role Mr. Obama might play internationally after the diplomatic opening with Cuba, the nuclear deal with Iran, the confrontations with Russia and the drawdown of American forces in Iraq and Afghanistan.

In an interview on the website Tumblr last year, Mr. Obama was asked what he expected to be doing in 10 years. The president took more than 30 seconds to respond, in a manner that suggested he had not yet settled on a good answer.

"I haven't projected out 10 years," he said, offering his standard promise to remain engaged in policy-making until his last days in the Oval Office. "I know what I'll do right after the next president is inaugurated. I'll be on a beach somewhere drinking out of a coconut."

Correction: August 18, 2015

An article about President Obama's future after he leaves office described incorrectly the business founded by Fred Eychaner, who donated $1 million to Mr. Obama's library. Mr. Eychaner founded Newsweb Corp., which owns community newspapers and radio stations; he did not found a Chicago "television empire." http://nyti.ms/1WfnOuV

XXVIII

THE DECLARATION OF INDEPENDENCE

In Congress, July 4, 1776,
The Unanimous Declaration of
The Thirteen United States of America

When in the Course of human events, it becomes necessary for one people to dissolve the political bands which have connected them with another, and to assume among the powers of the earth, the separate an equal station to which the Laws of Nature and of Nature's God entitle them, a decent respect to the opinions of mankind requires that they should declare the causes which impel them to the separation.

We hold these truths to be self-evident, that all men are created equal, that they are endowed by their Creator with certain unalienable Rights, that among these are Life, Liberty and the pursuit of Happiness – That to secure these rights, Governments are instituted among Men, deriving their just powers from the consent of the governed, – That whenever any Form of Government becomes destructive of these ends, it is the Right of the People to alter or to abolish it, and to institute new

Government, laying its foundation on such principles and organizing its powers in such form, as to them shall seem most likely to affect their Safety and Happiness, Prudence, indeed, will dictate that Governments long established should not be changed for light and transient causes; and accordingly all experience hast shewn, that mankind are more disposed to suffer, while evils are sufferable, than to right themselves by abolishing the forms to which they are accustomed. But when a long train of abuses and usurpations, pursuing invariably the same. Object evinces a design to reduce them under absolute Despotism, it is their right, it is their duty, to throw off such Government, and to provide new Guards for their future security. – Such has been the patient sufferance of these Colonies and such is now the necessity which constrains them to alter their former Systems of Government. The history of the present King of Great Britain is a history of repeated injuries and usurpations, all having in direct object the establishment of an absolute Tyranny over these States. To prove this, let Facts be submitted to a candid world.

He has refused his Assent to Laws, the most wholesome and necessary for the public good.

He has forbidden his Governors to pass Laws of immediate and pressing importance, unless suspended in their operation till his Assent should be obtained; and when so suspended, he has utterly neglected to attend to them.

He has refused to pass other Laws for the accommodation of large districts of people, unless those people would relinquish the right of Representation in the Legislature, a right inestimable to them and formidable to tyrants only.

He has called together legislative bodies at places unusual, uncomfortable, and distant from the depository of the public Records, for the sole purpose of fatiguing them into compliance with this measures.

He has dissolved Representative Houses repeatedly, for opposing with manly firmness his invasions on the rights of the people.

He has refused for a long time, after such dissolutions, to cause others to be elected; whereby the Legislative powers, incapable of Annihilation, have returned to the People at large for their exercise;

the State remaining in the meantime exposed to all the dangers of invasion from without, and convulsions within.

He has endeavoured to prevent the population of these States; for that purpose obstructing the Laws for Naturalization of Foreigners; refusing to pass others to encourage their migrations hither, and raising the conditions of new Appropriations of Lands.

He has obstructed the Administration of Justice, by refusing his Assent to Laws for establishing Judiciary powers.

He has made Judges dependent on his Will alone, for the tenure of their offices, and the amount and payment of their salaries.

He has erected a multitude of New Offices, and sent hither swarms of Officers to harass our people, and eat out their substance.

He has kept among us, in times of peace, Standing Armies without the Consent of our legislatures.

He has affected to render the Military independent of and superior to the Civil power.

He has combined with others to subject us to jurisdiction foreign to our constitution and unacknowledged by our laws; giving his Assent to their Acts of pretended Legislation:

For Quartering large bodies of armed troops among us:

For protecting them, by a mock Trial, from punishment for any Murders which they should commit on the Inhabitants of these States:

For cutting off our Trade with all parts of the world:

For imposing Taxes on us without our Consent:

For depriving us in many cases, of the benefits of Trial by Jury;

For transporting us beyond Seas to be tried for pretended offences:

For abolishing the free System of English Laws in a neighbouring Providence, establishing therein an Arbitrary government, and enlarging its Boundaries so as to render it at once an example and fit instrument for introducing the same absolute rule into these Colonies:

For taking away our Charters, abolishing our most valuable Laws, and altering fundamentally the Forms of our Governments:

For suspending our own Legislatures, and declaring themselves invested with power to legislate for us in all cases whatsoever.

He has abdicated Government here, by declaring us out of his Protection and waging War against us.

He has plundered our seas, ravaged our Coasts, burnt our towns, and destroyed the lives of our people.

He is at this time transporting large Armies of foreign Mercenaries to compleat the works of death, desolation and tyranny, already begun with circumstances of Cruelty & perfidy scarcely paralleled in the most barbarous ages, and totally unworthy the Head of a civilized nation.

He has constrained our fellow Citizens taken Captive on the high seas to bear arms against their Country, to become the executioners of their friends and Brethren, or to fall themselves by their Hands.

He has excited domestic insurrections amongst us, and has endevoured to bring on the inhabitants of our frontiers, the merciless Indian Savages, whose known rule of warfare, is in undistinguished destruction of all ages, sexes and conditions.

In every stage of these Oppressions We have Petitioned for Redress in the most humble terms: Our repeated Petitions have been answered only by repeated injury. A Prince whose character is thus marked by every act which may define a Tyrant, is unfit to be the ruler of a free people.

Nor have We been wanting in attention to our Brittish brethren. We have warned them from time to time of attempts by their legislature to extend an unwarrantable jurisdiction over us. We have reminded them of the circumstances of our emigration and settlement here. We have appealed to their native justice and magnanimity and we have conjured them by the ties of our common kindred to disavow these usurpations, which would inevitably interrupt our connections and correspondence. They too have been deaf to the voice of justice and of consanguinity. We must, therefore, acquiesce in the necessity, which denounces our Separation, and hold them, as we hold the rest of mankind, Enemies in War, in Peace Friends.

We, therefore, the Representatives of the united States of America, in General Congress, Assembled, appealing to the Supreme Judge of the world for the rectitude of our intentions, do, in the Name, and by Authority of the good People of these Colonies, solemnly publish and declare, That these United Colonies are, and of Right out to be Free and Independent States; that they are Absolved from all Allegiance to the British Crown, and that all political connection between them and the State of Great Britain, is and out to be totally dissolved; and that as Free and Independent States, they have full Power to levy War, conclude Peace, contract Alliances, establish Commerce, and to do all other Acts and Things which Independent States may of right do. And for the support of this Declaration with a firm reliance on the protection of divine Providence, we mutually pledge to each other our Lives, our Fortunes and our Sacred Honor.

Connecticut	Samuel Huntington
	Roger Sherman
	William Williams
	Oliver Wolcott
Delaware	Thomas Mckean
	George Read
	Caesar Rodney
Georgia	Button Gwinnett
	Lyman Hall
	George Walton
Maryland	Charles Carroll of Carrollton
	Samuel Chase
	William Paca
	Thomas Stone
Massachusetts	John Adams
	Samuel Adams
	Elbridge Gerry
	John Hancock
	Robert Treat Paine
New Hampshire	Josiah Bartlett
	Matthew Thornton
	William Whipple
New Jersey	Abraham Clark
	John Hart
	Francis Hopkinson
	Richard Stockton

	John Witherspoon
New York	William Floyd
	Francis Lewis
	Philip Livingston
	Lewis Morris
North Carolina	Joseph Hewes
	William Hooper
	John Penn
Pennsylvania	George Clymer
	Benjamin Franklin
	Robert Morris
	John Morton
	George Ross
	Benjamin Rush
	James Smith
	George Taylor
	James Wilson
Rhode Island	William Ellery
	Stephen Hopkins
South Carolina	Thomas Heyward, Jr.
	Thomas Lynch, Jr.
	Arthur Middleton
	Edward Rutledge
Virginia	Carter Braxton
	Benjamin Harrison
	Thomas Jefferson
	Francis Lightfoot Lee
	Richard Henry Lee
	Thomas Nelson, Jr.
	George Wythe

XXIX

THE CONSTITUTION OF
THE UNITED STATES

WE THE PEOPLE of the United States, in Order to form a more perfect Union, establish Justice, insure domestic Tranquility, provide for the common defence, promote the general Welfare, and secure the Blessings of Liberty to ourselves and our Posterity do ordain and establish this Constitution for the United State of America.

ARTICLE I.

Section 1. All legislative Powers herein granted shall be vested in a Congress of the United States, which shall consist of a Senate and House of Representatives.

Section 2. The House of Representatives shall be composed of Members chosen every second Year by the People of the several States, and the Electors in each State shall have the Qualifications requisite for Electors of the most numerous Branch of the State Legislature.

No Person shall be a Representative who shall not have attained to the Age or twenty five Years and have seven Years a Citizen of the United States, and who shall not, when elected, be an Inhabitant of that State in which he shall be chosen.

[Representatives and direct Taxes shall be apportioned among the several States which may be included within this Union, according to their respective Numbers, which shall be determined by adding to the whole Numbers of free Persons, including those bound to Service for a Term of Years, and excluding Indians not taxed, three fifths of all other Persons.] The actual Enumeration shall be made within three Years after the first meeting of the Congress of the United States, and within every subsequent Term of ten Years, in such Manner as they shall by Law direct. The Number of Representatives shall not exceed one for every thirty Thousand, but each State shall have at Least one Representative, and until such enumeration shall be made, the State of New Hampshire shall be entitled to chuse three, Massachusetts eight, Rhode Island and Providence Plantations one, Connecticut five, New York six, New Jersey four, Pennsylvania eight, Delaware one, Maryland six, Virginia ten, North Carolina five, South Carolina five, and Georgia three.

When vacancies happen in the Representation of any State, the Executive Authority thereof shall issue Writs of Election to fill such Vacancies.

The House of Representatives shall chuse their Speaker and other Officers; and shall have the sole Power of Impeachment.

Section 3. The Senate of the United States shall be composed of two Senators from each State [chosen by the Legislature] thereof for six Years; and each Senator shall have one Vote.

Immediately after they shall be assembled in Consequence of the first Election, they shall be divided as equally as may be into three Classes. The Seats of the Senators of the First Class shall be vacated at the Expiration of the second Year, of the Second Class at the Expiration of the fourth Year, and of the third Class at the Expiration of the sixth Year, so that one third maybe chosen every second year; [and if Vacancies happen by Resignation, or otherwise, during the Recess of the Legislature of any State, the Executive thereof may make temporary Appointments until the next Meeting of the Legislature which shall then fill such Vacancies].

No person shall be a Senator who shall not have attained the age of thirty Years, and been nine years a Citizen of the United States, and who shall not when elected, be an inhabitant of that State for which he shall be chosen.

The Vice President of the United States shall be President of the Senate, but shall have no Vote, unless they be equally divided.

The Senate shall chuse their other Officers and also a President pro tempore, in the Absence of the Vice President, or when he shall exercise the Office of President of the United States.

The Senate shall have the sole Power to try all Impeachments. When sitting for that Purpose they shall be on Oath or Affirmation. When the President of the United States is tried, the Chief Justice shall preside: And no Person shall be convicted without the Concurrence of two thirds of the Members present.

Judgment in Cases of Impeachment shall not extend further than to removal from Office and disqualification to hold and enjoy any Office of honor, Trust or Profit under the United States: but the Party convicted shall nevertheless be liable and subject to Indictment, Trial, Judgment and Punishment according to Law.

Section 4. The Times, Places and Manner of holding Elections for Senators and Representatives, shall be prescribed in each State by the Legislature thereof; but the Congress may at any time by Law make or alter such Regulations, except as to the Places of chusing Senators.

Section 5. Each House shall be the Judge of the Elections. Returns and Qualifications of its own Members, and a Majority of each shall constitute a Quorum to do Business; but a smaller Number may adjourn from day to day, and may be authorized to compel the Attendance of absent Members, in such Manner, and under such Penalties as each House may provide.

Each House may determine the Rules as its Proceedings, punish its Members for disorderly Behaviour, and, with the Concurrence of two thirds, expel a Member.

Each House shall keep a Journal of its Proceedings, and from time to time publish the same, excepting such Parts as may in their Judgment require Secrecy; and the Yeas and Nays of the Members of either House on any question shall, at the Desire of one fifth of those Present, be entered on the Journal.

Neither House, during the Session of Congress shall, without the Consent of the other, adjourn for more than three days, nor to any other Place than that in which the two Houses shall be sitting.

Section 6. The Senators and Representatives shall receive a Compensation for their Services, to be ascertained by Law, and paid out of the Treasury of the United States. They shall in all Cases, except Treason, Felony and Breach of the Peace, be privileged from Arrest during their Attendance at the Session of their respective Houses, and in going to and returning from the same; and for any Speech or Debate in either House, they shall not be questioned in any other place.

No Senator or Representative shall, during the Time for which he was elected, be appointed to any civil Office under the Authority of the United States, which shall have been created, or the Emoluments whereof shall have been increased during such time; and no Person holding any Office under the United States shall be a Member of either house during his Continuance in Office.

Section 7. All Bills for raising Revenue shall originate in the House of Representatives; but the Senate may propose or concur with Amendments as on other Bills.

Every Bill which shall have passed the House of Representatives and the Senate, shall, before it becomes a Law, be presented to the President of the United States. If he approves he shall sign it, but if not he shall return it, with his Objections to that House in which it shall have originated, who shall enter the Objections at large on their Journal, and proceed to reconsider it. If after such Reconsideration two thirds of that House shall agree to pass the Bill, it shall be sent, together with the Objections, to the other House, by which it shall likewise be reconsidered, and if approved by two thirds of that House, it shall become a Law. But in all such Cases the Votes of both Houses shall be determined by yeas and Nays, and the Names of the Persons voting for and against the Bill shall be entered on the Journal of each House respectively. If any Bill shall not be returned by the President within ten Days (Sunday excepted) after it shall have been presented to him, the Same shall be a Law, in like Manner as if he had signed it, unless the Congress by their Adjournment prevent its Return, in which Case it shall not be a Law.

Every Order, Resolution, or Vote to which the Concurrence of the Senate and House of Representatives may be necessary (except on a question of Adjournment) shall be presented to the President of the United States; and before the same shall take Effect, shall be approved by him, or being disapproved by him, shall be repassed by two thirds of the Senate and House of Representatives according to the Rules and limitations prescribed in the Case of a Bill.

Section 8. The Congress shall have Power to lay and Collect Taxes, Duties, Imposts and Excises, to pay the Debts and provide for the common Defence and general Welfare of the United States, but all Duties, Imposts and Excises shall be uniform throughout the United States;

To borrow Money on the credit of the United States;

To regulate Commerce with foreign Nations, and among the several States, and with the Indian Tribes;

To establish an uniform Rule of Naturalization and uniform Laws on the subject of Bankruptcies throughout the United States;

To coin Money, regulate the Value thereof, and of foreign Coin, and fix the Standard of Weights and Measures;

To provide for the Punishment of counterfeiting the Securities and current coin of the United States;

To establish the Post Office and post Roads;

To promote the Progress of Science and useful Arts, by securing for limited Times to Authors and Inventors the exclusive Right to their respective Writings and Discoveries;

To constitute Tribunals inferior to the Supreme Court;

To define and punish Piracies and Felonies committed on the high seas and Offences against the Law of Nations;

To declare War, grant Letters of Marque and Reprisal, and make Rules concerning Captures on Land and Water;

To raise and support Armies, but no Appropriation of Money to that Use shall be for a longer Term than two Years;

To provide and maintain a Navy;

To make Rules for the Government and Regulation of the land and naval Forces;

To provide for organizing, arming and disciplining, the militia, and for governing such Part of them as may be employed in the Service of the United States, reserving to the States respectively, the Appointment of the Officers, and the Authority of training the Militia according to the discipline prescribed by Congress;

To exercise exclusive Legislation in all Cases whatsoever, over such District (not exceeding ten Miles square) as may, by Cession of particular States, and the Acceptance of Congress, become the Seat of the Government of the United States, and to exercise like Authority over all Places purchased by the Consent of the Legislature of the State in which the Same shall be, for the Erection of Forts, Magazines, Arsenals, dock-Yards, and other needful Buildings – And

To make all Laws which shall be necessary and proper for carrying into Execution the foregoing Powers and all other Powers vested by this Constitution in the Government of the United States, or in any Department or Officer thereof.

Section 9. The Migration or Importation of such Persons as any of the States now existing shall think proper to admit, shall not be prohibited by the Congress prior to the Year one thousand eight hundred and eight, but Tax or duty may be imposed on such Importation, not exceeding ten dollars for each Person.

The Privilege of the Writ of Habeas Corpus shall not be suspended, unless when in Cases of Rebellion or Invasion the public Safety may require it.

No Bill of Attainder or ex post facto Law shall be passed.

No Capitation, or other direct, Tax shall be paid [unless in Proportion to the Census or enumeration herein before directed to be taken].

No Tax or Duty shall be laid on Articles exported from any State.

No Preferences shall be given by any Regulation of Commerce or Revenue to the Ports of one State over those of another; nor shall Vessels bound to, or from one State, be obliged to enter, clear, or pay Duties in another.

No Money shall be drawn from the Treasury, but in Consequence of Appropriations made by Law; and a regular Statement and Account of the Receipts and Expenditures of all public Money shall be published from time to time.

No Title of Nobility shall be granted by the United States: And no Person holding any Office of Profit or Trust under them, shall, without the Consent of the Congress, accept of any present, Emolument,

Officer, or Title, of any kind whatever, from any King, Prince, or foreign State.

Section 10. No State shall enter into any Treaty, Alliance, or Confederation; grant Letters of Marque and Reprisal; coin money; emit Bills of Credit; make any Thing but gold and silver Coin a Tender in Payment of Debts; pass any Bill of Attainder, ex post facto Law, or Law impairing the Obligation of Contracts, or grant any Title of Nobility.

No State shall, without the Consent of the Congress, lay any Imposts or Duties on Imports or Exports, except what may be absolutely necessary for executing its inspection Laws and the net Produce of all Duties and Imposts, laid by any State on Imports or Exports, shall be for the Use of the Treasury of the United States; and all such Laws shall be subject to the Revision and Control of the Congress.

No State shall, without the Consent of Congress, lay any Duty of Tonnage, keep Troops, or Ships of War in Time of Peace, enter into any Agreement or Compact with another State, or with a foreign Power, or engage in War, unless actually invaded, or in such imminent Danger as will not admit of delay.

ARTICLE II.

Section 1. The executive Power shall be vested in a President of the United States of America. He shall hold his Office during the term of four Years, and, together with the Vice President, chosen for the same Term, be elected as follows:

Each State shall appoint, in such Manner, as the Legislature thereof may direct, a Number of Electors, equal to the whole Number of Senators and Representatives to which the State may be entitled in the Congress: but no Senator or Representative, or Person holding an Office of Trust or Profit under the United States shall be appointed an Elector.

The Electors shall meet in their respective States, and vote by Ballot for two Persons, of whom one at least shall not be an Inhabitant of the same State with themselves. And they shall make a List of all the Persons voted for, and of the Number of Votes for each; which List they shall sign and certify and transmit sealed to the Seat of the Government of the United States, directed to the President of the Senate. The President of the Senate shall, in the Presence of the Senate and House of Representatives, open all the Certificates, and the Votes shall then be counted. The Person having the greatest Number of Votes shall be the President. If such Number be a Majority of the whole Number of Electors appointed; and there be no more than one who have such Majority; and have an equal Number of Votes, then the House of Representatives shall immediately chuse by Ballot one of them for President; and if no Person have a Majority, then from the five highest on the List the said House shall in like Manner chuse the President. But in chusing the President, the Votes shall be taken by State, the Representation from each State having one Vote; A quorum for this purpose all consist of a Member or Members from two thirds of the State, and a Majority of all the States shall be necessary to a Choice. In every Case, after the Choice of the President, the Person having the greatest Number of Votes of the Electors shall be the Vice President. But if there should remain two or more who have equal votes, the Senate shall chuse from them by Ballot the Vice President.

The Congress may determine the Time of chusing the Electors, and the Day on which they shall give their Votes; which Day shall be the same throughout the United States.

No person except a natural born Citizen, or a Citizen of the United States, at the time of the Adoption of this Constitution shall be eligible to the Office of President; neither shall any Person be eligible to that Office who shall not have attained to the Age of thirty five Years, and been fourteen Years a Resident within the United States.

[In Case of the Removal of the President from Office, or of his Death, Resignation, or Inability to discharge the Powers and Duties of the said Office, the Same shall devolve on the Vice President, and the Congress may by Law provide for the Case of Removal, Death, Resignation or Inability, both of the President and Vice President, declaring what Officer shall then act as President, and such Officer shall act accordingly, until the Disability be removed, or a President shall be elected.]

The President shall, at stated Times, receive for his Services, a Compensation, which shall neither be increased nor diminished during the Period for which he shall have been elected, and he shall not receive within that Period any other Emolument from the United States or any of them.

Before he enter on the Execution of his Office, he shall take the following Oath or Affirmation: – "I do solemnly swear (or affirm) that I will faithfully execute the Office of President of the United States and will to the best of my Ability preserve, protect and defend the Constitution of the United States."

Section 2. The President shall be Commander in Chief of the Army and Navy of the United States, and of the Militia of the several States, when called into the actual Service of the United States; he may require the Opinion, in writing, of the principal Officer in each of the executive Departments, upon any subject relating to the Duties of their respective Offices, and he shall have Power to grant Reprieves and Pardons for Offences against the United States, except in Cases of Impeachment.

He shall have power, by and with the Advice and Consent of the Senate, to make Treaties, provided two thirds of the Senators present concur; and he shall nominate, and by and with the Advice and Consent of the Senate shall appoint Ambassadors and other public Ministers and Consuls, Judges of the supreme Court, and all other Officers of the United States, whose Appointments are not herein otherwise provided for, and which shall be established by law; but the Congress may by Law vest the Appointment of such inferior Officers, as they think proper in the President alone, in the Courts of Law, or in the Heads of Departments.

The President shall have Power to fill up all Vacancies that may happen during the Recess of the Senate, by granting Commissions which shall expire at the end of their next Session.

Section 3. He shall from time to time give to the Congress Information of the State of the Union, and recommend to their Consideration such Measures as he shall judge necessary and expedient; he may, on extraordinary Occasions, convene both Houses, or either of them, and in Case of Disagreement between them, with Respect to the Time of Adjournment, he may adjourn them to such Time as he shall think proper; he shall receive Ambassadors and other public Ministers; he shall take Care that the Laws be faithfully executed, and shall Commission all the Officers of the United States.

Section 4. The President, Vice President, and all civil Officers of the United States, shall be removed from Office on Impeachment for, and Conviction of Treason, Bribery, or other high Crimes and Misdemeanors.

ARTICLE III.

Section 1. The judicial Power of the United States shall be vested in one Supreme Court, and in such inferior Courts as the Congress may from time to time ordain and establish. The Judges, both of the supreme and inferior Courts, shall hold their Offices during good behavior, and shall, at stated Times, receive for their Services a Compensation, which shall not be diminished during their Continuance in Office.

Section 2. The judicial Power shall extend to all Cases, in Law and Equity, arising under this Constitution, the Law of the United States, and Treaties made, or which shall be made, under their Authority; – to all Cases affecting Ambassadors, other public Ministers and Consuls; – to Controversies to which the United States shall be a party; - to Controversies between two or more States; –[between a State and Citizens of another State;] –between Citizens of different States; – between Citizens of the same State claiming Lands under Grants of different States, [and between a State, or the Citizens thereof, and foreign States, Citizens or Subjects.]

In all Cases affecting Ambassadors, other pubic Ministers, other public Ministers and Consuls, and those in which a State shall be Party, the Supreme Court shall have original jurisdiction. In all the other Cases before mentioned, the Supreme Court shall have appellate Jurisdiction, both as to Law and Fact, with such Exceptions, and under such Regulation Laws the Congress shall make.

The Trial of all Crimes, except in Cases of Impeachment, shall be by Jury; and such Trial shall be held in the State where the said Crime shall have been committed; but when not committed within any State, the Trial shall be at such Place or Places as the Congress may by Law have directed.

Section 3. Treason against the United States, shall consist only in levying War against them, or in adhering to their Enemies, giving them Aid and Comfort. No Person shall Be convicted of Treason unless on the Testimony of two Witnesses to the same overt Act, or on Confession in Open Court.

The Congress shall have Power to declare the Punishment of Treason, but no Attainder of Treason shall work Corruption of Blood, or Forfeiture except during the Life of the Person attainted.

ARTICLE IV.

Section 1. Full Faith and Credit shall be given in each State to the public Acts, Records and judicial Proceedings of every other State. And Congress may by general Laws prescribe the Manner in which such Acts, Records and Proceedings shall be proved, and the Effect thereof.

Section 2. The Citizens of each State shall be entitled to all Privileges and immunities of Citizens in the several States.

A person charged in any State with Treason, Felony, or other Crime, who shall flee from Justice and be found in another State, shall on Demand of the executive Authority of the State from which he fled, be delivered up, to be removed to the State having Jurisdiction of the Crime.

[No Person held to the Service or Labour in one State, under the Laws thereof, escaping into another, shall, in consequence of any Law or regulation therein, be discharged from such Service or Labour, but shall be delivered up on Claim of the Party to whom such Service or Labour may be due.]

Section 3. New States may be admitted by the Congress into this Union; but no new State shall be formed or erected within the Jurisdiction of any other State, nor any State be formed by the Junction of two or more States, or Parts of States, without the Consent of the Legislature of the States concerned as well as of the Congress.

The Congress shall have Power to dispose of and make all needful Rules and Regulations respecting the Territory of other Property belonging to the United States; and nothing in this Constitution shall be construed as to Prejudice any Claims of the United States or any particular State.

Section 4. The United States shall guarantee to every State in this Union a Republican Form of Government, and shall protect each of them against invasion; and on Application of the Legislature, or of the Executive (when the Legislature cannot be convened) against domestic Violence.

ARTICLE V.

The Congress, whenever two thirds of both Houses shall deem it necessary, shall propose Amendments to this Constitution, or on the Application of the Legislatures of two thirds of the several

States, shall call a Convention for proposing Amendments, which in either Case, shall be valid in all Intents and Purposes, as Part of this Constitution, when ratified by the Legislature of three fourths of the several States, or by Conventions in three fourths thereof, as the one or the other Mode of Ratification may be proposed by the Congress; Provided that no Amendment which may be made prior to the Year One Thousand eight hundred and eight shall in any Manner affect the first and fourth Clauses in the Ninth Section of the first Article; and that no State, without its Consent, shall be deprived of its equal Suffrage in the Senate.

ARTICLE VI.

All Debts contracted and Engagements entered into, before the Adoption of this Constitution, shall be as valid against the United States under this Constitution, as under the Confederation.

This Constitution, and the Laws of the United States which shall be made in Pursuance thereof; and all Treaties made, or which shall be made, under the Authority of the United Sates, shall be the supreme Law of the Land; and the Judges in every State shall be bound thereby, any Thing in the Constitution or Laws of any State to the contrary notwithstanding.

The Senators and Representatives before mentioned, and the Members of the several State Legislatures, and all executives and judicial Officers, both of the United States and several States, shall be bound by Oath or Affirmation, to support this Constitution; but no religious Test shall ever be required as a Qualification to any Officer or public Trust under the United States.

ARTICLE VII.

The Ratification of the Conventions of nine States shall be sufficient for the Establishment of the Constitution between the States so ratifying the Same.

Done in Convention by the Unanimous Consent of the State present the Seventeenth Day of September in the Year of our Lord one thousand seven hundred eighty seven and of the Independence of the United States of America the Twelfth In witness whereof We have hereunto subscribed our Names.

G. Washington
President and deputy from Virginia

Delaware	George Read
	Gunning Bedford Jun
	John Dickinson
	Richard Bassett
	Jaco: Broom
Maryland	James McHenry
	Dan of St Thos. Jenifer
	Danl. Carroll
Virginia	John Blair
	James Madison Jr.
North Carolina	Wm. Blount
	Richd. Dobbs Spaight
	Hu Williamson
South Carolina	J. Rutledge
	Charles Cotesworth Pinckney
	Charles Pinckney
	Pierce Butler
Georgia	William Few
	Abr Baldwin
New Hampshire	John Langdon
	Nicholas Gilman
Massachusetts	Nathaniel Gorham
	Rufus King
Connecticut	Wm. Saml. Johnson
	Roger Sherman

New York	Alexander Hamilton
New Jersey	Will Livingston
	David Brearley
	Wm. Paterson
	Jona: Dayton
Pennsylvania	B Franklin
	Thomas Mifflin
	Robt Morris
	Geo. Clymer
	Thos. FitzSimons
	Jared Ingersoll
	James Wilson
	Gouv Morris
	Attest William Jackson Secretary

AMENDMENTS TO
THE CONSTITUTIONS OF
THE UNITED STATES

Amendment I

Congress shall make no law respecting an establishment of religion, or prohibiting the free exercise thereof; or abridging the freedom of speech, or of the press, or the right of the people peaceably to assemble, and to petition the Government for a redress of grievances.

Amendment II

A well-regulated Militia, being necessary to the security of a free State, the right of the people to keep and bear Arms, shall not be infringed.

Amendment III

No Soldier shall, in time of peace, be quartered in any house, without the consent of the Owner, nor in time of war, but in a manner to be prescribed by law.

Amendment IV

The right of the people to be secure in their persons houses papers, and effects, against unreasonable searches and seizures, shall not be violated, and no Warrants shall issue, but upon probable cause, supported by Oath or affirmation, and particularly describing the place to be searched, and the persons or things to be seized.

Amendment V

No person shall be held to answer for a capital, or otherwise infamous crime, unless on a presentment or indictment of a Grand Jury, except in cases arising in the land or naval forces, or in the Militia, when in actual service in time of War or public danger; nor shall any person be subject for the same offence to be twice put in jeopardy of life or limb; nor shall be compelled in any criminal case to be a witness against himself, nor be deprived of life, liberty, or property, without due process of law; nor shall private property be taken for public use, without just compensation.

Amendment VI

In all criminal prosecutions, the accused shall enjoy the right to a speedy and public trial, by an impartial jury of the State and district wherein the crime shall have been committed which district shall have been previously ascertained by law, and to be informed of the nature and cause of the accusation; to be confronted with the witnesses against him; to have compulsory process for obtaining witnesses in his favor and to have the Assistance of Counsel for his defence.

Amendment VII

In Suits at Common law, where the value in controversy shall exceed twenty dollars, the right of trial by jury shall be preserved, and no fact tried by a jury, shall be otherwise re-examined in any Court of the United States, than according to the rules of the common law.

Amendment VIII

Excessive bail shall not be required, nor excessive fines imposed, nor cruel and unusual punishments inflicted.

Amendment IX

The enumeration in the Constitution, of certain rights, shall not be construed to deny or disparage others retained by the people.

Amendment X

The powers not delegated to the United States by the Constitution, nor prohibited by it to the States, are reserved to the States respectively, or to the people.

Amendment XI

The Judicial power of the United States shall not be construed to extend to any suit in law or equity commenced or prosecuted against one of the United States by Citizens of another State, or by Citizens or Subjects of any Foreign State.

Amendment XII

The Electors shall meet in their respective states and vote by ballot for President and Vice President, one of whom, at least, shall not be an inhabitant of the same state with themselves; they shall name in their ballots the person voted for as President and in distinct ballots the person voted for as Vice President, and they shall make distinct lists of all persons voted for as President, and of all persons voted for as Vice President, and of the number of votes for each, which lists they shall sign and certify, and transmit sealed to the seat of the government of the United States, directed to the President of the Senate; – the President of the Senate shall, in the presence of the Senate and the House of Representatives, open all the certificate and the votes shall then be counted; – the person having the greatest number of votes for President, shall be the President, if such number be a majority of the whole number of Electors appointed; and if no person have such majority, then from the persons having the highest numbers not exceeding three on the list of those voted for as President, the house of Representatives shall choose immediately, by ballot the President. But in choosing the president, the votes shall be taken by states, the representation from each state having one vote; a quorum for this purpose shall consist of a member or members from two-thirds of the states, and a majority of all the states shall be necessary to choose. [And if the House of Representatives shall not choose a President whenever the right of choice shall devolve upon them before the fourth day of March next following, then the Vice President shall act as President, as in case of the death or other constitutional disability of the President.] The person having the greatest number of votes as Vice President, if such number be a majority of the whole number of Electors appointed, and if no person have a majority, then from the two highest numbers on the list, the Senate shall choose the Vice President; a quorum for the purpose shall consist of two-thirds of the whole number of Senators, and a majority of the whole number shall be necessary to a choice. But no person constitutionally ineligible to the office of President shall be eligible to that of Vice President of the United States.

Amendment XIII

Section I. Neither slavery nor involuntary servitude, except as a punishment for crime whereof the party shall have been duly convicted, shall exist within the United States, or any place subject to their jurisdiction.

Section 2. Congress shall have power to enforce this article by appropriate legislation.

Amendment XIV

Section 1. All persons born or naturalized in the United States, and subject to the jurisdiction thereof, are citizens of the United States and of the State wherein they reside. No State shall make or enforce any law which shall abridge the privilege or immunities of citizens of the United States; nor shall any State deprive any person of life, liberty, or property, without due process of law; nor deny to any person within its jurisdiction the equal protection of the laws.

Section 2. Representatives shall be apportioned among the several States according to their respective numbers, counting the whole number of persons in each State, excluding Indians not taxed. But when the right to vote at any election for the choice of electors for President and vice President of the United States, Representatives in

Congress, the Executive and Judicial Officers of a State, or the Members of the Legislature thereof, is denied to any of the male inhabitants of such State, being twenty-one years of age, and citizens of the United States or in any way abridged, except for participation in rebellion, or other crime, the basis of representation therein shall be reduced in the proportion which the number of such male citizens shall bear to the whole number of male citizens twenty-one years of age in such State.

Section 3. No person shall be a Senator or Representative in Congress or elector of President and Vice President, or hold any office civil or military, under the United States, or under any State, who have previously taken an oath, as a member of Congress, or as an officer of the United States, or as a member of any State legislature, or as an executive or judicial officer of any State, to support the Constitution of the united States, shall have engaged in insurrection or rebellion against the same, or given aid or comfort to the enemies thereof. But Congress may by a vote of two-thirds of each House, remove such disability.

Section 4. The validity of the public debt of the United States, authorized by law, including debts incurred for payment of pensions and bounties for services in suppressing insurrection or rebellion, shall not be questioned. But neither the United States not any State shall assume or pay any debt or obligation incurred in aid of insurrection or rebellion against the United States, or any claim for the loss or emancipation of any slave; but all such debts, obligations and claims shall be held illegal and void.

Section 5. The Congress shall have the power to enforce, by appropriate legislation, the provisions of this article.

Amendment XV

Section 1. The right of citizens of the United States to vote shall not be denied or abridged by the United States or by any State on account of race, color, or previous condition or servitude –

Section 2. The Congress shall have the power to enforce this article by appropriate legislation.

Article XVI

The Congress shall have the power to lay and collect taxes on incomes, from whatever source derived, without apportionment among the several States, and without regard to any census or enumeration.

Article XVII

The Senate of the United States shall be composed of two Senators from each State, elected by the people thereof, for six years, and each Senator shall have one vote. The electors in each State shall have the qualifications requisite for electors of the most numerous branches of the State legislatures.

When vacancies happen in the representation of any State in the Senate, the executive authority of such State shall issue writs of election to fill such vacancies: Provided, That the legislature of any State may empower the executive thereof to make temporary appointments until the people fill the vacancies by election as the legislature may direct.

This amendment shall not be so construed as to affect the election or term of any Senator chosen before it becomes valid as part of the Constitution.

Amendment XVIII

Section 1. After one year from the ratification of this article the manufacture, sale, or transportation of intoxicating liquors within, the importation thereof into, or the exportation thereof from the United States, and all territory subject to the jurisdiction thereof for beverage purposes is hereby prohibited.

Section 2. The Congress and the several States shall have concurrent power to enforce this Article by appropriate legislation.

Section 3. This article shall be inoperative unless it shall have been ratified as an amendment to the Constitution by the legislature of the several States as provided in the Constitution within seven years from the date of the submission hereof to the States by the Congress.

Amendment XIX

The right of citizens of the United States to vote shall not be denied or abridged by the United States or any State on account of sex. Congress shall have power to enforce this article by appropriate legislation.

Amendment XX

Section 1. The terms of the President and the Vice President shall end at noon on the 20th day of January, and the terms of Senators and Representatives at noon on the 3rd day of January of the years in which such terms would have ended if this article had not been ratified and the terms of their successors shall then begin

Section 2. The Congress shall assemble at least once in every year and such meeting shall begin at noon on the 3rd day of January, unless they shall by law appoint a different day.

Section 3. If, at the time fixed for the beginning of the term of the President, the President elect shall have died, the Vice President elect shall become President. If a President shall not have been chosen before the time fixed for the beginning of his term, or if the President elect shall have failed to qualify, then the Vice President elect shall act as President until a President shall have qualified; and the Congress may by law provide for the case wherein neither a resident elect nor a Vice President shall have qualified, declaring who shall then act as President, or the manner in which one who is to act shall be selected, and such person shall act accordingly until a President or Vice President shall have qualified.

Section 4. The Congress may by law provide for the case of the death of any of the persons from whom the House of Representatives may choose a President whenever the right of choice shall have devolved upon them, and for the case of the death of any of the persons from whom the Senate may choose a Vice President whenever the right of choice shall have devolved upon them.

Section 5. Sections 1 and 2 shall take effect on the 15th day of October following the ratification of this article.

Section 6. This article shall be inoperative unless it shall have been ratified as an amendment to the Constitution by the legislature of three-fourths of the several states within seven years from the date of its submission.

Amendment XXI

Section 1. The Eighteenth Article of Amendment to the Constitution if hereby repealed.

Section 2. The transportation of importation into any State, Territory, or Possession of the United States for delivery or use therein of intoxicating liquors, in violation of the laws thereof, is hereby prohibited.

Section 3. This article shall be inoperative unless it shall have been ratified as an amendment to the Constitution by convention in the several states as provided in the Constitution, within seven years from the date of the submission hereof to the States by the Congress. [The 21st Amendment was ratified December 5, 1933]

Amendment XXII

Section 1. No person shall be elected to the office of the President more than twice, and no person who has held the office of President, or acted as President, for more than two years of a term to which some other person was elected President shall be elected to the office of President more than once. But this Article shall not apply to any person holding the office of President when this Article was proposed by Congress, and shall not prevent any person who may be holding the office of President, or acting as President, during the term within which this Article becomes operative from holding the office of President or acting as President during the remainder of such term.

Section 2. This article shall be inoperative unless it shall have been ratified as an amendment to the Constitution by the legislature of three-fourths of the several States within seven years from the date of its submission to the States by the Congress.

Amendment XXIII

Section 1. The District constituting the seat of Government of the United States shall appoint in such manner as Congress may direct:

A number of electors of President and Vice President equal to the whole number of Senators and Representatives in Congress to which the District would be entitled if it were a State, but in no event more than the least populous State; they shall be in addition to those appointed by the States, but they shall be considered, for the purposes of the election of President and Vice President, to be electors appointed by a State; and they shall meet in the District and perform such duties as provided by the twelfth article of amendment.

Section 2. The Congress shall have power to enforce this article by appropriate legislation.

Amendment XXIV

Section 1. The right of citizens of the United States to vote in any primary or other election for President or Vice President, for electors for President or Vice President, or for Senator or Representative in Congress, shall not be denied or abridged by the United States or any State by reason or failure to pay poll tax or other tax.

Section 2. The Congress shall have power to enforce this article by appropriate legislation.

Amendment XXV

Section 1. In case of the removal of the President from office or of his death or resignation, the Vice President shall become President.

Second 2. Whenever there is a vacancy in the office of the Vice President, the President shall nominate a Vice President who shall take office upon confirmation by a majority of both Houses of Congress.

Section 3. Whenever the President transmits to the President pro tempore of the Senate and the Speaker of the House of Representatives his written declaration that he is unable to discharge the powers and duties of his office, and until he transmits to them a written declaration to the contrary, such powers and duties shall be discharged by the Vice President as Acting President.

Section 4. Whenever the Vice President and a majority of either the principal officers of the executive departments or of such other body as Congress may by law provide, transmit to the President pro tempore of the Senate and the Speaker of the House of Representatives their written declaration that the President is unable to discharge the powers and duties of his office, the Vice President shall immediately assume the powers and duties of the office as Acting President.

Thereafter, when the President transmits to the President pro tempore of the Senate and the Speaker of the House of Representatives his written declaration that no inability exists, he shall resume the powers and duties of his office unless the Vice President and a majority of either the principal officers of the executive department or of such other body as Congress may by law provide, transmit within four days to the President pro tempore of the Senate and the Speaker of the House of Representatives their written declaration that the President is unable to discharge the powers and duties of his office. Thereupon Congress shall decide the issue, assembling within forty-eight hours for that purpose if not in session. If the Congress, within twenty-one days after receipt of the latter written declaration, or, of Congress is not in session, within twenty-one days after Congress is required to assemble, determines by two-thirds vote of both Houses that the President is unable to discharge the powers and duties of his office, the Vice President shall continue to discharge the same as Acting President; otherwise, the President shall resume the powers and duties of his office.

Amendment XXVI

Section 1. The right of citizens of the United States, who are eighteen years of age or older, to vote shall not be denied or abridged by the United States or by any State on account of age.

Section 2. The Congress shall have power to enforce this Article by appropriate legislation.

Amendment XXVII

Save
No law, varying the compensation for the services of the Senators and Representatives, shall take effect, until an election of representatives shall have intervened.

www.ingramcontent.com/pod-product-compliance
Lightning Source LLC
Chambersburg PA
CBHW062156270326
41930CB00009B/1547